Intellectual Property Law and Innovation

The rules of intellectual property law prevent competitors from imitating the innovative appearance or function of products. However, these rules are not derived from one single source, but are found in copyright law, designs law, patents law, trade secrets law and, when it comes to novel appearance, also in passing off and trade marks law.

Bringing together all these rules of intellectual property in a practical format, *Intellectual Property Law and Innovation* covers the areas of intellectual property law that are most relevant to both product and technological innovation. It surveys intellectual property law relevant to protecting or monopolising novel visual appearance, as well as the novel functions and substantive characteristics of products. It deals with central legal issues relating to copyright in computer programs, as well as in artistic works as relevant to the visual design of products; registered designs law; the equitable action for breach of confidence; patents law; *sui generis* regimes, including plant breeder's rights and the law relating to computer chip layouts; and particular aspects of trade marks law relevant to product appearance. It also examines the role of these different areas of the law from the perspective of innovation, including innovation strategy and public policy. In dealing with the law, the book focusses principally on Australia, but also refers occasionally to the law in other jurisdictions, principally in the English-speaking common law world.

This book places intellectual property law in the broader framework of innovation theory and strategy and will therefore benefit law students, legal practitioners, innovation managers, and all those working in the fields of intellectual property law and innovation management.

William van Caenegem is Professor of Law at Bond University.

Intellectual Property Law and Innovation

William van Caenegem

CAMBRIDGE
UNIVERSITY PRESS

University Printing House, Cambridge CB2 8BS, United Kingdom

One Liberty Plaza, 20th Floor, New York, NY 10006, USA

477 Williamstown Road, Port Melbourne, VIC 3207, Australia

314-321, 3rd Floor, Plot 3, Splendor Forum, Jasola District Centre, New Delhi - 110025, India

79 Anson Road, #06-04/06, Singapore 079906

Cambridge University Press is part of the University of Cambridge.

It furthers the University's mission by disseminating knowledge in the pursuit of education, learning and research at the highest international levels of excellence.

www.cambridge.org
Information on this title: www.cambridge.org/9780521837576

© William van Caenegem 2007

This publication is in copyright. Subject to statutory exception and to the provisions of relevant collective licensing agreements, no reproduction of any part may take place without the written permission of Cambridge University Press.

First published 2007

A catalogue record for this publication is available from the British Library

National Library of Australia Cataloging in Publication data
Caenegem, William van, 1961–
Intellectual property law and innovation.
Bibliography.
Includes index.
ISBN-13: 978-0-52183-757-6 paperback
ISBN-10: 0-52183-757-X paperback
1. Intellectual property (International law) – Textbooks.   2. Intellectual property – Australia – Textbooks.   3. Technological innovations – Law and legislation – Australia – Textbooks.   I. Title.
346.94048

ISBN 978-0-521-83757-6 Paperback

Reproduction and communication for educational purposes
The Australian *Copyright Act 1968* (the Act) allows a maximum of one chapter or 10% of the pages of this work, whichever is the greater, to be reproduced and/or communicated by any educational institution for its educational purposes provided that the educational institution (or the body that administers it) has given a remuneration notice to Copyright Agency Limited (CAL) under the Act.

For details of the CAL licence for educational institutions contact:

Copyright Agency Limited
Level 15, 233 Castlereagh Street
Sydney NSW 2000
Telephone: (02) 9394 7600
Facsimile: (02) 9394 7601
E-mail: info@copyright.com.au

Reproduction and communication for other purposes
Except as permitted under the Act (for example a fair dealing for the purposes of study, research, criticism or review) no part of this publication may be reproduced, stored in a retrieval system, communicated or transmitted in any form or by any means without prior written permission. All inquiries should be made to the publisher at the address above.

Cambridge University Press has no responsibility for the persistence or accuracy of URLs for external or third-party internet websites referred to in this publication, and does not guarantee that any content on such websites is, or will remain, accurate or appropriate.

Contents

Preface vii
List of acronyms xii
Table of statutes xiv
Table of cases xv

1 **Introduction** 1
   1 Intellectual property law and innovation 2
       Innovation, competition and IPRs 2
       IPRs and knowledge diffusion 6
       Property theory 10
       Theory and structure of rights 13
       Theory, policy and reality 15
   2 IP law trends relating to innovation 17
   3 The areas of intellectual property law included in this book 23

2 **Trade secrets** 25
       Introduction 25
   1 Policy context 26
   2 The equitable action for breach of confidence 31
       Introduction: doctrinal underpinnings 31
       The first element: information that is not in the public domain 35
       Demarcation and itemisation 40
       An implied or express obligation of confidence 42
       Use or disclosure of the confidential information 45
       Detriment and remedies in general 48
       Remedies against third parties 51
       Conclusions concerning trade secrets law 52
   3 The employment context 53
       Introduction 53
       The action for breach of confidence post-term 54
       Contractual extension of obligations of confidentiality 57

3 **Patents** 60
       Introduction 60
   1 Patent policy context 63
   2 Patents law: entitlement 70
       Patentable subject matter 71

                Novelty and inventiveness   80
                    Novelty   80
                    Inventiveness   84
                Utility, secret use and section 40 requirements   87
                    Section 40 requirements   87
                    Utility   89
                    Secret use; prior user rights   89
        3   Standard patents and innovation patents   90
        4   Ownership of patents   93
                The inventor's entitlement to a patent   93
                Employer entitlement to inventions and patents: some policy issues   94
                The law of ownership of employee inventions in Australia   96
        5   Rights and infringement   99
        6   The nature and extent of the exploitation right   104

4   **Copyright and designs**   110
        Introduction   110
            Policy context   110
            The legal regimes covered in this chapter   115
        1   Copyright   116
                Introduction   116
                Subsistence of copyright   117
                Infringement of copyright: reproduction of works   121
        2   Registered designs   129
                Introduction and policy context   129
                Designs law in Australia: entitlement   135
                    Introduction   135
                    Requirements for a valid design   136
                    The novelty test   143
                    Nature of the design right   148
                Infringement of a registered design   150
        3   The copyright–designs overlap   162

5   *Sui generis* **regimes and trade mark registration**   174
        Introduction   174
        1   Computers   178
                Computer program copyright   179
                Patents for computer programs   186
                Circuit layouts   188
        2   Plant varieties   192
                Introduction   192
                The *Plant Breeder's Rights Act 1994*   195
        3   Reliance on trade marks registration to monopolise new product shapes?   200

Bibliography   205
Index   214

Preface

Innovation is both a central aspect of industry policy and a crucial management issue for individual firms. Governments strive to devise policy settings that encourage innovation in industry; and no individual firm can ignore the innovation imperative in its decision-making. The distinct factors that determine the shape and size of the innovation spend are many and varied, complex in their interaction and challenging to conceptualise. Inventive individuals, firms and institutions are motivated by incentives ranging from the purely personal to the structural, including the competitive imperatives of market dynamics. In industry, a firm's R&D investment decisions are influenced by its perceived ability to capture sufficient returns from innovative products introduced into a competitive market where consumers determine commercial success. By deploying various strategies, individually or in combination, an innovative firm can profit from innovation even in the presence of avid imitators. Many available strategies are practical (for instance keeping an invention secret, or relying on imitation lag), and are considered in the broader innovation management literature. This book focusses on the role of law, ie of reliance on the various rights and remedies of intellectual property law to prevent or limit imitation and increase returns from innovation.

The subsistence, structure, scope and interaction of relevant intellectual property rights impacts on individual decisions to invest in innovation, so they are a significant topic of study and evaluation from the innovation and technology policy perspective. At the same time, they are controversial, in that there is considerable disagreement both in industry and in academe about the real impact on innovation of exclusive legal rights. But the relevant intellectual property (IP) regimes are also an inherently interesting subject matter because they are so closely intertwined with aspects of our broader culture, with its historical emphasis on progress, technological prowess and inventiveness. Innovation is a central theme of our times, and within it IP law plays a significant, if difficult to evaluate role.

The separate treatment of the areas of intellectual property law relevant to innovation in this book also accords with the growing recognition of that subject as a distinct area of study. Innovation policy, technology policy, innovation management and commercialisation of IP are dealt with as coherent and integrated topics for teaching, research and publication in books and journals. Encouraging innovation and using intellectual property law to capitalise on investment in innovation are topics well rehearsed and frequently addressed in public forums by government bodies, public institutions and private advisers.

This book focusses only on those selected legal regimes that play a role in industrial innovation. This includes IP law relevant both to what is referred to below as *technological* innovation, ie innovation in function, and to what is referred to below as *product* innovation, ie innovation in product appearance. Areas of intellectual property law that are not concerned with useful products and processes, but with topics such as art, literary, dramatic and musical entertainment, thus fall outside the confines of this book. Traditionally the treatment of intellectual property law is divided either into individual 'regimes', or into two parts: *intellectual* property, ie mostly copyright law, and *industrial* property, which comprises designs, patents, trade secrets, trade marks and passing off, as well as minor *sui generis* regimes; in short, the law relevant to industry rather than to arts and entertainment. This book cuts across this division: it does not address industrial property law as a whole, but only those aspects relevant to innovation in industry: trade marks law and passing off, naturally significant to industry, are therefore largely (but not wholly) ignored. But some aspects of copyright law are *included*; in particular, copyright in artistic works, as relevant to the original appearance and manufacturing of new products, and copyright in computer programs as functional processes.

The core regimes relating to the novel *appearance* of products are copyright (although based on the concept of originality rather than novelty) and designs (either by registration or as an 'unregistered design'). Naturally copyright includes far more subject matter than is considered here: although in part relevant to the innovation in product appearance, it mainly concerns other things, related to entertainment (music, theatre, literature) or other forms of communication. In relation to *functional* innovation, the core regime is patents law, although the narrower *sui generis* regimes mentioned above also play a significant role, as does copyright for computer programs. Trade secrets law is also crucially important as a default regime applicable to all forms of innovation.

Intellectual property law relating to innovation consists largely of regimes that are technology-neutral, ie the criteria for protection are abstract and do not identify the subject matter by its concrete technological nature or visual character. Patents law, designs law, copyright and the law of trade secrets all fall within this class, and form the bulk of the subject matter considered in this book. But a few regimes concern only specific and narrow technologies or products: principally plant breeder's rights and computer chip layouts. These are considered in a single chapter (Chapter five), which also covers computer programs. This is because, although strictly speaking no *sui generis* protection regime covers them, with both copyright and patents law playing a role, arguably something *akin* to a *sui generis* regime has been elaborated within copyright law to cope with the special nature of computer programs: they are functional and fundamentally differ from all other copyright subject matter. The theoretical choice between *sui generis* protection and a technology-neutral approach to innovations is a fundamental theoretical question, and is also addressed in Chapter five. That chapter also includes a brief appraisal of the role of trade marks registration in product innovation, which although limited and merely incidental has generated considerable interest in practice and industry.

The structure and content of intellectual property law is, at one level, a matter of policy, ie it results from public debate that is political in nature. Concrete outcomes, modulated by governments, are influenced by multiple, time-bound and often competing interests. On another level, it is a question both of legal theory, the logical structuring and organisation of legal rules and principles, and of specific application: how given rules of law operate in a particular factual matrix, and evolve in the context of real disputes. Although the latter is a matter more for lawyers than for policy-makers, in fact law and policy in IP are always closely intertwined. Lawyers active in intellectual property tend to be well acquainted with underlying policy debates, much as innovation managers keep a wary eye on legal developments. This book attempts to bridge the gap between the specifics of law and underlying theory and policy questions, something that is now increasingly attempted in the literature. Therefore each chapter covers both aspects of policy and theory and core legal issues, with the intention of informing and challenging that growing but varied body of readers (students, teachers, professionals, policy-makers and managers) with a common interest in innovation policy and law, but who, because of different training and experience, bring varying perspectives to specific issues.

As indicated above, the book covers IP related both to innovation in function and innovation in appearance. The law itself tends to observe this distinction between form and function: if an innovation is in essence functional, patents law is primarily applicable; if in essence related to appearance, then copyright and/or designs law applies. Nonetheless, some hybrid forms of protection exist: for instance, computer programs as functional products are protected by copyright as well as by patents. In truth the division between form and function is in any case conceptually tenuous, because products that are novel in appearance often also provide some functional advantage, and vice versa. Nonetheless the law requires the pigeonholing of every innovation, or innovative aspect, in a specific regime, so as to generate a remedy (or remedies: sometimes several areas of law will apply in relation to one product or process). A significant issue, addressed in this book, is thus identifying which legal regimes are relevant to a certain product or process, and also how the various regimes interrelate and sometimes offer cumulative or alternative legal protection. Products also do not necessarily match rights, in that different aspects of a single product may attract the grant of multiple and distinct rights, possibly held by different owners, and often of a different nature (thus rather than having 'one product one patent' a single product may attract patent, design and copyright protection in its different aspects). This requires looking at an innovative product with an informed eye, which can recognise legally relevant categories: for instance, a personal computer (PC) is not a category of subject matter as such in any Act; but its novel appearance (eg an unusual shape), its new functionality (eg exceptional speed) and its characteristic user interface may each fall within the scope of protection of one or another regime (designs, patents and copyright respectively in this case). These questions of the interrelationship between regimes are an important theme running through this book, both from a practical perspective, but also from the angle of policy and theory.

Apart from its specific focus on innovation and IP, other choices have shaped this book. Consideration of substantive issues rather than procedural and formal matters lies at its heart. For instance, the book features no detailed discussion of the application process for patents, but contains a substantial discussion of what can and cannot be patented, what novelty really means, who owns an invention, etc. The underlying intention is also to cut through to core questions interesting the majority of readers, rather than providing comprehensive detail on the latest decisions concerning every narrow legal question which may happen to arise; therefore the number of case references is limited. The reading list provides one way of discovering more about specific areas of interest; in other cases only a detailed analysis of the law will provide a satisfactory answer – either by accessing other monographs on intellectual property, of which there are now many, mostly current, in which up-to-date case references can be found; or by seeking the advice of professionals with the necessary skills! The book is also mostly limited to Australian law, although it occasionally refers to other jurisdictions, because that provides informative contrasts between local and foreign solutions. Although there is much harmony between national regimes now compared to the past, there are also still many areas of sometimes striking difference.

Some reasons for writing this book are given above; but most importantly it is a vehicle for sharing ideas and insights with the increasing number of students and professionals both within the law, within management and within the innovation policy disciplines who are equally fascinated with all aspects of the complex process of technological innovation and change. The text condenses and brings together the results of research conducted over a number of years, which has in part found its way into some previously published articles. But it does not pretend to provide definitive answers or final conclusions: for that the diversity of well-reasoned opinion in the literature is far too great. A chapter-based bibliography provide both reference detail about sources of information and inspiration, and starting points for further reading. The lists are not intended to be comprehensive, but include such articles and works as I have found particularly informative or interesting, either because of clarity of exposition or innovativeness of ideas. The scholarly output concerning relevant aspects of innovation policy is in fact vast; some of it is too mathematical for most lawyers and others not trained in economics, but much of it is quite accessible. Some is specifically directed at legal issues, while other literature, though principally engaged with technology policy, also has relevance for intellectual property lawyers. As will become apparent from perusal of the reading lists, certain journals tend to publish exactly the kind of articles that lawyers, managers and policy-makers interested in innovation policy are concerned with, and in an accessible form. They amply reward regular review, as does the output of some recently established Australian research institutions, principally the Intellectual Property Research Institute Australia (IPRIA) at the University of Melbourne and the Australian Centre for Intellectual Property in Agriculture (ACIPA).

This book originated in the idea that with the exponential growth of the subject matter a series of distinct works on sub-categories of intellectual property law was warranted. Dividing the subject matter into IP and innovation, IP and entertainment, and IP and reputation seemed like a logical approach. The process of first developing the concept and then structuring the book began quite a while ago. Jill Henry of CUP was interested, supportive and patient throughout, for which I am most grateful. I have also benefited from the encouragement and support of many colleagues, who gave me the opportunity to air and discuss my thoughts and publish ideas in past years. In particular Ulf Petrusson of the University of Gothenburg inspired me with his passion for the subject. Always encouraging and willing to discuss, Peter Drahos of ANU was an example of academic rigour and a source of relevant leads, as was Peter Hall of UNSW/ADFA. Pierre-Yves Gautier's words of encouragement spurred me on at a few critical moments. I am also grateful to Dean Duncan Bentley of the Bond Law Faculty for his continual support, and my other colleagues there for their cheerful willingness to listen to my accounts of progress (or lack thereof). My thanks also to an anonymous reviewer who provided useful comments. My family also has been patient and a wonderful relief and support whenever required. My research assistant Rachel Norden, whose work was funded by a Faculty Research Grant, also made an excellent contribution.

William van Caenegem
July 2006

List of acronyms

3D – Three Dimensional
ABS – Australian Bureau of Statistics
ACCC – Australian Competition and Consumer Commission
ACIP – Advisory Council on Intellectual Property
ALRC – Australian Law Reform Commission
AUSTLII – Australian Legal Information Institute
CAD – Computer Aided Design (sometimes also: Computer Assisted Drafting)
CLA – Circuit Layouts Act 1989 (Cth)
CRC – Collaborative Research Centre
CSIRO – Commonwealth Scientific and Industrial Research Organisation
DUS – Distinctive Uniform and Stable
EDV – Essentially Derived Variety
EL – Eligible Layout
EPC – European Patent Convention
EU – European Union
FRG – Federal Republic of Germany
GMO – Genetically Modified Organism
IP – Intellectual Property
IPAC – Industrial Property Advisory Committee
IPAustralia – Intellectual Property Australia; Australian Government agency responsible for administering patents, trade marks, designs and Plant Breeder's Rights.
IPRs – Intellectual Property Rights
IVF – In Vitro Fertilisation
NDA – Non Disclosure Agreement
NGO – Non Governmental Organisation
NRDC – National Research Development Corporation (predecessor of CSIRO)
PBR – Plant Breeder's Right
PCT – Patent Cooperation Treaty
PSA – Person Skilled in the Art
PV – Plant Variety
R&D – Research and Development
RAM – Random Access Memory
SME – Small and Medium Enterprise

TMA – Trade Marks Act 1995 (Cth)
TPA – Trade Practices Act 1974 (Cth)
TPC – Trade Practices Commission (forerunner of the ACCC)
TRIPS – Trade Related Intellectual Property rights
UPOV – (International) Union for the Protection of New Varieties of Plants
USFTA – United States–Australia Free Trade Agreement
VDU – Visual Display Unit
WIPO – World Intellectual Property Organization
WTO – World Trade Organization

Table of statutes

Statute of Monopolies 1609 (UK)   73, 72, 75, 93
Designs Act 1906 (Cth)   112, 128, 134, 150, 166, 167, 188
Copyright Act 1911 (UK)   169
Patents Act 1949 (UK)   76
Registered Designs Act 1949 (UK)   149, 151
Copyright Act 1962 (NZ)   120
Copyright Act 1968 (Cth)   23, 26, 39, 111, 115, 116, 117, 121, 124, 134, 139, 140, 150, 162, 163, 164, 165, 167, 168, 178
Trade Practices Act 1974 (Cth)   21, 178
Patents Act 1977 (UK)   76
Semiconductor Chip Protection Act 1984 (US)   189
Copyright, Designs & Patents Act 1988 (UK)   149
Circuit Layouts Act 1989 (Cth)   23, 140, 174, 178, 188, 189, 191, 199
Copyright Amendment Act 1989 (Cth)   166
Therapeutic Goods Act 1989 (Cth)   48
Patents Act 1990 (Cth)   23, 38, 48, 63, 64, 70, 90, 107, 134, 150
Plant Breeder's Rights Act 1994 (Cth)   23, 174, 193, 195–200
Trade Marks Act 1994 (Cth)   203
Trade Marks Act 1995 (Cth)   23, 105, 133, 201
Copyright Amendment (Computer Programs) Act 1999 (Cth)   184, 191
Copyright Amendment (Digital Agenda) Act 2000 (Cth)   179, 184
Patents Amendment (Innovation Patents) Act 2000 (Cth)   90
Patents Amendment Act 2001 (Cth)   134
Prohibition of Human Cloning Act 2002 (Cth)   76
Designs Act 2003 (Cth)   23, 112, 116, 128, 133, 134, 135, 140, 161, 163, 189

Table of cases

Accounting Systems 2000 (Developments) Pty Ltd v CCH Australia Ltd (1993)   126, 180
Admar Computers Pty Ltd v Ezy Systems Pty Ltd (1997)   181
Allen John Wilson v Hollywood Toys (Australia) Pty Ltd (1993)   157
Allen Manufacturing Company Ltd v McCallum Co Ltd [2001]   137
Altoweb, Inc [2002]   141
American Cyanamid Co v Alcoa of Australia Ltd (1993)   41
Anaesthetic Supplies Pty Ltd v Rescare Ltd (1994)   73, 107
Apple Computer Inc v Computer Edge Pty Ltd (1984)   176, 179
Apple Computer Inc v Design Registry (2001)   141
Arrow Pharmaceuticals Ltd v Merck & Co, Inc [2004]   86, 105
Aus Fence Hire Pty Ltd v Thomas [2004]   91
Australian Broadcasting Corporation v Lenah Game Meats Pty Ltd [2001]   34, 53
Australian Video Retailers Association Ltd v Warner Home Video Pty Ltd [2001]   185
Autodesk Inc v Dyason [No 2] (1993)   125, 179, 180, 181, 182
Azuko Pty Ltd v Old Digger Pty Ltd (2001)   90, 103

Baygol Pty Ltd v Foamex Polystyrene Pty Ltd [2005]   103
Bristol-Myers Squibb Co v F H Faulding & Co Ltd [2000]   75, 76, 108
British Leyland Motor Corporation Ltd v Armstrong Patents Co Ltd [1986]   161, 162
British Reinforced Concrete Co v Lind (1917)   98

Canon v Green Cartridge [1997]   161
Cantor Fitzgerald International v Tradition (UK) Ltd [2000]   180, 181
Catnic Components Ltd v Hill & Smith Ltd (1982)   101, 102
CCOM Pty Ltd v Jiejing Pty Ltd (1994)   74, 88, 186
Centronics Systems Pty Ltd v Nintendo Co Ltd (1992)   189
Christopher Russel John Hansly (1988)   167
Coca-Cola Co (1986)   204
Coco v AN Clark (Engineers) Ltd [1969]   31, 46
Compagnie Industrielle de Precontrainte et D'Equipment des Constructions SA v First Melbourne Securities Pty Ltd [1999]   124, 125, 128
Comshare Incorporated Applications (1991)   141
Concrete Ltd's Application (1939)   167
Conrol Pty Ltd v Meco McCallum Pty Ltd & Anor (1996)   131, 137
Coogi Australia Pty Ltd v Hysport International Pty Ltd & Ors [1998]   125, 127, 169, 170, 171, 179
Cultivaust Pty Ltd v Grain Pool Pty Ltd [2005]   197

TABLE OF CASES

D Sebel & Co Ltd v National Art Metal Co Pty Ltd (1965)   144
Darwin Fibreglass Pty Ltd v Kruhse Enterprises Pty Ltd [1998]   120, 168
Data Access Corp v Powerflex Services Pty Ltd [1999]   176, 180, 181, 182, 183, 184, 187
Datadot Technology Ltd v Alpha Microtech Pty Ltd [2003]   91
Diamond v Chakrabarty (1980)   77
Doric Products Pty Ltd v Lockwood Security Products Pty Ltd (2001)   103

Eagle Homes Pty Ltd v Austec Homes Pty Ltd (1999)   124, 125, 128
Eastland Technology Australia Pty Ltd v Whisson [2005]   99
Electrolux Ltd v Hudson [1977]   99

Faccenda Chicken v Fowler [1987]   56
Ferrero's Design Application (1978)   137
Fine Industrial Commodities Ltd v Powling (1954)   98, 99
Firmagroup Australia Pty Ltd v Byrne & Davidson Doors (Vic) Pty Ltd (1987)   114, 138, 153–154, 156
Fisher & Paybel Healthcare Pty Ltd v Avion Engineering Pty Ltd (1992)   113
Foggin v Lacey [2003]   150, 151, 155
Fractionated Cane Technology Ltd v Ruiz-Avila (1988)   45
Franchi v Franchi (1967)   35
Frank Winstone (Merchants) Ltd v Plix Products Ltd (1983–1985)   122
Franklin v Giddins [1978]   34, 45

G Ricordi & Co (London) Ltd v Clayton & Waller Ltd [1928–1935]   125
Galaxy Electronics Pty Ltd v Sega Enterprises Ltd (1997)   185
Grain Pool of WA v The Commonwealth [2000]   193
Grant v Commissioner of Patents [2005]   73
Greater Glasgow Health Board's Application [1996]   98
Greenfield Products Pty Ltd v Rover-Scott Bonnar Ltd (1990)   120, 121
Griffin v Isaacs (1938)   91
Grosse [2003]   53
Grove Hill Pty Ltd v Great Western Corporation Pty Ltd [2002]   83, 88

Harris' Patent [1985]   98
Harvard College v Canada (Commissioner of Patents) [2002]   200
Herbert Morris Ltd v Saxelby [1916]   58
Hosakawa Micron Pty Ltd v Michael Fortune (1991)   166

Ibcos Computers Ltd v Barclays Mercantile Highland Finance Ltd (1994)   181
Improver Corporation v Remington Consumer Products Ltd [1990]   102, 103
Independent Management Resources v Brown (1987)   41, 42
Interlego AG v Croner Trading Pty Ltd (1992)   120, 161, 163, 166
International Business Machines v Smith, Commissioner of Patents (1992)   79, 176, 186

Kenman Kandy Australia Pty Ltd v The Registrar of Trade Marks [2001]   202
Kenman Kandy Australia Pty Ltd v The Registrar of Trade Marks [2002]   202, 203
Kevlacat Pty Ltd v Trailcraft Marine Pty Ltd (1987)   165

TABLE OF CASES   xvii

Kipling v Genatosan Ltd [1917–1923]   125
Kirin-Amgen Inc v Hoechst Marion Roussel Ltd [2004]   100, 101, 102, 103
KK Suwa Seikosha's Design Application (1982)   141
Koninklijke Philips Electronics NV v Remington Products Australia Pty Ltd [2000]
  114, 202, 203, 204
Kwan et al v The Queensland Corrective Services Commission [1994]   97

L.B. (Plastics) Ltd v Swish Products Ltd (1979)   120, 122, 123, 124
Lincoln Industries Ltd v Wham-O Manufacturing Co (1984)   120
Lockwood Security Products Pty Ltd v Australian Lock Company Pty Ltd [2005]
  137, 138, 150
Lockwood Security Products Pty Ltd v Doric Products Pty Ltd [2004]   88
Luminis Pty Ltd & Fertilitescentrum AB (2004)   76–77

Macrae Knitting Mills Ltd v Lowes Ltd (1936)   153
Maggbury Pty Ltd v Hafele Australia Pty Ltd [2001]   44, 59
Mainbridge Industries Pty Ltd v Gordon Whitewood (1984)   127
Malleys Ltd v J.W. Tomlin Pty Ltd (1961)   151, 152, 154
Mars UK Ltd v Teknowledge Ltd [2000]   35
Marsden v The Saville Street Foundry and Engineering Co Ltd (1878)   93
Masport Ltd v Bartlem Pty Ltd [2004]   91
Minnesota Mining and Manufacturing Co v Beiersdorf (1980)   72
Moorgate Tobacco Ltd v Philip Morris Ltd (1984)   33
Muscat v Le [2003]   139, 169, 172

N V Philips Gloeilampenfabrieken v Mirabella International Pty Ltd (1995)   72, 86,
  176, 186, 187
National Research Development Corporation v Commissioner of Patents (1959)
  69, 71, 177, 186, 187
Nesbit Evans Group Australia Pty Ltd v Impro Ltd (1997)   103
Neurizon Pty Ltd v Jupiters Ltd (2004)   103
Nintendo Ltd v Centronics Systems Pty Ltd (1994)   191
Norbrook Laboratories Ltd v Bomac Laboratories Ltd [2004]   41, 46
Nordenfelt v Maxim Nordenfelt Guns & Ammunition Co Ltd [1894]   58

O'Brien v Komesaroff (1982)   41

Peter Szabo and Associates Pty Ltd [2005]   73
Pharmacia Italia SPA v Mayne Pharma [2005]   104
PhotoCure ASA v Queen's University at Kingston [2005]   103
Plix Products Ltd v Frank M Winstone (Merchants) Ltd (1983–1985)   122, 124, 127
Polyaire Pty Ltd v K-Aire Pty Ltd [2003] [2005]   138, 152, 153
Populin v H. B. Nominees Pty Ltd (1982)   101, 103
Printers and Finishers Ltd v Holloway [1965]   56

RL Crain v Ashton [1950]   36
Rolls Royce Ltd's Application (1963)   76
Root Quality Pty Ltd v Root Control Technologies Pty Ltd (2000)   102–103
Rufus Riddlesbarger's Application (1935)   76

xviii   TABLE OF CASES

Seager v Copydex [1967]   47
Secton Pty Ltd v Delawood Pty Ltd (1991)   39
Sega Enterprises Ltd v Galaxy Electronics Pty Ltd (1996)   184
Sheldon v Metrokane [2004]   169, 171
SKF Laboratories (Aust) Ltd v Registrar of Trade Markes (1967)   201
Smith Kline and French Laboratories v Secretary, Department of Community Services and Health (1990)   33
Smith Kline and French Laboratories v Secretary, Department of Community Services and Health (1991)   47
Solar Thomson Engineering Co Ltd v Barton [1977]   161
Spencer Industries Pty Ltd v Anthony Collins and B&J Manufacturing Company [2002]   98
Stack v Davies Shephard [2001]   93, 94
Stephen John Grant [2004]   84
Stevens v Kabushiki Kaisha Sony Computer Entertainment [2005]   185
Sullivan v Sclanders [2000]   34
Sun World International Inc (Formerly Sun World Inc) v Registrar, Plant Breeder's Rights [1998]   195–196
SW Hart Co Pty Ltd v Edwards Hot Water Systems (1985)   118, 122, 125–6, 127
Swarbrick v Burge [2003]   120
Sydney Cellulose Pty Ltd v Ceil Comfort Home Insulation Pty Ltd (2001)   103

Talbot v General Television Corporation Pty Ltd (1980)   38
Tamawood Limited v Henley Arch Pty Ltd [2004]   125, 126, 182
Tefex Pty Ltd v Bowler (1981)   168
Terrapin Ltd v Builders' Supply Co (Hayes) Ltd (1967)   37, 50
The Antaios [1985]   101
Thomas Marshall v Guinle [1978]   36
Triplex Safety Glass Co Ltd v Scorah [1938]   57, 98
Tu v Pakway Australia Pty Ltd [2004]   156
Turbo Tek Enterprises Inc v Sperling Enterprises Pty Ltd (1989)   138, 154, 155

United Indigo Chemical Company Ltd v Robinson [1931]   56

Victoria University of Technology v Wilson [2004]   97–98

Wanem Pty Ltd v John Tekiela (1990)   152
Welcome Real-Time SA v Catuity Inc (2001)   74, 79
Wham-O Manufacturing Co v Lincoln Industries Ltd [1984]   119, 120
Whang (2004)   76, 77
Wheatley's Patent Application (1984)   90
Wheatley v Drillsafe Ltd [2001]   102
Worthington Pumping Engine Co v Moore (1902)   98
Wright v Gasweld Pty Ltd (1991)   56, 58

1

Introduction

[This chapter] This chapter concerns the relationship between intellectual property (IP) law and innovation in technology and product design in general. Further chapters return to this topic but within the specific confines of particular legal regimes, such as patents, designs or copyright. A major premise underlying this book is that innovation and imitation are predictable competitive behaviours in a market economy. The choice between the two strategies, in the absence of rule constraints, seems to favour imitation: innovation is uncertain, requires diversion of scarce resources from other activities, and risks immediate subversion by competitive imitation. Imitators on the other hand tread a known path, avoid all the risk and expense of innovation, and can enjoy the full benefit of their natural advantages. Nonetheless, to innovate is a natural ambition, and non-legal strategies allow innovators to capture greater returns from innovation than imitators. Naturally, even though we speak of imitation and innovation as alternatives, they are often closely intertwined processes: firms innovate but also imitate, or imitate but also innovate, and the competitive process may not be accurately identified as entirely one or the other.

[Law, innovation and imitation] Certain parts of intellectual property law act to recast the parameters within which imitation/innovation decisions are made. These rules constrain imitation as a competitive conduct. The central argument justifying this normative interference is that greater social welfare results where the 'natural' balance between imitation and innovation is disturbed to favour the latter. The harm flowing from lessening competition-by-imitation is said to be outweighed by the advantage flowing from more innovation. It is in this context that the relationship between intellectual property and competition law must be seen: the rules of intellectual property construct a framework of permitted restraints on competition; naturally, competition law cannot therefore operate with its normal force to destroy these restraints, whether genuinely monopolistic or not. Its normal operation may have to be modified where uses of intellectual property are concerned.

[Alternative approaches to intellectual property] This innovation/imitation framework is far from the only prism through which intellectual property law can be viewed. Property theory, the economics of knowledge and information, communications theory, or philosophical (for instance Lockean) approaches are all well established in the literature. But a central focus on innovation/imitation as competitive conduct in industry is peculiarly apt for this book, concerned as it is with intellectual property laws in the realm of industrial production, rather than of artistic expression or communication *per se* (not that these are separated by an unbridgeable chasm). While it provides a macro-framework for analysis of law and policy in this area, it also comfortably accommodates the micro-level of individual, competitive decision-making which is the bread and butter of industry in a knowledge economy.

1 Intellectual property law and innovation

Innovation, competition and intellectual property rights

[Curiosity and the search for knowledge about the human condition] Knowledge accumulation, flowing from curiosity and the inherent need to understand the human condition, occurs naturally; only its direction and extent vary with time and place. Knowledge does not necessarily have a scientific basis, it may be religious or mythological; it may be widespread within a community, or jealously guarded by an elite; it may be received or discovered, sacrosanct or open to question. Cultural and religious norms and attitudes will determine the rate and direction of *new* knowledge accumulation. Societal acceptance of scientific method as a valid source of knowledge results in the accumulation of a body of knowledge which is open to free and general testing and debate, is vindicated by predominant acceptance, and is constantly growing and evolving.

[Intellectual property and our belief in progress] One common factor in industrialised nations with a heritage of such free scientific inquiry *and* a relatively long history of intellectual property law is the concept of progress. Belief in progress rejects a world view which prioritises stability and stresses the preordained nature of human living conditions; rather, it is premised on humans' ability to modify them. Knowledge is not simply accumulated for its own sake, but with a view to applying it to practical ends: not only for the sake of *explanation* but also for the sake of *application*. In this environment innovation not only results from doing and improving, but from conceptual advances: inventions, innovations, new products are conceived *from* or *in* theory rather than arrived at by trial and error in-the-doing. Rule structures such as those of intellectual property law that reduce risk for actors engaged in applying scientific knowledge to practical ends are perfectly attuned to a *progressivist* world view.

[The innovation dynamic] Belief in progress also results in a closely integrated mutual dynamic, as innovation (the application of knowledge to new products and processes) feeds the theoretical knowledge base and vice versa. Practical applications also spawn the development of tools that permit more accurate observation and collection of scientific data thus further accelerating accumulation of knowledge. Applied technologies also require further compatible technologies to function efficiently. The injection of scientific knowledge and processes into practical innovation thus undermines predictability, accelerates substitution and obsolescence, and therefore both accentuates risk and drives up innovation costs.

[How to manage innovation risk] Natural risk-aversion militates against investing in innovation. But various mechanisms help to manage risk and mitigate its effects. One is to regulate innovation by some mechanism of state planning, thus coordinating all research and development and reducing the risk of wastage by subversion and by duplication. Whatever innovations are produced can then be shared freely by all economic actors. But the planning and *a priori* determination of resource allocation from above for innovation also engenders costs; in particular, wastage caused by the difficulty of predicting consumer choice and demand in relation to products and technologies that are by definition unknown. It is also inherently difficult to 'plan' innovation, since serendipity, cross-fertilisation, imagination, etc are activities that can only be projected or planned with limited efficiency.

[Open markets and consumer choices] An alternative is to subject innovation decisions and risk management to market mechanisms: to encourage the development of alternative products and technologies by multiple independent and uncoordinated actors, and to subject those alternatives to *ex post* assessment by consumer choices, rather than an *a priori* determination. Markets thus become a mechanism determining the rate and direction of innovation; not necessarily the *only* such mechanism, but at the very least an alternative to centralised planning of innovation. Intellectual property – the private ownership and control of knowledge – is then the institutional mechanism which enables this process of market determination of innovation investment.

[The disadvantages of markets for innovations] Creating this institutional mechanism – determining ownership, scope and interaction of various exclusive or monopolistic (property) rights – comes at a cost to the economy and the community. It is neither cheap nor easy to demarcate knowledge, to erect and police *barriers* between knowledge 'items'. Furthermore, competition results in duplication – ie resources are expended on innovation in competitive conditions which militate against the sharing of information. Where research and development is conducted in secret, firms may continue to invest in innovation that a competitor's unpredicted introduction of a substitute product renders redundant. Others, of whose progress an actor is ignorant, may win the race to obtain exclusive rights. The law may again be able to mitigate this duplication effect of competitive innovation, but only to a limited extent. Legal rights will never be able to perfectly match the level of monopolisation of knowledge an individual actor may desire.

[Innovation as an unavoidable risk] In conditions of (partial) secrecy, ie where a firm has imperfect knowledge of competitors' innovative activity, and of partial legal protection, the innovation dynamic in markets takes on a different quality. The question is rather how to manage innovation, rather than whether to engage in it at all. Managing the risk of competitors innovating will inevitably require *some* innovation strategy on the part of every firm, even if only to maximise the opportunities to imitate (since it is difficult to imitate in the absence of an internal knowledge base). Technological and product innovation then merely takes its place amongst other forms of strategic behaviour that are the bread and butter of competitive conduct: innovation and change on organisational, marketing, advertising, legal, financial or other levels. In this sense innovation is a risk-management strategy attuned to the competitive environment as a whole.

[Risk reduction] Reliance on intellectual property rights (IPRs) helps to reduce risk in a competitive market, by allowing firms to capture higher returns from investment in innovation, and denying its advantages to others. Higher returns can also be captured by market behaviour and managerial strategies, of course, and certain innovation activity would remain attractive in the absence of intellectual property law; private investment in innovation would be modified rather than annihilated by abolishing IPRs. Secrecy, market power, lead time, network effects and complexity are all factors that will reduce or delay imitation. Risk can also be reduced by building non-product-specific *goodwill*. Consumer choices can be influenced or manipulated to favour *whatever* product or technology a firm chooses to introduce. The law promotes this risk-reduction strategy by protecting reputation, which encourages consistency and predictability in product innovation: if consumers come to trust a certain firm's *brand* then they are more likely to favour that firm's every new product. To some extent a firm can absorb the risk of constant product innovations by depending on the continuity of its underlying reputation; at the same time, it can leverage consumer perception of recurrent innovations into a continuous reputation for technological leadership.

[R&D and interdependence] One result of the transfer of knowledge from the public to the private domain in a property-based innovation system is increased fragmentation. Competitors are not able to possess all required knowledge resources, or access them from a common pool. Knowledge is fenced in, requiring an exchange mechanism to access it, either based on barter or valuable consideration. The need for access to fragmented and dispersed knowledge results in interdependence which in turn encourages cooperation between firms. This mitigates the duplication-of-research problem, and also the fact that private investment tends to focus on downstream innovation, avoiding upstream, theoretical, blue-sky research, where risk and delay to market are too great. This can be addressed by public funding for such research, but *some* level of coordination and cooperation between firms in upstream research is also appropriate. Increasing product complexity also necessitates a level of cooperation between disparate rights holders at the downstream, commercialisation level. Legal structures peculiar to IP support such cooperation: for example, flexible ownership rules (for instance, provision for joint ownership of intellectual property, and for ownership limited in time and space), assignments and above all licensing. But in this context the law must address the balance between collaboration and monopolisation: while it may be in the public interest that private actors, or public and private actors collaborate at some stage of research, this risks destroying the very market mechanisms that private knowledge ownership intends to support. Collaboration in upstream research cannot be allowed to contaminate competition in downstream product markets, and must not erect unacceptable barriers to entry for actors outside the collaborative cartel; in other words, a finely calibrated system of rules and rights is required.

[Innovation and scarcity of resources] Innovation is not just a matter of strategic choice for individual actors. In conditions of growing scarcity of resources in consumption-oriented societies, efficiency gains from innovation may be a *necessity*. From this perspective, efficiency-enhancing innovation equals increased output from otherwise steady or decreasing inputs of capital, natural resources, energy and labour. Therefore in circumstances of growing scarcity of some inputs, measures that encourage private R&D expenditure, or conversely reduce the risks of innovation in the private sector may be called for. However, here a private property rights-based innovation mechanism faces a dilemma because competitive innovation itself – as opposed to its products – is, for various reasons, wasteful. One significant reason is duplication in the race for property rights; another is the inherent unpredictability of the innovation exercise, resulting in wasted investment in dead-end trajectories; and yet another is secrecy, which prevents firms from adequately estimating risk flowing from substitute products or technologies at the time of investment. Therefore although a proprietary system may result in a better approximation between consumer needs and innovation investment, a system that over-incentivises investment in innovation may be counterproductive in terms of overall economic efficiency. Again a finely calibrated system of rules, rights and incentives is required.

[Competition, innovation and the calibration of rights] Intellectual property law subjects imitation and knowledge transfer to legal restraints, thus modifying the rate and direction of innovation. It amends the balance between factors that encourage and factors that discourage investment in innovation. There can be little doubt that IPRs enable and accelerate a competitive dynamic, Schumpeter's 'gale of creative destruction': that is, competition with innovation and substitution at its core. On the downside, IPRs potentially *reduce static efficiency*, in that products are made available at higher than marginal cost because they are protected from competition-by-imitation. But on the upside they potentially *increase dynamic efficiency*: more substitute products are introduced, enhancing consumer choice. IPRs do form barriers to market entry, certainly if the market is conceived of as that for the product protected by IPRs (eg a certain copyrighted song) rather than a more broadly defined product category (eg all songs).

But whether this barrier has a benign economic effect crucially depends on the *innovation threshold*, ie the novelty of the object of IP protection. If barriers to entry are erected against suppliers of *known* products, prices will rise without the benefit of greater choice. Conversely, if a proper novelty requirement is instituted and policed then barriers to entry are apt to encourage the creation and introduction of new products. Crucial also is the *scope of rights*: earlier entrants' IPRs that are too broad will prevent new players from entering markets. But new entrants' IPRs can subvert existing actors' dominance only if they themselves are sufficiently broad, so a fine balance is required.

The two central characteristics of statutory IPRs, the *innovation threshold* and the *scope of protection*, lie at the heart of the continuous development of intellectual property law. Existing rules are constantly reinterpreted by decision-makers and frequently revisited by policy-makers. Certainty appears to be an elusive goal, as empirical evidence about the IPR/innovation relationship tends to be inconclusive and the technological future unpredictable.

IPRs and knowledge diffusion

[IPRs and diffusion of knowledge] Other than interfering with the 'natural' balance between innovation and imitation, IPRs also modify knowledge flows. The pursuit of knowledge is of course valued for its own sake, but knowledge can also be turned to account. Potential applications increase with the growth in knowledge, and with its wider availability (ie with its 'diffusion'). But in a competitive market individual actors seek to deny access to knowledge – so stymieing diffusion. They can achieve this in *practical* ways, mainly by hiding it, but this interferes with practical applications. IPRs offer a way out of this dilemma, by *prohibiting* some, but not all further uses of the information disclosed in the course of commercialising practical applications. Generally IPRs make a distinction between accessing and learning knowledge, which competitors can legitimately do, and putting such knowledge to certain directly competitive uses, which, for a limited term, is prohibited. This is often a difficult line to draw, and one that is much fought over in intellectual property law.

[Secrecy] In the absence of IPRs, there is a disincentive to invest in creating knowledge whose practical application results in disclosure. Even if knowledge can be kept secret *and* exploited (for instance a novel production process hidden in a factory), there still may be a disincentive to invest if there is a significant risk of independent invention by others. By contrast, in the absence of a significant risk of independent invention, if the innovator *can* exploit knowledge while retaining secrecy it is sensible to do so. But even though secrecy may be a practicable strategy for an individual actor, it is not necessarily beneficial to the innovation effort as a whole.

Secret knowledge is not diffused so others cannot benefit or learn from it. The cumulative and interconnected evolution of knowledge is disturbed by secrecy: knowledge generation does not occur in a vacuum but depends on access to other knowledge, as stepping stones, for serendipitous connection, for improvements, etc. Thus there is good reason to replace the vicious dynamic of secrecy with a benevolent dynamic of publicity, and IPRs attempt to achieve this in two ways: by linking exclusive rights to disclosure; and giving nuanced legal protection to trade secrets. In the patent system, legal restraints on imitation depend on an 'enabling disclosure', and the scope of a patentee's monopoly is strictly limited leaving many derivative uses free. And although the law does protect secrets, it does so only to a limited extent: whereas breaches of confidence are actionable, reverse engineering (eg taking apart a product) of secret information is not.

[Diffusion of tacit knowledge] In the presence of IPRs, knowledge is partly diffused by free transfer from public domain sources, and partly by proprietary exchanges, primarily on the basis of assignments and licences. Nonetheless some knowledge is not amenable to either method of diffusion, either because it is difficult to express precisely – is too costly to codify and record – or because it is too subtle to be transferred in a proprietary or 'dehumanised' form. Thus a lot of knowledge is instead diffused as tacit knowledge in the mind of people migrating between firms, countries, etc. Here also the law, through trade secrets and contract principles, plays a role by encouraging knowledgeable individuals to disclose and exploit their 'tacit' knowledge – thus aiding diffusion – but maintaining firms' rights over 'true' trade secrets. In particular, the law encourages individuals to share their knowledge with any firm they work for. It discourages broad claims by previous employers over knowledge that is not sufficiently itemised nor strictly a trade secret, and views with suspicion restraints of trade or non-competition clauses that limit the rights of employees to transfer to other firms with all their knowledge and experience.

[The disclosure dilemma] Publicity (for instance through a patent register) concerning the knowledge inventories of individual firms also benefits cooperation and coordination of research efforts. In an era where research is expensive and complex, and may bring together disparate areas of science or technology in highly complex systems, this is very significant. Secrecy, on the other hand, hampers coordination of research effort and results in unnecessary duplication. Unfortunately, publicising knowledge stocks presents something of a dilemma: it is often impossible to disclose knowledge without potentially destroying its commercial value. Thus it makes sense to encourage the sharing of knowledge by recognising and enforcing by law the conditions surrounding its disclosure imposed by the confidor. Thus the two legal mechanisms, the law of trade secrets which enables conditional disclosure, and the law of patents, which requires public disclosure in return for exclusive rights, encourage publicity and exchange of information about private knowledge inventories, and thus coordination and cooperation of innovation effort. This will also enhance the introduction of complex products: knowledge of complementary technologies encourages complexity and sophistication.

[The incentive to publish] In other words, reliance on secrecy as a practical method of appropriating the advantages flowing from private investment in innovation has significant drawbacks: it skews private R&D investment towards technologies that can indeed be kept secret (eg process development rather than product development); and it encourages duplication and more generally reduces coordination of research strategies. Secretive innovators send no signals to competitors indicating research results obtained or directions under consideration. By contrast, publicity concerning knowledge inventories will limit duplication of research and enhance coordination between diverse actors interested in similar fields – so some incentive or legal guarantee attaching to disclosure may be beneficial, as addressed above. However, a key difficulty lies in the size and nature of the incentive to disclose hitherto secret knowledge. In the context of trade secrets law this incentive is infinitely variable, simply a matter for the parties to negotiate. But in relation to patent disclosures a universal standard must be devised. Various options are available: it may be advantageous to encourage disclosure *early* in the innovation cycle, when researchers first recognise *potential* practical uses of new knowledge, but specific technical applications have not been accurately described. However, then the scope of exclusive rights would be correspondingly broad; maybe *too* broad, as it may be beyond the capacity of the patentee to effectively coordinate the downstream development of multifarious applications and improvements. The patent may become a dead hand and chill independent development. If disclosure *later* in the innovation cycle (in relation to some concrete application of knowledge) is encouraged then the monopoly on offer as an incentive will be narrower and less of a potential obnoxious constraint on downstream development. However, duplication and lack of coordination of research effort will be more prevalent, since the signal to desist will only be received at a later date. Rent-dissipation theory attempts to reconcile all these factors. The law must devise a balance between the two, and patents law tends more towards the latter of the two options, by requiring detailed description of a concrete application with clear and present utility.

[Public and private sectors] As pointed out above, public funding and direction can compensate for the natural reluctance of private actors to invest in R&D in the absence of legal protection. But such funding has a significant role even where proprietary rights over knowledge do exist. Public funding makes sense where returns from research are too distant or uncertain to attract private investment (ie for 'blue-sky' or basic research). The short-term exigencies of business tend to discourage investment in highly speculative research, but nonetheless such research often turns out to be highly productive. Public funding also makes sense in areas of research with high need, but low returns: for instance, in relation to so-called 'orphan drugs' (rare diseases with high mortality rates). But at a more fundamental level, given its speculativeness, its intricacy, its multifaceted nature, and its widely dispersed knowledge base, scientific research must almost inevitably be conducted in the public sphere. The production and distribution of science through research and education can realistically only be undertaken on a non-proprietary basis, ie organised around teaching, publication and peer review.

But where public and private spheres intersect, conflicts tend to develop requiring modulating rules. Various legal mechanisms come into play here. Firstly, there are those that set limits on appropriation, ie which delineate potential private rights and thus define the public domain. Secondly, there are those that formally regulate cooperation between public and private actors, and that regulate the transition of knowledge from the public to the private sphere. Contractual mechanisms such as joint ventures, spin-offs, CRCs, etc play a role in this area, but so also do the legal rules that determine conflicts over ownership of knowledge: between those who privately fund public research and the state; between researchers and institutions, etc. This area has evolved considerably in recent times, mainly because of increased integration and cooperation between public entities and private actors. New funding models for public institutions have encouraged appropriation at the institutional level, and in conjunction with commercial actors. The impetus for these changes has been partly fiscal, and partly policy driven: a perception exists that closer integration has better results in terms of commercialisation.

[The law's considerable impact on the innovation matrix] Depending on the priorities and value system of any given society a certain mix will develop between *a priori* bureaucratic decision-making and *ex post* market-based determination of new knowledge production. It is this 'matrix' that makes up the core of the innovation system. The law is one of the factors that influence the shape of the matrix, and that in many different ways. For instance, the exact scope of exclusive rights or the threshold requirements for their subsistence will co-determine the dividing line between public and private innovation resource allocation. The law also plays a crucial role in determining the balance between the secretive and the public stages of research and development, encouraging competitors to desist from duplicative research or seek a mutually satisfactory accommodation at certain junctures. The law will also be influential in determining the scale of the organisation of innovation. Anti-trust or competition law rules determine how far cooperation in R&D can go. Cooperation must be allowed to enable complex technologies to evolve and the stock of proprietary knowledge to be used efficiently; but on the other hand, research-based cartels must not result in counterproductive barriers to competition.

Whether innovation occurs inter- or intra-firm will also be determined in part by legal rules; in particular, those rules that determine the rights of employees over their knowledge and ideas, both in terms of ownership of what is legally construed as an individual invention, and in relation to trade secrets. These rules have an effect on the organisational scale and autonomy of innovation efforts: the spin-off, start-up, specialised R&D firm-model vs the integrated model of innovation, where firms are not specialised in innovation but integrate the whole process from conception through development to actual marketing. Furthermore, as diffusion of technology and of innovation is a good, it makes sense to encourage investment in development, refinement and market-responsive adaptation of known technologies. The law will co-determine who undertakes these adaptations of technology to consumer demand: the original innovator or second comers. Thus the law will influence the innovation matrix in this sense as well.

[Unfair competition torts as a regulatory tool] If imitation is viewed as a form of competition which must be regulated in the public interest, then rather than develop a complex constellation of disparate legal responses, or proprietary rights, it may seem desirable to integrate the policing of imitation within the confines of a single legal standard of wide application, such as a tort of 'unfair competition'. Such a tort exists in one form or another in numerous jurisdictions, although not as such in Australian law. There is some conceptual difficulty with this approach if one accepts that imitation is not inherently unfair, but a normal and benign incident of competition. If such is the case, then when does imitation become so unfair that it should be restrained?

Despite greater flexibility, the inherent disadvantages of this kind of approach are twofold. The first is that it does not offer any great transactional advantages – in the absence of *a priori* established, delineated and recognised proprietary rights there is nothing around which to construct knowledge transactions with any certainty. The second is uncertainty resulting from its broad remit and vague standard ('unfairness'). Uncertainty in innovation decisions is exactly what the law might seek to *reduce*. In terms of innovation decisions, there is a definite advantage in clarity and certainty concerning what imitations or derivations will be allowed and what not. Furthermore, such an action also results in unpredictable and potentially major costs flowing from *ex post* resolution of conflicts concerning actionable vs permissible imitation. It may therefore be more attractive to adopt a system which will increase the *a priori* certainty as to what imitations will be allowed and what not, by creating clear and universal rules about object (the nature and scope of the innovation protected) and rights (what is an actionable innovation). But that will only be possible through some form of *a priori* and admittedly costly bureaucratic intervention. This leads us naturally in the direction of property rights as an alternative which may offer greater certainty and a universal transactional structure. Such a property approach lies at the other end of the legal spectrum from an unfair competition approach.

Property theory

[*A priori* determination] The alternative to a broad action for unfair competition is a system of defined rights in knowledge 'units' itemised on the basis of predetermined parameters. This model has come to be known as a system of 'intellectual property' rights (IPRs). Many and varied parameters could be tested prior to grant; for instance, the level of investment in development of the new knowledge, the social utility of an invention, its moral value, the extent to which exclusive rights are necessary to prevent imitation, etc. But such investigations would be time-consuming, expensive and often self-defeating, as the ultimate result would be an interventionist bureaucratic system that would withdraw innovation from market discipline. So a bureaucratic system must seek to balance certainty and cost, by limiting the extent of investigations surrounding the grant of IPRs. This contains the expense of administering the system, but drives up potential costs to the innovator by generating uncertainty and an increased incidence of demarcation disputes. What the innovator requires is a system that is value-neutral, quick, efficient and consistent.

[Demarcation of subject matter] Uniform standards must therefore be set at a level of generality and universality that allows relatively quick and easy testing. Critical to the efficient operation of any system of *ex ante* determination is that knowledge units are accurately itemised and catalogued, and that units of knowledge be sufficiently distinct to reduce demarcation disputes. If transaction costs are to be reduced it must be easy to identify and distinguish what one actor owns from the intellectual property of another, or from the public domain. Equally it makes no sense to grant exclusive rights over technologies that already exist – no incentive is required and no free-rider problem exists. So some test for distinguishing the relevant subject matter from existing knowledge must be devised: novelty, inventiveness, originality, distinctiveness, etc. Tests of this kind can be applied by comparison with public reference material (ie without dependence on information only available to the applicant).

However, in an era of knowledge fragmentation, rapid transformation and constant innovation, testing against even apparently straightforward standards is a fallible process. Testing can only limit and cannot exclude uncertainty about demarcation and validity of rights – validity cannot be guaranteed. Because of the fallibility of the testing process, it makes sense to allow competitors to intervene (by 'opposition', applications for revocation, counterclaims for invalidity, etc). The opposite – of having perfect procedures resulting in perfect grant – is practically speaking impossible; the cost of complete certainty would be exorbitant. It should not be forgotten that expenditure on acquiring property rights may be entirely wasted because the market is never interested in the innovation concerned. Costs of acquisition of property rights in multiple innovations may have to be absorbed by those few that generate a proper return.

[The property analogy] The term 'property' is used in this context to mean ownership of knowledge or information, by analogy with personal or real property. Although in truth this analogy is somewhat misleading, property theory is apposite because of its emphasis on a mechanism for cooperation and exchange based on *a priori* demarcation, certainty, utility and transaction cost mitigation. But knowledge does have different characteristics from physical things: it is an inexhaustible public good, in the sense that it can be transferred without loss to the transferor and can be infinitely replicated. In terms of physical property possession is 9/10ths of the law – in other words, physical control is the starting premise. Arguably the opposite applies to knowledge, as it is slippery, fuzzy and easily transferred; erecting a fence around a piece of land is much easier than around a unit of knowledge. In no dimensions are property rights ever truly absolute, but this is most true when it comes to ownership of knowledge or intangibles. Physical property does not lapse or revert to the public domain, whereas this is an almost invariable characteristic of *intellectual* property.

Furthermore, exclusive rights in knowledge are limited and closely circumscribed, partly again to limit transaction costs and avoid demarcation problems, and partly to accommodate beneficial flow-on or spill-over effects while still allowing knowledge to be turned to account. Physical ownership is much less finely tuned and subtly modulated than ownership of knowledge: because knowledge has such multiple and varied uses, it is possible to monopolise its exploitation in one way while allowing it to diffuse and serve a useful purpose to competitors in others.

[Transaction, organisation and the firm] Nonetheless, a system which accurately documents and delineates knowledge, prevents overlapping and demarcation disputes, and circumscribes exclusive rights delivers increased predictability. This permits planning and execution of innovation over time, moderating its inherent uncertainty. IPRs form a structured basis for collaboration in research, and for networks of knowledge exchange; but IPRs are also the mechanism around which the firm itself collects complementary resources to organise innovation. The structure and limits of property rights will affect the innovation models firms adopt. The firm can be seen as a collection of diverse property rights, and for the innovative firm a significant proportion of those rights will adhere to intangibles.

The nature of property rights in intangibles will thus affect the structure of the firm. For instance, the extent to which a firm integrates upstream and downstream research and development will be influenced by the scope of the rights in intangibles the law permits it to acquire; the extent to which it conducts rather than out-sources research will depend on the predictability of the validity of its rights; and the structure of its R&D efforts will be affected by the extent of legal control over employees' ideas. Property rights thus mitigate the risks inherent in innovation and structure organisation and investment in developing new knowledge. Predictable and stable rights encourage firms to acquire complementary resources to develop, organise and exploit knowledge.

[Abuse of property rights] Intellectual property rights may well be carefully modulated but they are nonetheless amenable to abuse. Competition law counteracts such abuses to some extent, although its application to IPRs is somewhat unresolved. Rights holders cannot be commanded to exploit their rights in any given way, or effectively prohibited from suppressing knowledge, although copyright, patents and design legislation provides for compulsory licences and public or 'Crown' use. Property rights can also be accumulated or amassed, so that the careful modulation of individual rights can be subverted by the acquisition of contiguous rights in many closely related units of knowledge (eg so-called 'patent portfolios').

How to deal with such accumulations is currently debated in the literature: *is* it a problem? and if so how can it be counteracted? or does it have organisational and transactional advantages for the firm which should not be disturbed – a new reality to which we must adjust? Property rights also render markets vulnerable to lobbying and capture – bureaucrats and politicians who ultimately construct and bestow such rights (rather than independent courts) will be the target of rent-seeking and self-serving behaviour by firms, which may distort the system. Having amassed property rights, firms may be motivated to divert resources away from genuine innovation to leveraging and manipulation of rights in their existing knowledge base. The system must be resistant to these types of influences, conserving conceptual and policy integrity while being flexible enough to respond to emerging trends in science, technology and innovation management.

Theory and structure of rights

[Structuring rights in knowledge: *ex post* vs *ex ante*] Adequately structuring proprietorial rights in knowledge is predicated on devising and implementing taxonomical rules, and then documenting, demarcating and classifying knowledge units accordingly. This task lies at the core of *ex ante* statutory IPRs, such as the patent, designs and registered trade mark systems; precision and certainty are essential but costly and difficult to achieve. It is also required in non-proprietary areas such as breach of confidence (trade secrets), but only *ex post*: the common law and equity equally predicate the grant of a legal remedy upon precise identification and documentation of relevant knowledge, but this need only be done at the time when a dispute actually needs to be resolved.

The debate concerning the cost and utility of *ex ante*, bureaucratic structuring and grant of property rights is well illustrated by recent reforms in patents and designs law. The cost of up-front examination is often a dead loss, because the rights granted in inventions and designs are in fact never exploited or never infringed. Taking this into account, laws were recently amended to introduce grant *without* prior substantive examination for designs and for innovation patents. However, enforcement is conditional upon examination; in other words, the costs of substantive examination can be deferred until the time when infringement threatens, which may in fact never come. The debate concerning such an approach centres on the trade-off between certainty (an unexamined patent is of uncertain value) and cost (but it costs little to issue it). An important factor in the equation is the unpredictable, indeterminate and often inchoate nature of knowledge-in-the-making: its precise application, relevance and utility are not perfectly known *ab initio* and may only become apparent over time.

[Property rights and the innovation process] A significant question is where along the path from theory to application to 'locate' property rights over knowledge? Should they attach to a theoretical concept or idea or only to its concrete and specific applications? The question is best illustrated by the patent scope issue, as already referred to above: should patents be awarded for discoveries (laws of physics, mathematics or biology) or only for precisely described practical inventions? Discoveries may be more readily documented and delineated, so awarding rights might be simple, cheap and clear. It might also provide a strong incentive for theoretical research, depending on the precise extent of the attached monopoly. But will the efficiency of the search for practical applications not suffer? The grantee would control a potentially very large, multifarious, divergent, literally 'unimaginable' sphere of applications. So large and multifarious in fact that the grantee can never coordinate and organise search, development and commercialisation effectively or efficiently.

Thus a possible gain in ease of documenting knowledge is countered by a loss of efficiency in the process of generating useful applications and actual products. Devising applications of theoretical knowledge requires the active engagement of many independent minds and resources from disparate areas of commercial and practical life, experience and activity. The 'owner' of *theoretical* knowledge is likely to become a mere rent-seeker, neither burdened by the risks and costs of product development and commercialisation, nor making a significant contribution to the efficient organisation of actual innovation. Furthermore, the potential size of the reward flowing from the grant of broad rights shifts investment into theoretical research to the detriment of resources available for the development and commercialisation of actual, useful practical applications. Taking into account also that an arguably effective, *academic* recognition and reward model already exists for the publication of speculative and theoretical research, it is not surprising that law makes revelation of some *concrete* application a principal condition of patent grant; on the other hand, it does not go so far as to attach rights only to products first made commercially available. The appropriate balance between secret development and public revelation is a closely related issue. The broader, more theoretical the knowledge or idea in which a property right can be obtained the earlier knowledge will be revealed publicly, since the grant of rights is unavoidably conditional upon the revelation of the subject matter concerned. If the early publication of knowledge is advantageous because it encourages rapid diffusion and adoption by others, then granting rights with broad scope in the earlier theoretical or conceptual stages of the development process makes sense. Again the main countervailing factors are the likely inefficiency of the downstream coordination of R&D and the distortion of investment because of the size of the 'prize'.

[The object of rights] If the object of rights is not a theoretical or purely conceptual advance, but some concrete application then is it to be circumscribed by reference to form or function or in some other way? Property rights must be relevant to the way the innovator conceptualises a breakthrough: where it lies in the *appearance* of a product, exclusive rights can be circumscribed by reference to some concrete *representation* (a drawing, photo or model). This is what is required for design registration. But where it lies in *function*, or utility of a product or process, the description and delineation of the 'object' of rights becomes more difficult. A representation of the appearance is inadequate: the shape of an aspirin is irrelevant to its therapeutic advantages. Functional utility is usually described, explained and claimed in *language* (in the broad sense), not graphically represented. Rights come to be constructed around words and formulae, which must be sufficiently precise without being overly constraining. Exclusive rights in an invention should not be readily set at nought by minor changes, so a specific example or 'embodiment' may too narrowly circumscribe the scope of entitlement. Settling appropriately balanced language is the essential task of a patent attorney. Although opting exclusively for form or function may often be highly artificial, IPR systems have come to be focussed around one or the other, with the option of cumulating rights. In Australian law, design rights give exclusive rights in appearance but not in function, but purely functional designs can be registered. On the other hand, patents give rights in function not appearance; but some products combining form and function can be registered as both or either.

[Monopoly vs anti-copying rights] A further critical issue concerning the structure of rights in intangibles relates to the owner's rights of action against independent creators. Should the law grant monopolistic rights, ie rights of action against a person who has arrived at the same result without ever *actually* copying? Should a genuine innovator who is not a 'free-rider' be deprived of the advantages of some product or process of their own devising just because, unbeknownst to them, another actor has earlier obtained a statutory right to prohibit them from doing so? The difficulty with monopoly rights is wastage – investment in development by third parties is wasted if another wins the race to obtain the right and then interdicts their exploitation by all comers. We saw above that this problem can be mitigated by making grant dependent on the early and sufficient publication of relevant information – the earlier in the innovation cycle this occurs, the sooner competitors will get the signal to desist from same-track research. Critically therefore, potential wastage is mitigated by the instigation of a central register or repository, which can be readily accessed by the public and in particular those embarked on similar research paths. The difficulty with the alternative – anti-copying rights, or independent invention as a defence – is that where the risk of independent invention by third parties is *high*, limiting exclusive rights to prohibiting copying reduces the incentive to invest in R&D. The prize or incentive will not be a monopoly, but coexistence in the market with an unknown number of independent inventors.

Theory, policy and reality

[Theory and practice, concept and detail] Conceptual analysis of the place and structure of IPRs in competitive markets, while it provides a *framework* for addressing specific legal issues, is rarely conclusive *per se*. Translating theoretical conclusions or policy precepts into detailed rules is not even a simple task; theoretical conclusions about policy direction do not necessarily provide sufficient guidance to this process. In practice, trade-offs between countervailing policy imperatives in the constantly mutating field of innovation and technology compel the law towards unimaginable rule-density and technicality. On the one hand, the law exists and develops in contests between disputing parties – its rationality is born not so much of theoretical thought as of careful examination of previous experiences, and adversarial argument. Its own continuous internal dynamics thus partly explain its present state. On the other hand, political influences govern its development through the interventions of bureaucracy, government and parliament, concerned as those institutions are with exercising political power, rather than pursuing theoretical consistency. This realisation must temper an inclination to discover consistent theoretical rationality in the law. But the law is not static, nor does it evolve in a closed cycle, and revisiting it from an innovation policy, competition and market theory perspective contributes to its dynamic evolution and interpretation. This chapter has focussed on imitation and competition as one way of approaching the relationship between innovation and IPRs; but this neither provides the only legitimate framework for analysis of the law nor directs its every aspect.

[Personality-based IPRs] One alternative is to adopt the focus on the personality-theory said to underpin IPRs in civil law jurisdictions. Apt as this is in copyright where artistic works can readily be seen as embodying the author's innermost personality, it appears somewhat strained in relation to industrial property rights for invention and the like. Alternatively, exclusive rights can simply be seen as the natural reward for the intellectual effort and talent of the individual. But this approach suffers from the same handicap of providing only limited guidance for the translation of theory into the detail of specific rules. In particular, rights-based theories tend to lack inherent restraints, other than the fact that one person's rights are limited by every other person's equivalent rights. By contrast, in market-based theory the arguments favouring the grant of exclusive rights are inherently muted by the need to preserve competition. Nonetheless a focus on personal human contributions is not entirely out of place in industrial property law, even in a market-oriented framework. Innovation is evidently concerned with *new* products and processes, and the law requires some level of novelty for all grants of rights. Truly new things can only be invented by the human mind, and thus the requirement of novelty naturally gravitates towards a focus on the mental processes of individuals (for instance, through the requirement of inventiveness in patents law).

[History vs theory] Whatever the theoretical framework one adopts, it is an inescapable fact that protection of IPRs in various forms emerged in a specific historical context and was driven by political factors, personalities, immediate needs, compromises, etc. The considered theoretical analysis that we are so familiar with today did not always exist. But although the mantle of coherent theory has only been thrown over IPRs in more recent times, there has been considerable continuity in the underlying fundamentals of norm structures and principles over relatively long periods.

There are two central concerns with imposing theory on history: first, that the theory comes after the fact rather than vice versa, ie that our theoretical analysis is more informed by the historically formed nature of the rules than we realise. Theory becomes justification rather than explanation. This can result in narrowness of perspective and a lack of creativity in norm-construction and adaptation. Secondly, history and theory can become so mixed that we are left with a sense of historical inevitability – a sense of pervasive improvement towards a nirvana of perfectly efficient rules. This is of course a misleading perspective both in relation to IPRs and in relation to history and law as such, but maybe more in relation to IPRs because of the predominant role (economic) theory has come to play in this field.

[Manipulating theory?] A further problem is that imposing any form of theoretical framework (be it social, economic or philosophical) is in some ways dangerous as it is a potential smokescreen for rent-seeking, and gives a false sense of certainty and security. Although empirical proof of many propositions relating to law and innovation is non-existent, the uninitiated are nonetheless bamboozled with graphs and figures and technical terminology. Reforms and amendments are often a stab in the dark, and quickly overhauled by unexpected technological or industrial developments. Perverse or unintended side-effects are common, and it is therefore not surprising that intellectual property law is a movable feast, with pervasive change and constant amendment. Nonetheless, IPRs relating to innovation *are* concerned with markets and their operation, with improving efficiency by substitution of new products and processes in the competitive clash between private rights. IPRs are central tools that shape the way the competitive knowledge economy operates as much as the economy shapes them. Thus the terminology of competition, imitation and market operation lies comfortably at the core of a natural discourse about IPRs and innovation.

2 IP law trends relating to innovation

[General] A volatile innovation scene, structural shifts in resource allocations to private and public sector R&D and the emergence of radically new science-based technologies continue to give rise to vigorous debate concerning IPRs. A constant tension between traditional structures, policies and goals of IPR protection and contemporary trends informs these debates. The core systemic question is to what extent established principles and policies of intellectual property law – if indeed they exist – should be relinquished in the new environment, or whether they are so robust and significant that they should be allowed to *shape* the contemporary innovation landscape in their own image. Some significant changes to intellectual property law *have* indeed resulted from changes in the innovation system, ie the manner in which innovation is organised and conducted across all sectors of the economy. But in other ways traditional principles have proved surprisingly resilient and influential. At the same time there have been significant changes in the mechanisms of policy formulation and 'norm-setting' in innovation-related IPRs. Whereas this was once a predominantly local and technical process dominated by the legal profession, now global debates linked to numerous other issues, such as trade and industrial development, conducted by diverse professionals and NGOs in multifaceted organisations determine the shape of the international treaties that strongly influence municipal rule formulation. The 'main game' in intellectual property policy formulation has shifted from Canberra to Geneva (where the World Intellectual Property Organization (WIPO) and the World Trade Organization (WTO) are based).

[Science and innovation] The exponential growth of fundamental scientific knowledge is probably the most significant development of the last 50 years. Scientists hold the keys to vast reservoirs of useful information which can now be systematically tapped, revealing numerous potential downstream applications. Pure science and IPRs thus come into closer and more frequent contact. The changing role of universities also promotes integration between theoretical science and practical innovation. Previously providers of public knowledge largely uninterested in proprietary rights, universities now actively seek to recoup the costs of scientific research by acquiring IPRs and commercialising them in collaboration with industry, further encouraging the incursion of IPRs into the domain of pure science. However, IPRs, particularly patent laws, are traditionally structured to reward the non-obvious results of individual human ingenuity rather than to protect large investments in systemic data-crunching *per se*. Therefore, in a technological and industrial environment requiring massive systems-based private investment, the law comes under pressure to adjust. This has resulted in the formulation of novel systems of rights, in particular the protection of databases (by copyright or by special 'database rights', as in the EU). Various aspects of patents law have also experienced stress, but with mixed outcomes, as is investigated further in the chapter on patent rights below.

[The R&D business] Recent decades have experienced a shift in funding for R&D from the public to the private sector. Australian Bureau of Statistics (ABS) figures show that government funding for R&D fell from 64% to 46% between 1988–89 and 2000–01.[1] Traditionally, publicly funded universities and research institutions contributed knowledge to the public domain, while innovation-active corporations integrated all stages of product development, from R&D to commercialisation. Two significant developments have now added layers of complexity: first, public institutions take a more proprietary approach to knowledge production, often collaborating closely with corporations and financiers. Secondly, a layer of specialised R&D firms has emerged, some of them spin-offs and start-ups rooted in public institutions or major corporations. Their skills and activities are focussed on financing and carrying out R&D, more than on actual commercialisation of products. Major corporations still conduct R&D in-house but increasingly acquire innovation externally by corporate acquisitions or licensing, both from public sector institutions and from R&D-based firms. They have developed skills in

---

[1] ABS, 1370.0, *Measures of Australia's Progress*, 2004.

identifying, monitoring and acquiring innovations from a relatively large number of R&D specialist firms. They are supported by complex and flexible contractual models drawing on their advisers' expertise in banking, corporate and tax law and centred on the principal asset of these exchanges: intellectual property. At the same time, increased collaboration with foreign corporations and institutions in global markets has added a further layer of complexity.

[Harmonisation] As indicated above, the principal intellectual property policy forums are now multilateral international organisations, above all WIPO and WTO/TRIPS (Trade Related Intellectual Property), but more recently also bilateral trade negotiations such as the recent Australia–United States Free Trade Agreement (USFTA). These global negotiations about IPRs have resulted both in greater harmonisation of domestic IP standards and an expansion of the geographical coverage of IPRs. Simultaneously, partly because the international norm-setting process is a step removed from domestic political scrutiny, and therefore more vulnerable to lobbying by vested interests, both protected subject matter and the scope of rights have expanded. In other words, there is an ongoing multi-pronged extension of the realm of intellectual property law. This has a positive and a negative side: the positive is that because of more effective levels of protection and enforcement around the world, individual businesses can be more confident in investing in IPRs and exploiting them globally. Trade opportunities increase and greater revenues provide an added incentive for further investment in innovation. On the negative side, knowledge becomes too densely populated by proprietary claims, adding cost and complexity to the acquisition and creation of new knowledge, both at the product level and at the level of research inputs.

[The shrinking public domain?] This expansion is hard to stem or reverse, but more recently active concern about the resulting shrinkage of the 'public domain' (ie freely available knowledge) has slowed the growth dynamic. A 'healthy' public domain of knowledge and information, which can be preserved by limiting the scope and term of rights or granting exceptions and derogations (eg fair dealing in copyright or experimental use exceptions in patents law), is advanced as a precondition for real and sustainable innovation. As the public domain shrinks and more knowledge becomes proprietary, the costs of entry into dynamic fields of research certainly rise. Such higher barriers to entry hamper competition – and that in an age where small start-ups and spin-offs are seen as a force countering the often innovation-unfriendly internal dynamics of large corporations. A crimping of the public domain also drives up the cost of public-sector and blue-sky research because basic research tools (eg in gene technology) and inputs must be acquired from commercial entities rather than being freely adopted from the academic literature. Partly however this trend has actually been accelerated by the public sector itself: research institutions' own insistence on a proprietary approach to the knowledge *they* generate puts them in a difficult position when simultaneously arguing for free access to knowledge and information held by others. However, although the public domain is obviously crucial to the evolution of science and technology, no universally accepted empirical method can as yet determine its ideal 'size'.

[Intellectual property, development and technology transfer] The public domain also shrinks with the global expansion of IPRs, for instance the introduction of patents for pharmaceuticals, or copyright on educational works in countries that did not previously recognise IPRs. Where copying was free, royalties due to overseas rights-owners drive up the costs of knowledge acquisition in countries with no meaningful indigenous knowledge-generating capacity. Adoption of the higher standards of IP protection in WTO/TRIPS and various WIPO-administered instruments promised greater R&D investment and secure technology transfers, resulting in more domestic R&D, technological advancement and economic growth. However, arguably *overestimation* of what IPRs by themselves (ie without sufficient infrastructure in education, healthcare, transport, communications, etc) can achieve and *underestimation* of the short-term cost implications of increased IPR protection have resulted in a post-TRIPS review of the impact of IPRs on development. The mandatory IP standards in WTO/TRIPS have never been matched by *mandated* technology transfer or R&D investment in developing countries or LDCs (Least Developed Countries) – this is purely a matter for private sector decision-making. The resulting imbalance has seen calls to link intellectual ownership to national control over source-resources: the genetic biodiversity which the biotech industry requires is overwhelmingly located in developing countries and LDCs; so is much of the 'traditional knowledge' on which pharmaceutical companies rely to find relevant genes. But there is considerable resistance in developed nations to making patent acquisition conditional upon prior informed consent and source disclosure. The resulting tensions have bedevilled the negotiations concerning a new Substantive Patent Law Treaty under the auspices of WIPO. More radical alternatives based on communities of interest who bypass traditional IPRs have also developed, with 'open-source' movements in computer programs, copyright works in the sphere of literature and the arts and now also for biotech. The lack of empirical certainty about the economic effect of IPRs, even in developed economies, has also encouraged this trend to explore everything from mild tweaking to radical substitution. Historical models add grist to the mill: the period of patent abolition in Switzerland, the Soviet system, the rapid industrialisation of north Asian economies and high rates of innovation in certain industry sectors in the absence of meaningful IP standards all challenge traditional incentive theory.

[Overlapping and interaction of regimes] Expansion of its scope and increased awareness of its competitive potential have drawn attention to the organisation of intellectual property law. Corporations are now very alert to the opportunities that cumulative reliance on *multiple* protection regimes offers. As a result the boundaries between the various regimes (copyright, designs, patents, trade marks, etc) have become more blurred, the nature of the field and its subdivisions more closely questioned. Proposals for radical overhauling, abolition or substitution with rights of action more homogeneous in principle and uniform in remedy are commonplace. The subject matter and rules of each IP regime are diverse – doubt as to whether they should even be treated as a single legal discipline at all are quite legitimate.

Nonetheless they do have a common core. All are concerned with an additional layer of value resulting from intellectual effort and going beyond the primary worth of a physical carrier or record. Intellectual property traditionally approaches this intangible value as based in three separate categories: reputation (trade marks and passing off); visual expression (copyright and designs); and utility (patents). But often intangible value is in fact multifaceted: a useful innovation adds to reputation (think '*Vorsprung durch Technik*' advertising for Audi cars); a successful book vests a valuable reputation in fictional characters (think Harry Potter merchandise); or a functionally superior product has a distinctive and attractive appearance (think Apple iPod). Intellectual property law has traditionally policed the borders between regimes, allowing cumulative protection in some cases but not others. But this strict policing has been relaxed, and complex legal and conceptual questions of overlap and cumulation result more frequently. The most striking example relevant to product innovation is the relationship between copyright, designs and now also trade mark registration for distinctive shapes, which is considered in detail in later chapters.

[IPRs and trade practices] Perceived growth in the scope and application of intellectual property laws has refocussed attention on the nature of the relationship between intellectual property and competition law (as largely contained within the provisions of the *Trade Practices Act 1974* (Cth) (*TPA*) in Australia). If intellectual property law represents an *inherently benign* trade-off between dynamic (ie substitution-based) and static (ie price-based) competition, then competition law appears to have no role to play as either an internal constraint (eg by making grant of rights dependent on Australian Competition & Consumer Commission (ACCC; then TPC) approval),[2] or as an external one. IPRs that excessively lessen competition should be amended, rather than modified in practice by application of the *Trade Practices Act*.

For most knowledge goods, monopoly pricing is tempered by the availability of at least partial substitutes (eg the patentee's monopoly price for paracetamol is tempered by the availability of aspirin as a substitute). But does market behaviour based on the exercise of IPRs therefore never warrant the intervention of competition law? By virtue of section 51 (3) of the *TPA* contractual terms relating to the exercise of IPRs themselves are privileged from the application of provisions concerning misuse of market power (section 46 and 46A) and resale price maintenance (section 48). Other provisions of the Act apply normally (eg in relation to tying), but substantial lessening of competition resulting from abuse of market power derived from accumulated IPRs (eg patents) could arguably not be

---

[2] See Australian Law Reform Commission (ALRC), Report No 74 *Designs* (1995), Recommendation No 165.

countered effectively on the basis of *TPA* provisions. The IPR/*TPA* relationship has come under scrutiny in recent times: for instance, by the Intellectual Property and Competition Review Committee (IPCRC).[3] But despite proposals to the contrary the protection of section 51 (3) continues to apply; amendments inspired by particular competition concerns have rather been to rules of intellectual property law themselves, in particular relating to parallel importation of copyright materials, where restrictions have largely been removed (unlike in most other jurisdictions). Cases considering the application of the *TPA* to intellectual property are very rare, but this does not necessarily indicate that there is no abuse of IPRs.

[Pressure on 'established' principles] Developments in science and technology constantly challenge the established principles of intellectual property law, as do new business models and norm-setting environments. In conclusion, two recent developments that radically question basic policy presumptions command some attention, one related to the nature of the innovations governed by IPRs, and another to the standard of innovation required.

Exclusive rights have traditionally been connected to some technological or practical innovation. Organisational, service or pure business innovations have not been 'protected' by IPRs (other than in certain circumstances as trade secrets). Yet such innovations are more relevant to the services-based economies of most developed nations today. Unsurprisingly therefore the technology bias of the system has spawned vigorous debate, mostly centred on the patentability of so-called 'business method inventions' and computer programs. Digitalisation is in some measure an organisational tool, and the line between the technical and the organisational blurs in the internet environment (think eBay: is it a new business scheme or a technological breakthrough or both?). Therefore, some have argued that in the service economy organisational innovations merit the grant of exclusive rights: this is a significant issue that will be further explored in the context of patents law below.

Another consistent hallmark of intellectual property law has been that exclusive rights are only granted for creating something new. *Existing* knowledge is in the public domain. However, for traditional custodians of communal knowledge and technologies, the 'public domain' is a byword for dispossession by others. Should newness then be abandoned as a universal requirement, so that rights extend to traditional knowledge and technology? Although this would fly in the face of traditional notions of incentive and innovation in IP law, it may support both traditional culture and development in societies lacking industrial methods of knowledge acquisition and attribution. Most significantly, recognising the systems of rights and controls over knowledge that exist in other communities alerts us to the fundamentally cultured and historic nature of the current system of IPRs.

---

[3] Intellectual Property & Competition Review Committee (IPCRC), *Review of Intellectual Property Legislation under the competition Principles Agreement* (Final Report, 30 September 2000).

3 The areas of intellectual property law included in this book

[Innovation related] Ultimately, intellectual property law is the legal mechanism by which knowledge goods are subjected to the rigours of the market. But only those areas of intellectual property law that are relevant to process and product innovation in the broad sense are covered in this book. Use of the term 'innovation' is intended to limit the field in a number of ways: first, the book focusses on *industrial* products and processes only. In other words, arts and entertainment products (the copyright industries) are not addressed. Secondly, it focusses on *new* products and processes, whose novelty results from intellectual activity. Within those parameters, it encompasses both innovation in *appearance* and innovation in *function*, which sometimes coalesce in a single product, but not in every case; in other words, it covers both 'product innovation' and 'technological innovation'. Therefore copyright in categories of artistic works relevant to industrial production and in computer programs is included. Also covered are some aspects of trade marks law and passing off, in particular the registration of product shapes as trade marks, which opens up limited opportunities for the monopolisation of the appearance of goods by reference to consumer perception of their distinctive shape. All the areas of law covered relate to the investments firms make to render new and useful products or processes more enticing to consumers. In other words, all these areas concern rights that are of interest to firms engaged in developing, making and selling new products.

[Areas of IP law covered] The area of IP directly concerned with technological innovation is primarily patents law (*Patents Act 1990* (Cth)), which naturally forms a significant part of this book. But some technology is covered by other forms of IPRs: original computer programs, as well as being patentable if new and inventive, are also protected by copyright (*Copyright Act 1968* (Cth)). Computer chips are covered by special legislation, the *Circuit Layouts Act 1989* (Cth), which effectively protects the design of the circuitry on the chip. Plants, as well as being patentable, can also be registered under the *Plant Breeder's Rights Act 1994* (Cth), which is also covered in this book. The protection of trade secrets by way of the action for breach of confidence extends to any form of information not in the public domain, including information relevant to innovative products or processes, in which context it is also covered. As to product innovation, ie the novel appearance of products, the relevant aspects of copyright law – primarily copyright in artistic works created in the course of industrial production – are included, as well as the core regime of designs registration (*Designs Act 2003* (Cth)). In Australia this regime extends to designs determined by function as well as by aesthetics. Finally, some aspects of trade marks law (*Trade Marks Act 1995* (Cth)) with brief reference to passing off concerned with imitation of product shapes are also covered.

[The relationship between regimes] Although intellectual property law segments various aspects of innovation into diverse regimes, products or technologies are not conceived with a view to fitting them into one or another regime – they might fit in one, but they might fit in several. Various complex issues result, including: uncertainty of legal categorisation in terms of protection; applicability of multiple regimes to a single product; confusion about the purpose and extent of protection in a certain product category; and overlap and cumulation of rights. For the individual firm this presents both opportunity (potential of multiple avenues of protection) and risk (complexity and risk of error resulting in exclusion from given regimes). In terms of understanding the law it is crucial to come to terms with the fact that a single product or process can be viewed from different perspectives: for instance, a functional innovation (patents) may also be aesthetically pleasing (designs or copyright) and so distinctive as to become associated with one supplier (trade marks or passing off). Different legal issues and threshold tests arise depending on the perspective from which one approaches the product: does the product operate in a new manner; has it appeared in public before; do consumers associate the shape with one trader; and so on. Therefore some flexibility of approach, imagination and an open mind to the options presented by various regimes is required; an appreciation of the relationships between various regimes is also important. It must also be accepted that the edges between regimes are often fuzzy and not as distinct as the law intends to present them.

2

Trade secrets

Introduction

[This chapter] This chapter concerning trade secrets or 'confidential information' consists of two main parts. The first part initially focusses on policy context, and then on the elements of the equitable action for breach of confidence itself; the second on a significant sub-category of confidential information: knowledge acquired by employees. This topic merits separate attention: first, because of the frequency of conflict about and the density of contractual terms concerning the dividing line between employers' trade secrets and employees' private knowledge. Secondly, because portability of employee knowledge impacts significantly on knowledge diffusion and therefore on innovation as a whole.

[Trade secrets?] This book is primarily concerned with technical trade secrets, ie information related to product and process innovation in a broad sense. But the applicable action in Australian law, the equitable action for breach of confidence, has a far broader remit, covering *all* confidential information, whatever its nature: from private confidences, to commercial or business secrets, to what is sometimes known as 'know-how', ie those technical secrets associated with patented inventions. Section 1a below considers some policy issues concerning the legal protection of trade secrets, against the background of a significant strategic choice for the innovative firm: between trade secrets protection and patenting. As will be further addressed in the next chapter, patents law is a system of monopolistic proprietary rights in inventions, based on application and grant on the basis of threshold tests of novelty and inventiveness, and with a limited monopoly term of 20 years. Breach of confidence actions by contrast are not based in property, are not predicated upon *ex ante* bureaucratic demarcation of subject matter and determination of rights and will generally lie for as long as the information concerned has not entered the public domain.

[The patents–trade secrets dichotomy] Although the choice between patenting and reliance on trade secrets protection pervades this chapter, commercial reality does not present such a simple choice. A firm seeking to appropriate greater returns from knowledge creation may choose to disregard both secrecy and patents or combine them (see below, Chapter three). Strategic factors may make this a sensible option: for instance, the strength of the firm's market position; the number of competitors; product lead time to market; reverse engineering barriers to competition; systems-embeddedness of the technology concerned; network effects, etc. These factors form a relevant backdrop, but are not the primary focus of this work, which primarily addresses legal issues, rather than the broader strategic parameters of the marketing and commercialisation of innovations.

[Relationship with contract and other areas of law] Because trade secrets law is concerned with such a wide spectrum of knowledge, a close relationship exists with other areas of law, most significantly contract law. Equitable remedies for breaches of confidence are largely residual, available in the absence of remedies for breach of contractual terms. However, the courts impose some public policy restraints on contractual provisions relating to trade secrets, so that occasionally they override contract. Further, apart from the significant relationship with patents, an interesting overlap exists between trade secrets and copyright law, and also with the related statutory protection for non-original databases (in jurisdictions where it exists, principally in the EU, but not in Australia). Can a compilation of data selected from the public domain amount to a trade secret; and/or does it amount to a copyright-protected literary work (a category which includes 'compilations' by virtue of section 10 of the *Copyright Act 1968* (Cth))? In a more general sense, copyright may also protect works that have been produced in secret by a firm (eg technical or engineering drawings used in manufacturing), and provide either a fallback protection or a first line of defence against imitators.

1 Policy context

[Secrecy: its limitations] A firm can appropriate greater returns from new products or processes it has created or obtained by keeping them secret – this strategy prevents imitation. The law assists a firm in preserving secrecy by supporting the self-help measures it deploys to that end with legal remedies in certain circumstances. However, this legal support has significant limitations. In particular, the innovative firm relying on secrecy faces two uncontrollable and irremediable hazards: reverse engineering and independent invention. Reverse engineering of a product by a competitor is a risk stemming either from the impracticality and cost of maintaining some secrets or from the practical impossibility of maintaining secrecy *while commercially exploiting* a product. If a product is put on the market then, in the absence of a patent, the law does not restrain any person from reverse engineering it, accessing and using the knowledge embodied within (at least the residual equitable rules don't: contract may to some extent). By making its product public the firm surrenders the protection of trade secrets law. While it is often said that knowledge has public good characteristics this is not strictly speaking the case (nothing forces us to divulge unique knowledge) – but when it is embodied in products or processes supplied to the market, it certainly does.

[Independent invention] Independent invention may also undermine the position of a firm as the unique possessor of new knowledge. Trade secrets law provides no remedy against a third party who independently arrives at the same secret knowledge or invention – again, unlike in patents law. The patent monopoly *does* extend to prohibiting both reverse engineers and independent inventors from exploiting the patented invention during the term of protection. Furthermore, the action for breach of confidence depends on *maintaining* secrecy: once knowledge becomes public, unless skulduggery is involved, there is no legal remedy against those who choose to adopt it from any public source. These limitations underscore the fact that trade secrets law is, in the eyes of the courts in Australia, based on a policy of safeguarding against abuses of the underlying relationship between confidor and confidee, and not on a right of property in knowledge, information or innovations.

[Secrecy: why firms might choose it] Nonetheless a firm might still decide to rely on secrecy, supported as it is by the law, as a mechanism to appropriate higher returns from innovation. One determinant, hinted at above, is simple enough: can the knowledge be kept secret and exploited at the same time? If a secret is embodied in a product that is to be released to the market, then this may be impossible. However, it may take a competitor, who does not have the embodied knowledge in readily usable form, considerable time to reverse engineer the product, isolate relevant knowledge, manufacture a copy and then market it. This may still allow the firm considerable lead time over free-riders, a period during which price setting is less constrained by competitive imitation. In such circumstances and, certainly where the life of the technology is short, the expense of patenting may not be justified. Another determinant, where a product or process *can* be secretly exploited, is the firm's estimation of the risk that others will independently arrive at the same thing. If the chance is remote, then relying on secrecy may have the additional advantage of extending the effective monopoly *beyond* the patent term – at no stage is there a legal obligation to relinquish trade secrets to the public domain. Furthermore, a patent will only be granted for an invention which has been fully disclosed to the public in the application. Such disclosure supplies information from which competitors can learn even in the presence of a monopoly right. In spite of that, where a firm cannot reliably estimate the commercial life of the technology or the likelihood of independent invention, it may choose the more secure option of a patent. Recent times have seen a steady migration from trade secrets to patenting because so much innovation relates to new applications of generic technologies with a commonly known underlying scientific canon. This either increases the risk of independent invention or renders it difficult to estimate; examples of such generic technologies are computer programs, computer implemented inventions, biotechnology, pharmaceuticals, etc. Also, in a knowledge-based economy, factory secrets secured behind high walls are less central to wealth creation, and thus the ability to *physically* hide secrets is reduced. Systematic patents acquisition resulting in large portfolios has also become the norm in many innovative sectors, and patenting is heavily promoted by various stakeholders.

[Patents and trade secrets: why have differential legal protection?] Why does the law not protect technical trade secrets more comprehensively? Or to put this question in legal terms: why no property rights in trade secrets (which would mean no reverse engineering would be allowed)? Landes and Posner offer an explanation: the law effectively places a different value on a unit of knowledge depending on how obvious it is[1] – in other words, how likely it is that another person will independently arrive at it. The less obvious, the greater its contribution to the progress of technology – ultimately what the law intends to encourage. If it is obvious then no legal protection is available; if it is less than obvious, but is likely to occur to a number of parties independently, then it deserves trade secrets protection. Such protection is limited in the sense that any other party that *does* independently arrive at it may use it. If it is not obvious, yet it is not impossible that another party should arrive at it, and it can be readily reverse engineered, then a patent is appropriate; and if it is totally non-obvious, so that nobody else is likely to come up with it independently, and it cannot be reverse engineered, then trade secrets protection, potentially permanent as it is, is again appropriate. In the latter case the law effectively says: because it is so inventive (and hence represents such advancement on the known art), the inventor can appropriate it for the life of the technology, however long that may be.

[Secrecy and publicity] The legal mechanism of trade secrets protection is thus finely modulated to allow a potentially perpetual monopoly in very inventive new knowledge that cannot be reverse engineered; and a more limited term monopoly for knowledge that is likely to be independently discovered by others or can be reverse engineered. But this protection based on secrecy has two public policy drawbacks: first, potentially valuable knowledge is kept secret from the rest of society, preventing beneficial diffusion. And secondly, secrecy prevents competitors from becoming aware of competitors' relative position in the R&D race, resulting in wastage by duplication of expenditure on research. A patent, on the other hand, flags to others that they should consider discontinuing certain R&D; duplication is thus restrained. The patentee can contribute to the coordination of downstream innovation because other firms will have to acquire licences to use the patented invention (the so-called prospect theory of Kitch[2]).

However, there are some mitigating factors. On the one hand, if knowledge does not reach the standard of non-obviousness that patents law requires, its lack of public diffusion as a trade secret is not of any great consequence. Further,

---

[1] Landes WM and R Posner, 'Trademark law: an economic perspective' (1987) 30 *J of Law & Eco* 265.
[2] Kitch EW, 'The nature and function of the patent system' (1978) *J of Law & Eco* 20, 165.

as Friedman, Landes and Posner point out,[3] the secret use of an invention at least does not prevent a patent being obtained over it by another independent inventor, although the secret user is excluded from obtaining a patent (as we shall see below, patent law provides that a person who has secretly used an invention cannot obtain a patent for it himself; but others who were secretly using it at the time of application can continue to use it notwithstanding the grant of a patent). Posner also suggests that since independent invention and reverse engineering of trade secrets are allowed, the potential return from trade secrets protection is smaller than that from patent protection with its winner-takes-all rules. Thus trade secrets protection does not have the same tendency to encourage a blind race to invent as does the patent system, thereby avoiding wasteful duplication.

[Transaction issues with trade secrets protection] One advantage of patents law, as a system of proprietary rights, is that it provides solid foundations for knowledge transactions, ie in relation to the sale and acquisition of knowledge assets. Property rights based on a system of *ex ante* demarcation (or itemisation) of knowledge units to which monopoly rights are extended assist certainty and predictability. This process addresses the apparent fuzziness, seamlessness and interconnectedness of knowledge, which makes it an otherwise difficult commodity to trade in. Patents law generates and applies organising principles; but this comes at a considerable bureaucratic cost, which is often wholly wasted because the patented invention turns out to have little commercial value. However, the patents system does afford interested parties an early independent assessment, a kind of limited quality assurance, flagging at least *potential* commercial value. The trade secrets system, by contrast, leaves it entirely up to private entities to undertake the tasks of demarcation and evaluation, either in the context of contract, or of litigation. It is up to a purchaser to assess the value of such knowledge entirely independently or alternatively to risk reliance on the vendor's representations. It is up to the litigant at the time of litigation to itemise claimed knowledge, to prove that the standards for protection are met, and then to prove 'ownership' – all of which are difficult tasks. Nonetheless the value of a patent grant should not be overestimated: it is only an indication and not a guarantee that the knowledge concerned attains a certain standard (ie that the patent is valid), and is not a very reliable predictor of commercial value.

[Demarcation and trade secrets law] Demarcation disputes concerning knowledge units must be resolved in some manner, and the law of trade secrets uses two main mechanisms: to seek out some physical record that can serve to delineate the trade secret; and/or to insist, as suggested above, that the plaintiff clearly itemises knowledge in concrete and substantive terms, not just by reference to abstract categories (such as 'the trade secrets', 'the confidential information'). The two demarcation mechanisms are interlinked: a claimant who is not able to circumscribe trade secrets by reference to some physical record (eg a

---

[3] Friedman D, W Landes and R Posner, 'Some Economics of Trade Secret Law' (1991) *Journal of Economic Perspectives*, 5, 1, 61–72.

certain document, or a certain computer disk) will often face difficulties in itemising them sufficiently. The same holds true in terms of commercial dealings in trade secrets: it is not coincidental that in trade they are often referred to as 'property', and often acquire that precision in contractual delineation associated with property rights (but not always: contracts often contain ambit claims in abstract terms). Again most often contractual identification is by reference to some record or containment, or else by association with a certain product, process or patent.

[**Tacit knowledge in trade secrets actions**] Because of difficulties in demarcation, secret knowledge which is not recorded in some documentary form will often be difficult to appropriate. This is particularly true of knowledge acquired by employees in the course of their work. An employer faces considerable hurdles when attempting to restrain an (ex-)employee's use or disclosure of knowledge allegedly amounting to a trade secret, partly because it can be difficult to itemise, circumscribe and distinguish from contextual knowledge and information. Chances of an effective remedy are improved where a firm can identify the trade secret allegedly taken by reference to some specific record removed by the employee: a documented client list, a confidential catalogue, technical drawings, documented commercial data, instruction books, etc. Where an employee has departed with such recorded knowledge, even post-term an employer can sometimes succeed not just on the basis of breach of the narrow obligation of confidence, but of the broader duty of fidelity that binds every employee during their term of employment (as further explored below). But where the allegation is that unrecorded, tacit knowledge (ie existing only in the mind) has been taken, not contained in some identifiable record, legal outcomes are difficult to predict.

[**Unpredictable outcomes in trade secrets cases**] The unpredictability of employee trade secrets cases is but one instance of the problems with demarcation and itemisation; contradictory policy goals; vague standards and weak conceptual underpinnings that bedevil trade secrets law. The action for breach of confidence serves critical useful purposes in rather subtle and sometimes unpredictable ways – it is a most fact-driven area of the law. The action for breach of confidence does not erect a complete mechanism of protection organised by the state, as does patents law, but merely aims to underpin or support the self-help measures that individuals take to protect their secrets. In any case, the rules of law are default rules; the vagaries of trade secrets law can thus be addressed as much by contractual provisions as by effective practical measures.

[**Trade secrets and competition**] Breach of confidence law is not exclusively concerned with innovative products or processes – with technical data. Many cases concern *client* data – know-who rather than know-how. In such cases the significance of trade secrets law as a tool whereby firms attempt to control information flows in a competitive market is starkly revealed. Courts are repeatedly called upon to draw a line between legitimate protection of a trade secret, and illegitimate attempts to limit competition by hampering competitors' access to what in truth is public domain information. Not all commercially valuable information a firm possesses amounts to a trade secret which it can appropriate by force of law. For instance, client details are not routinely considered to be trade secrets; nor are details concerning useful or reliable suppliers: after all, information about potential clients or suppliers is publicly available to be ascertained with some slight effort.

The realisation that to constrict the flow of knowledge is to deny fuel to competition also inspires cases relating to technical trade secrets. Courts' insistence on itemisation and demarcation and on the claimant adequately proving that knowledge is indeed secret deter speculative actions and ambit claims which would chill competition. Normal processes of observing, obtaining, even spying out relevant commercial information, including information concerning competitors' new products and processes, must be preserved: they lie at the heart of competition. Nonetheless, there is a line of proper conduct and respect for confidential interaction that should not be crossed if a market is to operate efficiently. Thus trade secrets law in Australia can be conceptualised as a balancing act between the need to preserve the free flow of information on the one hand, and to sanction standards of trust and confidence in commercial interaction on the other. Both are crucial ingredients of welfare-enhancing, genuinely competitive markets.

[**The 'unknowability' problem**] Trade secrets suffer from 'unknowability'; in other words, commercial interaction is hampered by the risk attached to disclosing trade secrets fully to a potential counterpart before a binding bargain has been sealed. Efficient pricing and valuation of trade secrets depends on disclosure, but disclosure carries the inherent risk of complete devaluation of the secret. A productive bargain thus requires agreed parameters within which otherwise unknowable secrets can be safely revealed. The limited purpose for which information is supplied provides these parameters, and the action for breach of confidence polices and enforces these with appropriate remedies.

2 The equitable action for breach of confidence

Introduction: doctrinal underpinnings

[**The focus of the action: standards of interaction**] The mechanism the law uses to protect trade secrets is not property rights in knowledge or information. Instead, the law focusses on proper standards governing the interaction or communication between parties within which knowledge is shared. It enforces standards of propriety and good faith, which when absent means the effective circulation of knowledge, both within organisations and between economic actors, would be severely hampered. As Megarry J (as he then was) points out in *Coco v AN Clark (Engineers) Ltd* [1969] RPC 41 at pp 46–47: 'The equitable jurisdiction in cases of breach of confidence is ancient; confidence is the cousin of trust'.

By its nature knowledge is dispersed, possessed by diverse actors, so efficient cooperation and exchange are essential to innovation. Cooperation may be centred around formal exchange of proprietary information, but equally around *collaborative* relationships between diverse actors (firms, institutions, individuals) in the economy, within which information circulates on agreed terms. The law in general tends to focus on relationships, categorising them and policing standards of conduct it sees as appropriate to their nature and intensity. An ongoing relationship between employer and employee, for instance, is conceived of as one of '*fidelity*'. A relationship of *confidence* is of a lesser quality – it does not rest on a community of interest; usually the interests of both parties, more arm's-length actors, are understood to be divergent. But even where actors are rivals they must have the ability to exchange information *on the basis of trust*, and the law cannot countenance abuse of such trust or good faith. The parameters of the relationship are the foundations on which the action for breach of confidence is built.

[*Coco v Clark*: elements of the action for breach of confidence] The elements of the modern action for breach of confidence were first articulated in the landmark case of *Coco v Clark* (see above). They are:

1   information that is not in the public domain;
2   communication of the information in confidence;
3   some unauthorised use or disclosure;
4   resulting in actual or apprehended damage.

Each of these threshold requirements is formulated in broad and abstract terms – their application to myriads of varied factual circumstances is often challenging and unpredictable. The second element is described in *Coco* as information having been *communicated in circumstances importing* an obligation of confidence, but this formula is peculiar to the factual circumstances of that case. The obligation of confidentiality need not always be implied from the circumstances – it can be agreed or communicated in express terms. Below, itemisation is dealt with as an additional requirement, but they can also be seen as being contained within the first element: to prove that it was not in the public domain the information claimed must first be identified clearly.

[Third parties and industrial espionage] Founding the remedy on enforcing proper standards of interaction between parties, rather than on property rights in information, gives rise to significant problems. First, what is the basis for granting a remedy where no relationship between a confidor and confidee exists, because they have never actually communicated any information, never relevantly interacted? In other words, how to deal with cases of industrial espionage, unconscionable or illegal acquisition of knowledge? And secondly, can a remedy still be fashioned against a third party who obtains a trade secret, but with whom the original confidor has no direct relationship (so-called third-party liability)? The latter problem can be reasonably well accommodated by extending the obligation of confidence to third parties who are, or ought to be, conscious of the relationship of confidence between the original confidor and the confidee from whom they have obtained information. Those knowingly taking advantage of a breach of confidence should then be held accountable. The first problem is harder to resolve in the absence of property rights in information. Yet the courts have not hesitated to fashion a remedy in equity in situations where a person knew or ought to have known that information was secret, used illegal or unconscionable means to obtain it, and then handled it in a manner detrimental to the original 'owner'. The doctrinal difficulties that this gives rise to have mostly been ignored.

[Doctrinal basis: property and equity] Which takes us back to the question: 'how significant are questions relating to the doctrinal basis of the remedy?'. Observing the courts' flexible approach, the answer must be: not very. Further, in practice, although the law bases the remedy in equity, commerce commonly deals with trade secrets as *property*. Even the courts themselves often use the terminology of 'property', and 'ownership' of trade secrets. Trade secrets are bought, sold, assigned and licensed, frequently in association with other intellectual property such as patents. That tends to reinforce the notion that the formal doctrinal basis is of little consequence; in any case, where information is passed between contracting parties it is the implied or express terms of the contract rather than equity which will determine the availability and nature of the remedy. Nonetheless, there is no doubt that in terms of granting an equitable remedy in an action for breach of confidence, the courts have rather continued to reject than grown to accept the notion of property rights in knowledge as the appropriate doctrinal framework.

[Unconscionability and restitution for wrongs] In fashioning standards for interaction courts tend to fasten on the conscience of the parties. Dean J commented in *Moorgate Tobacco Ltd v Philip Morris Ltd* (1984) 156 CLR 415 that the Court's intervention is based on 'the notion of an obligation of conscience arising from the circumstances in or through which information was communicated or obtained'.[4] His Honour's statement was adopted in later cases, such as *Smith Kline and French Laboratories v Secretary, Department of Community Services and Health* (1990) 22 FCR 73 (at FCR 112). In this view, unconscionable conduct becomes the basis for the award of a remedy; and with that approach, remedies in industrial espionage and third-party cases (as referred to above) are more readily accommodated, because the problem of referring back to actual interaction between confidor and confidee is removed. If wrongful conduct is the basis for awarding a remedy, then restitutionary principles will inform such awards, since these are based on restitution for wrongs.[5] However, it may often be difficult to define unconscionability in this context without reference to some underlying relationship or interaction – after all, it is commonly the affront to this relationship that renders the conduct unconscionable.

---

[4] At CLR 438; as referred to by Dean R, *The law of trade secrets and personal secrets*, 2nd edn, LBC, 2002, at p 59 [2.160].
[5] See eg Friedmann D, 'Restitution for wrongs: the basis of liability' in WR Cornish et al (eds), *Restitution: Past present and future*, Hart, 1998, at p 150.

[Industrial espionage cases: illegality and invasion of privacy] In industrial espionage-type cases, the difficulty is how to delineate the sort of conduct that is actionable in equity, given that vigorous information-gathering is a competitive process which should arguably be nurtured. It is well accepted that illegality (whether in terms of civil trespass or criminal offences, like theft or break and enter) is a sufficient basis; the Queensland case of *Franklin v Giddins* [1978] Qd R 72 has stood unchallenged for this proposition. But short of illegality where is the line to be drawn? An interesting issue is whether breach of privacy is categorised as a wrong, in terms of the law, given that the common law world is edging ever closer to universal acceptance of such a tort, although for the time being the High Court continues to reject it in Australia: see *Australian Broadcasting Corporation v Lenah Game Meats Pty Ltd* [2001] HCA 63. If a breach of privacy were accepted as the kind of unconscionable conduct for which an equitable remedy under the umbrella of breach of confidence is awarded, then the two actions become very closely aligned – *Sullivan v Sclanders* [2000] SASC 273 (18 August 2000) presents an interesting example of the kind of conduct offending common notions of privacy that may yet not be illegal in the absence of a tort of invasion of privacy. But then there are also cases of tricks, deceptions, etc which fall short of illegality, and which may also not encompass invasions of privacy.

[Industrial espionage: where to draw the line] Freedman lists cases where:

> various conduct based standards have been proposed in the context of the equitable action of breach of confidence – amongst them that the act of acquisition was itself unlawful, surreptitious, reprehensible, unconscionable, wrongful, and on the basis that the act falls under some generalized principle of liability grounded in the flexible nature of the equitable jurisdiction itself.[6]

Freedman at the same place rightly refers to the risk of uncertainty flowing from the imposition of 'highly idiosyncratic' judicial views on general and commercial morality. If efficiency-enhancing competition encourages vigorous information-gathering and analysis, then there are strong arguments against extending the scope of remediable unconscionable conduct too far, or leaving its outer limits too uncertain. A distinction must be drawn between conduct which is merely wrong, immoral, offensive or unpleasant, and conduct which is of such a degree of impropriety as to warrant a remedy. The easiest way to do this is to categorise only conduct that traverses established legal rights (for the time being not including a right to privacy!), or is criminal, as conduct sufficiently reprehensible to attract an equitable remedy. In other words, within those parameters 'industrial espionage' should be permitted as benefiting desirable diffusion of knowledge. A nice analogy here is with the resistance in Australia against a general tort of unfair competition: broad concepts of unfairness could be used to base a remedy, but vagueness and idiosyncrasy would result in an unacceptable level of

---

[6] Freedman CD, 'The Extension of the Criminal Law to Protecting Confidential Commercial Information: Comments on the Issues and the Cyber-Context', 14th BILETA Conference: 'CYBERSPACE 1999: Crime, Criminal Justice and the Internet', at p 5 (available at www.bileta.ac.uk); the author gives case references for each category.

unpredictability. Consider also the case of reverse engineering:[7] to date reverse engineering is recognised as not being unconscionable; if the product reverse engineered is not stolen, the legitimate acquirer has full property rights, extending to the entitlement to pull it apart and learn its hidden secrets, and then use them to its own advantage. But no doubt plenty of firms find the practice thoroughly objectionable and mightn't hesitate to call it unconscionable . . .

[Is criminalisation the alternative?] Arguments such as those raised by Freedman, in favour of criminalisation of industrial espionage, are certainly in harmony with the general trend towards extending IPRs. But they tend to discount the value of free circulation of knowledge where innovation is a central competitive pursuit. In civilian jurisdictions criminalisation of trade secrets breaches is nothing new[8] although it tends to be limited to misuse of trade secrets by employees during the term of employment. Freedman makes the point that the criminal law can assist where the plaintiff is indigent, for instance has lost everything due to the misappropriation. Nonetheless, arguably criminalisation should not extend beyond special positions of trust, such as trusted employees during employment and some governmental officers. The net of criminal sanctions too widely cast may have too much of a chilling effect on legitimate information-gathering. Investigating competitors' activities provides useful signals to firms as to whether to persist or desist with existing R&D programs, thus preventing waste. Furthermore, knowledge of others' innovations is not only necessary to advance one's own technological base, but also to predict rapidly changing market conditions; for instance, due to the unpredictable introduction of new technologies.

The first element: information that is not in the public domain

[The relative standard] Secrecy is a relative concept in the law of confidence. That knowledge should not be in the public domain does not equate to requiring that it not be available to any member of the public anywhere. By contrast an application for a patent must be rejected if information disclosing the invention is available to the public, no matter how obscure its location and irrespective of how few people actually access it. Such a high threshold requirement does not apply here. The crucial question in breach of confidence cases is not whether information is notionally available to the public at large but whether it is *actually* known to the *relevant* public. However, apart from knowledge being public because it can be shown that it circulates within a relevant group, it may be treated as public simply because of its inherent qualities – it is public in the sense that it is obvious, or banal or unoriginal – anybody could come up with it. But the standard of 'non-obviousness' in this context is again not subject to the strict and particular rules that adhere in patents law.

---

[7] See eg *Mars UK Ltd v Teknowledge Ltd* [2000] FSR 138.
[8] As noted by the Law Commission of England and Wales: 'Legislating the Criminal Code: Misuse of Trade Secrets', Consultation Paper 150, 1997.

[Not known to the relevant public] But who is the relevant public, when technical trade secrets, such as new products or processes, are at issue? Dean refers to a number of cases to support the proposition that '[T]he public domain in trade secret cases is usually not the world at large but the trade in which the plaintiff competes'.[9] The information must be judged 'in the light of the usage and practices of a particular industry or trade concerned', a phrase Dean quotes from Megarry J's judgment in *Thomas Marshall v Guinle*.[10] However, it is not clear that Megarry J intended to say that the correct question is whether the information concerned is known in the relevant trade. It may be that he intended rather to indicate that the customs of the trade as to how it would treat information of that kind are relevant; that is, whether members of the trade would consider it a secret or not. Dean also refers to *RL Crain v Ashton* [1950] 1 DLR 601,[11] in which it was said that certain details concerning the manufacture of a machine were not trade secrets once 'they became known to others who were interested in the construction or sale of such [machines], that is to say, became known to the trade,[...].'

[The standard] Whatever the case may be, the standard is relative in this sense: on the one hand, it is not necessary to show that it is known at large before it can be said to be in the public domain; but on the other hand, notional public availability is not necessarily enough to undermine confidentiality either. Conversely, if information is of a kind that is normally sourced by a certain group 'interested in the [subject matter]' within the jurisdiction, it will lose its secret character, even though the source of the information may be obscure and not actually accessed by those not so interested. This is so even if the group is limited, with special membership, as in *Franchi v Franchi* (1967) RPC 149, where it was held that UK patents attorneys could be expected to ascertain a source of patent publications in Belgium. So there is geographical relativity: the knowledge may be public in some other jurisdiction in some other place, but would only be public for breach of confidence purposes here if the relevant trade would normally be expected to ascertain it nonetheless. Again the standard is lower than that of worldwide novelty that prevails in patents law. The evidence of members of the trade as to their usual information-gathering practices will be crucial.

[Relative secrecy: is it possible to develop it independently?] A trade secret may also still be a trade secret even though it is possible with some effort or expenditure of resources to arrive at it by accessing and compiling knowledge from various public sources. The crucial issue will be how extensive is the effort required, and thus what advantage the defendant derives from having avoided the same search efforts as the plaintiff – from taking a shortcut. This is an issue that frequently arises in the know-how cases relating to customer information. It is open to any person to identify customers, by approaching potential candidates

---

[9] Dean, *The Law of Trade Secrets*, p 92 [3.180].
[10] This phrase appears in the All ER's at p 210 rather than 209 as indicated in Dean's footnote (the case itself is at [1978] 3 All ER 193).
[11] Without a page reference; presumably the author is referring to a passage at 609.

or accessing published materials, and ascertaining what their requirements might be. That information is in the public domain, and seeking out and approaching potential clients is basic competitive conduct. However, a compiled list in documentary or digital form, with all details of identity, contact details, requirements, price discounts, etc compiled in an immediately usable form and maybe over an extended period of time may amount to a trade secret: in that form the information is not in the public domain and considerable investment in time and resources would be required to compile it in such a readily usable format.

[Reverse engineering] More relevant to product and process innovation is reverse engineering. It may be that certain secret knowledge is embodied in a product that has been put on the market. But that does not mean that the underlying knowledge as such is in the public domain – considerable resources may be required to ascertain the information in a form in which it is usable in competition with its progenitor. Again, nominally the knowledge is available but it will take time and effort to isolate it and turn it to account. In practical terms this means that a person who had previously received the underlying secret knowledge in confidence will not simply be able to rely on it for some unintended purpose from the moment the product is made public or put on the market, by arguing that the information is now in the public domain.

[The connection between secrecy and remedy] A close connection exists between the question of sufficient secrecy and that of a sufficient remedy. The benchmark remedy for breach of confidence lies in equity: an injunction prohibiting further use or disclosure of the knowledge concerned, often granted at the interim stage on an interlocutory basis. However, by the time of trial, it may be that what was previously secret has become public, either autonomously because of the breach complained of, or because of the actions of the plaintiff – for instance by putting the previously secret product or process on the market. Should the courts simply refuse a remedy at trial because the information is by then, in theory at least, in the public domain? If so, the defendant may benefit from his own abuse of confidence, gaining an unfair advantage, either from his own wrongdoing that resulted in the publication, or by taking a shortcut that is unavailable to those not in the confidence of the plaintiff.

In the original 'Springboard' case, *Terrapin Ltd v Builders' Supply Co (Hayes) Ltd* (1967) RPC 375, the plaintiff *did* obtain a remedy at trial – a limited term injunction against the defendant who had used a trade secret for a purpose not contemplated by the confidor, although by the time of trial the plaintiff had put the product embodying the trade secret on the market: it could be ascertained by reverse engineering. Normally, once the information is public, a party should not be put at a special disadvantage vis-à-vis every competitor who now has access to it, simply because he abused the confidence of the plaintiff. The compromise solution arrived at in the Springboard case and since emulated in many other cases was to impose a temporary restraint – for as long as it would take an interested person to reverse engineer the plaintiff's product and bring a resulting product of his own to market. Hence the *relative* secrecy of the confidential information – ie that some effort was still required to ascertain it although the product embodying it was in the public domain – provided the hook upon which satisfaction of the first requirement could be hung.

[Relative secrecy: an original twist] It is well established in Australian law that in breach of confidence the quality or characteristics of the information concerned are irrelevant in legal terms, as long as they are sufficiently circumscribed. It need not meet the threshold test of non-obviousness that adheres in patents law; it need not be a good idea, inventive or striking, creative or original *per se*. However, these qualities may be relevant because they take the information outside the public domain: an original or creative concept is not common knowledge, nor the kind of thing any knowledgeable person could come up with. It is sometimes said that the knowledge, idea or concept concerned must be shown to have commercial value, but this suggests a distinction between trade secrets (ie commercial secrets) and other forms of confidential information such as private data, a distinction which Australian law does not make – the term 'trade secret' is not here a term of art, unlike in the United States, otherwise perhaps than in the context of employment (see further below). However, in Australia, although not as a separate requirement, commercial value may indeed have some relevance. First, absence of commercial value will tend to be consistent with ideas that are too vague and uncertain to attract the protection of equity; and secondly, the commercial value of some concept or idea may derive from its *uniqueness*, which goes some way towards establishing that it is not in the public domain.

[A low originality threshold] The rather low standard of originality which suffices to take some idea outside the public domain is well illustrated by the 'format' cases; for instance, *Talbot v General Television Corporation Pty Ltd* (1980) VR 224. In that case an idea for a TV show that would seem to most ordinary people rather banal – *a fortiori* so to trade insiders – was considered a trade secret, as it had a slight original twist. In relation to technical knowledge, such a 'twist' need not meet the standard of inventiveness prescribed for a patentable invention, which makes sense given the lesser protection obtained by trade secrets. Sometimes doubts arise about inchoate ideas or schemes, or overly vague or general propositions. The proper approach is to focus on two separate issues: first, whether the idea or concept is sufficiently precise to enable a court to determine whether it is in the public domain or not; and secondly, whether it has some special element of inventiveness, originality or creativity which takes it outside the realm of things commonly known. In terms of comparison with patentable inventions, whereas the standard of inventiveness for standard patents is relatively high, it is lower for the newly introduced innovation patent: there only a more than insubstantial contribution to the working of the invention need be proven (see *Patents Act 1990* (Cth), section 7 (4)). Arguably some products or processes previously only qualifying as trade secrets are now suitable for the grant of an innovation patent, in particular some relating to mechanical inventions that are easy to reverse engineer.

[The relationship with copyright] There is an interesting relationship between trade secrets law relating to concepts or ideas, such as in *Talbot*,[12] and the legal protection available under copyright law. A twist or original idea that takes a concept or format, whether artistic, technical or commercial, outside the public domain is often expressed in some document, which itself amounts to an original literary or artistic work. However, copyright protection does not extend to original ideas or concepts *as such* – only to their expression in some particular form, for instance as plans, drawings, manuals, etc. Copyright is unsuited to the monopolisation of a concept, scheme or idea *as such*, because any person is entitled to extract and use an idea as long as the form of expression is not copied in the process. By contrast, as long as the document is not made public, trade secrets protection does provide residual protection of *content*. The fact that the threshold test of originality in copyright in Australia is very low, compared to many other jurisdictions, really is of little assistance if it is an underlying idea, concept or technical breakthrough that a firm wants to monopolise, as opposed to the working out of the idea in a specific form of its own devising. Commonly this occurs in cases where intermediate copyright items such as technical drawings play a significant role in developing manufacturing processes, key elements of which may also be kept secret within the confines of the firm.

[Copyright, trade secrets and compilations] Copyright may also arise in private collections of units of knowledge that are individually in the public domain, as 'compilations' and thus literary works (see section 10 of the *Copyright Act 1968* (Cth)). With the low standard of originality in Australia, industrious collection of pre-existing data will suffice to vest copyright in compilations. But this protection does not extend to individual items, only to the manner and form of their compilation in the work as a whole. An infringement of copyright will occur if a substantial part of the compilation as such is reproduced, rather than simply by the reproduction of individual items. As indicated above, a breach of confidence may occur in such circumstances, if the compilation of materials requires investment and is presented in a particularly useful form. Access and extraction of multiple data compiled in a useful format may then constitute a breach of confidence too.

[Relative secrecy: technical trade secrets] In the case of technical trade secrets, to prove that certain knowledge constitutes a trade secret is a potentially expensive, time-consuming and hazardous task. Where the information is properly documented the risks and evidentiary difficulties are somewhat mitigated. But where knowledge is inchoate, ie at the stage of a broad idea, concept, research pathway or desideratum, and not precisely outlined and contained within some available record, difficulties multiply. First, the precise nature and outline of the concept must be clearly identified – if it is inchoate and unrecorded (eg where it has only ever been raised in conversation) that presents inherent difficulties. Then to demonstrate that it is not obvious, was not prevalent or had not been

---

[12] Mentioned above; see also *Fraser v Thames Television* [1983] 2 All ER 101 (the 'Rock Follies' case).

arrived at by other members of the relevant scientific community might require the presentation of expert evidence. Where this must be done in an adversarial setting, cases tend to become expensive, unpredictable, the outcome not necessarily conclusively favouring either party. *Secton Pty Ltd v Delawood Pty Ltd* (1991) 21 IPR 136 illustrates the difficulties inherent in cases concerning inchoate and insufficiently documented concepts; it is said to be one of the longest in Victorian legal history. Such cases concerning inchoate ideas frequently occur between employer and ex-employee, a matter considered in some further detail below.

[Relative secrecy: within the firm] That knowledge is shared between multiple parties does not necessarily mean it is in the public domain, if its circulation is within defined and controlled parameters. A common difficulty is to prove that information that circulates within a firm still amounts to a trade secret. The line to be drawn is between information whose circulation is so free and unrestricted that a conclusion that it is in the public domain is inevitable, even though it may not actually be known outside the firm; and information which may circulate widely within a firm, but whose circulation is restricted in relevant ways. Thus even information known quite widely within a firm can still be 'jealously guarded' and therefore a trade secret, if additionally it does not circulate amongst the relevant public outside the confines of the firm. To prove that it is a 'jealously guarded' trade secret, a plaintiff might establish: the existence of a restricted list of the initiated; the physical or contractual measures taken to keep the information secret; warnings and notices placed or distributed amongst staff and visitors; relevant provisions in contracts of employment; etc. A close connection exists between this test and the requirement of communication in confidence – it may be that information is unique to the firm, but is treated in such a cavalier fashion, that it can be said not to have been disclosed in circumstances implying that a duty of confidence attaches to it.

Demarcation and itemisation

[Demarcation of knowledge] Demarcation or itemisation is not a separate component of the *Coco* formula. But Dean rightly points out that the requirement has been elevated to 'an importance equal to the nature of the information itself'.[13] Knowledge is inherently an amorphous and closely interrelated mass. For the purposes of commercial transactions and enforcement of rights, knowledge must be demarcated and particularised. This can be done *ex ante* by way of a bureaucratic mechanism, as underlies the bestowal of property rights in patented inventions. But in the context of confidential information, the process is *ex post*, in the sense that it takes place at the time a dispute occurs or a transaction is concluded. The most straightforward method of demarcation is by reference to the record or container which contains the relevant knowledge: documents, computer disks, directories, catalogues, etc. But where this method is not available, courts require a

---

[13] See Dean, *The Law of Trade Secrets*, at p 106, [3.245].

substantive itemisation of the information, which they can keep confidential during proceedings if need be. In other words, ambit claims to knowledge described by reference to abstract categories (such as 'trade secrets in the defendant's possession') are not sufficient – what the information is must be sufficiently particularised, not merely described in global terms.

O'Brien v Komesaroff (1982) 150 CLR 310 identifies the supporting rationale in terms of the administration of justice: 'confidential information which is sought to be protected must be described by a plaintiff with sufficient particularity to enable it to be identified and to be embodied in an order of the court granting an injunction'.[14] Judges identify the issue as one of fairness to respondents who must comply with court orders, and should not be placed at risk of being unintentionally in contempt (be 'embarrassed'). It is crucial that information which is claimed to be a trade secret can be severed from surrounding and interconnected information, so that an order for injunctive relief can be properly complied with.

[Other reasons for particularisation] But appropriate particularisation is also relevant to the second element of the action as prescribed in *Coco*. In *Independent Management Resources Pty Ltd v Brown* (1987) VR 605 at 609 the Court put it as follows:

> The more general the description of the information which a plaintiff seeks to protect, the more difficult it is for the court to satisfy itself that information so described was imparted or received or retained by a defendant in circumstances which give rise to an obligation of confidence.

Furthermore, the plaintiff should not be allowed to shift the onus onto the defendant to show that information in some broad and abstract category has *not* been misused. As the New Zealand Court of Appeal said in *Norbrook Laboratories Ltd v Bomac Laboratories Ltd* [2004] NZCA 56 (5 May 2004; at [27]) in relation to a contractual obligation of confidence, and as would *a fortiori* apply in the absence of contract:

> Nor do we accept that contractual obligations of confidentiality in a commercial context require that there should be a legal or evidential onus on a party in possession of confidential information to satisfy the Court that it has not misused it. Any other approach would unduly inhibit competition [. . .].

The Court pointed out that an obligation of confidence is thus not equivalent to a fiduciary obligation such as might exist between solicitor and client.

[Practical difficulties] This requirement of itemisation can be a real hurdle where the plaintiff cannot, by dint of the circumstances, identify with precision that which the defendant is alleged to have misappropriated. In situations which concern tacit knowledge, existing only in the mind, or inchoate ideas, particularly involving employees, clearly separating confidential knowledge from public domain know-how is often an insuperable problem. Evidence of the exact nature

---

[14] See also *American Cyanamid Co v Alcoa of Australia Ltd* (1993) AIPC 91-032; (1993) 27 IPR 16.

and demarcation of trade secrets will be very difficult to provide, and in any case courts err on the side of caution, inspired by general policy concerns about competition and freedom of labour. Only the confidee knows exactly what the information concerned is and how he has misused it – but he is not exactly co-operating with the plaintiff. This can work unfairly against the confidor but, on the other hand, could tend to indicate that the information at issue is either so raw, or so irrelevant as to defy any need for a remedy.

[The importance of demarcation] So demarcation and particularisation are significant in various ways, so that the courts can satisfy themselves of the fact that information concerned is not in the public domain; see *Independent Management Resources v Brown* mentioned above. Further, they are important so that the courts can ascertain whether the information was imparted in circumstances implying an obligation of confidence; so that an injunction can be framed that will not be embarrassing to the respondent; so that under the guise of claims to trade secrets protection firms can't illegitimately disturb competition; and so that employees are free from ambit claims concerning trade secrets when engaging in competition post-term. The requirement will most easily be satisfied where the information concerned is contained in a defined record, a particular document or storage device, etc. It is far more difficult where what is allegedly removed is an idea or concept, for instance of a technical kind. If it is too vague or uncertain it will simply not amount to an actionable trade secret. It is therefore important for firms to document and record trade secrets wherever possible – as well as this being a useful due diligence tool wherever resources are committed to innovation, such records will be easy to refer to in contractual terms, and will also allow demarcation of a firm's own terrain if conflict about confidences arises later.

An implied or express obligation of confidence

[The basis for holding a recipient accountable] Information is frequently imparted with the intention of spreading it far and wide: there are gains to be had from publicising and diffusing knowledge. Ordinarily communications do not take place under the cloak of confidentiality – the norm in society is openness rather than secrecy. But in a commercial context knowledge is valuable and is customarily treated with greater circumspection. Furthermore, many transactions will only be possible if a firm engaged in commerce can reveal knowledge on a conditional basis confident that it will neither be used for some incompatible purpose, nor be publicly revealed so as to destroy its commercial value. Secret information is at risk of catastrophic disclosure, as well as of misuse. But if recipients' use of imparted knowledge is to be confined within limited parameters, the circumstances of the communication must make it reasonable that they be so restrained at law. So the law requires that it be apparent to the confidee from the circumstances that the information is imparted for a *limited* use – and not for him to divulge or use in any way he sees fit. In other words, the information is received on a conditional basis, and the circumstances must support the conclusion that the confidee is or ought to have been aware of that fact.

[The standard tests] Two alternative tests are usually advanced as applicable in the absence of an implied or express contractual obligation of confidence: the reasonable person test, and the limited purpose test. The latter holds that if it was or ought to have been sufficiently clear to a recipient that information was communicated for a specific purpose, the confidee is under an obligation of conscience to use it for no other purpose; and it will be enforceable at law. The limited purpose may emerge from express statements to that effect, but it is not essential that the confidor spell it all out. In other words, the circumstances of – including the lead-up to – the communication may imply restrictions. The relevant distinction is between the 'man on the Clapham omnibus' who loudly describes his brilliant invention because he wants to tell everybody how clever he is (circumstances that do not imply confidentiality), and the employed researcher disclosing a breakthrough at a scheduled meeting with financial backers for the sake of evaluation (circumstances that do). The courts are flexible in the sense that the antecedents of a meeting (eg correspondence setting out the purpose of a technology demonstration), the general nature of a meeting (eg business rather than a social gathering), commercial custom (eg the usual nature of format disclosures in the TV industry), the way in which a meeting is conducted, etc are all circumstances from which a limited and specific purpose can be implied. While the limited purpose test has a narrow focus on the purpose of the communication, the reasonable person test is more general and flexible. But although in theory other circumstances may be relevant, generally a reasonable person would realise that if information is provided for a specific purpose, an obligation attaches not to use it for any other. Generally, therefore, the reasonable person test is hardly distinguishable from the limited purpose test, which can be conceived of as one of its sub-categories.

[Technical trade secrets] When it comes to technical knowledge, inventions and innovations, the manner in which knowledge is communicated is a crucially significant issue, not only for the purposes of trade secrets law. The person who discloses hitherto hidden ideas in an unguarded manner will have to suffer the consequences both in terms of the action for breach of confidence, but also as far as patent applications are concerned. Revealing an invention in public without restraint before the date of lodging an application for a patent (ie the priority date) will constitute 'anticipation' and result in refusal for lack of novelty. At the same time, no recourse in equity against a recipient for using it will lie. But if the invention is communicated under the cloak of confidence (ie for a limited purpose), there is no anticipation and the option of filing for a patent remains. However, the potentially severe consequences of unfettered public disclosure have been mitigated by the recent introduction of a grace period (ie an 'amnesty' in relation to disclosures by the applicant during the 12 months prior to lodging of the application; see further below in Chapter three) for patent applications. Where the communication takes place in the commercial sphere, there will usually be little difficulty in implying confidence attaches, but obviously this does not apply to academic publications, either at conferences or in journals and the like. An invention thus published may benefit from the grace period for the purpose of patenting, but in terms of breach of confidence, the information would be neither secret nor communicated in confidence.

[Contractual obligation of confidence] An obligation of confidence may not arise in equity, but on the basis of a contract or deed. In commercial circles Non-Disclosure Agreements normally precede any disclosure of valuable commercial knowledge. Confidentiality clauses – whether general or specific – may also be included in general contracts, whether concerned with technology transfer, collaborative R&D, licensing of patents or other matters. Alternatively, the obligation of confidence may arise by implication from the terms and nature of the contract. If the obligation of confidence arises in a contractual relationship, remedies lie in breach of contract rather than in equity. Normally such a contractual obligation of confidence ceases when the information at some later date enters the public domain. But can the parties expressly agree that the obligation persists even after that time? On the one hand, once information is public any other competitors can use it, and it appears an unjustified restraint of trade that only the confidee is limited in the uses they can make of it. On the other hand, there is arguably no reason why a party to a contract should not agree and be held to an agreement, freely arrived at, not to use certain information, whether it be confidential or not. In *Maggbury Pty Ltd v Hafele Australia Pty Ltd* [2001] HCA 70 the High Court held that a clause, which imposed restraints on the use by the recipient *ad infinitum*, irrespective of whether the information remained in the public domain, was invalid. Since it no longer served the purpose of protecting a genuine trade secret once the information was public, the clause constituted an illegitimate restraint of trade which offended against public policy.

An associated issue is how to identify in the contract the information to which an obligation of confidence attaches – in abstract terms or particularised and identified in substance. The former may give rise to litigation and difficulty in proving what is covered, in particular, in distinguishing genuine trade secrets from mere know-how, not subject to any obligation of confidence. Particularisation on the other hand may not be possible, either because the nature of trade secrets that may emerge is unpredictable, or because it is simply impracticable to do so. The risk remains that broad terms relating to obligations of confidence may be struck down either for being too uncertain, or for going beyond the proper confines of genuine trade secrets into information that is in the public domain and whose use should not be restrained by contract.

[Referability to the obligation of confidence] If an agreement exists between parties in relation to the treatment of certain information, then contract prevails, as already mentioned above. But the information disclosed must be referable to the obligation – in other words, it must be some piece of knowledge to which the obligation applies. This is also the case where the obligation is based in equity rather than in contract. So if information revealed at some point is of a kind that the confidor did not previously have in contemplation, then no obligation of confidence will attach. This is what happened in the case of *Fractionated Cane Technology Ltd v Ruiz-Avila* (1988) 1 Qd R 51: unexpected results revealed during a demonstration of a piece of machinery related to processing of sugarcane for the purposes of stock feed were not covered by an obligation of confidence. In the circumstances, the confidees could not be held to an obligation relating to information which nobody even had in contemplation when they agreed to attend the demonstration to evaluate the machine for a different purpose. The circumstances did not warrant importing an obligation of confidence.

[Third parties and industrial espionage] That the circumstances of the communication should be such as suggests to reasonable persons that they are under an obligation of confidence is again somewhat artificial in cases of industrial espionage. This has not impeded courts' willingness to grant a remedy, based on the spy's obligations of conscience. Nonetheless, it must be shown that there were sufficient indications that the information concerned was indeed a trade secret. If there is clear evidence that a defendant has embarked on a course of deliberate, deceitful, illegal or surreptitious conduct to obtain information, the facts tend to speak for themselves. It may also be that it is known that the plaintiff considered certain information to be proprietary – he might have put it about in the district, as in *Franklin v Giddins* (see above). Or it may be that it is clear to any reasonable person, from the protective measures taken, that the plaintiff treats the information as his and his alone, and that it was therefore unconscionable to make off with it. It may be different where a person coincidentally comes across information of value and then uses it, or where it is inadvertently blurted out; that is a very different scenario from one where a person deliberately sets out by foul means to access and acquire clearly confidential data.

Use or disclosure of the confidential information

[Not from another source] The obligation of the confidee is to abstain from using or disclosing trade secrets for some purpose other than that for which they were provided. The exact purpose for which the information was imparted must be established from all the circumstances; and then whether what was done falls within or outside it. But a further question which often arises is whether it was the information imparted by the confidor that was actually used to arrive at some result, or rather other information in the possession of the confidee or available from other sources. The confidee might argue that no recourse was had to the confidential information the subject of the dispute, to produce some product that appears to embody it. Care must be taken that the onus of proof is not transferred by the confidor pointing to similarities in the confidee's concepts developed or products made, and requiring the latter to prove that some trade secret was not abused in the process; nor should the confidee be allowed to refer to some abstract category, like 'the trade secrets', then requiring the confidor to prove that nothing contained within it was misused. It may well be that the confidee's response just hides actual abuse of confidence; but in fact it may reflect the difficult position of a confidee if information they have received in confidence becomes public, or is of a kind they would have arrived at in the normal course of affairs and by their own efforts anyway.

This is not uncommon in an era of science-based research where multiple organisations are pursuing similar research paths, often based on common generic techniques or data, and also exchange information and research data to a certain, if carefully ring-fenced degree. A balance must be struck between allowing normal processes of competitive research within the confines of a market-based innovation system, and the necessary legal support for proper conduct in this branch of business.

[Independent development or misuse of confidential information] The following extended passage from *Norbrook Laboratories Limited v Bomac Laboratories Limited* [2004] NZCA 56 (5 May 2004) at [35] and [36] usefully addresses the issues referred to in the previous paragraph:

> The misuse of confidential information will sometimes be relatively straightforward to prove. A chain of documentation may establish misuse, or there may be other clear independent evidence. Where, however, proof depends on the drawing of an inference from similarity between what it is that the defendant has disclosed or done and the confidential information, more difficult questions may arise. It is helpful to begin from some basic principles. First, the possession of confidential information does not of itself preclude a person from developing a product equivalent to that which is protected, provided that the confidential information or element is not misused. Secondly, the fact that a person is aware, when receiving information from an independent source, that it conforms with the confidential information, does not in itself give rise to misuse. Nor does the mere fact that the person takes comfort from that knowledge. It is only if the knowledge or comfort causes the person to do, or to omit to do, something that there is conduct amounting to misuse. Normally this will take the form of a person avoiding having to undertake some part of the process required to develop the product. Were the rule to be otherwise, it would be virtually impossible for those possessing confidential information ever to be involved in developing equivalent competing products. It must be borne in mind that the purpose of the protection of confidences in law and equity is to prevent disclosure and misuse, not to disqualify people from competing. Megarry J said in *Coco v A N Clark* [1969] RPC 41:
>
>> I also recognise that a conscientious and law-abiding citizen, having received confidential information in confidence, may accept that when negotiations break down the only honourable course is to withdraw altogether from the field in question until his informant or someone else has put the information into the public domain and he can no longer be said to have any start. Communication thus imposes on him a unique disability. He alone of all men must for an uncertain time abjure this field of endeavour, however great his interest. I find this scarcely more reasonable than the artificiality and uncertainty of postponing the use of the information until others would have discovered it (p 49).
>
> We share the view that there it would be unreasonable for the law to place such a 'unique disability' on those who possess confidential information.

The disability referred to would be 'unique' because neither the confidor nor any other competitor would labour under it. However, the Court of Appeal's reasoning does not rule out inferring breach from similarity altogether, in the absence of a trail of documentary proof. As the Court went on to say (at [36]):

> In determining whether to draw an inference from similarity between confidential information, and what the defendant has disclosed or done, the ultimate test will often be, as Lord Denning MR put it in *Seager v Copydex* [1967] 1 WLR 923, 931, whether: 'The coincidences are too strong to permit of any other explanation'.

[Risks from accepting confidential information] Nonetheless there are risks inherent in receiving confidential information, which make firms increasingly reluctant to receive information under the cloak of confidence, unless they have deliberately sought it out, or have an established relationship with the confidee. The first risk is that recipients may be forced out of a field of research by concerns about litigation where there is a close connection between information received and their own R&D, even if they prudently isolate proprietary research (eg by using 'clean rooms' or 'Chinese walls'). Secondly, in an environment of unpredictable outcomes, providers of (allegedly) confidential information may be encouraged to seek by (threats of) litigation what they fail to obtain by negotiation. Courts have shown some inclination to favour those who provide innovative ideas from an apparently weak bargaining position. One instance of this is the adoption of the concept of *subconscious* use of a trade secret: accepting that a witness is truthful when testifying that he cannot remember receiving some idea or information in confidence, but still finding a breach has occurred through some subconscious mental process. Such reasoning exposes recipients of new knowledge to inestimable risk, even though it may be mitigated by their dominant market position, or their influence in the industry concerned. In seemingly wishing to protect the position of the under-resourced and vulnerable confidee, the courts have not necessarily adopted a policy that encourages the kind of free exchange and diffusion of ideas that would promote innovation. The conundrum of unknowability (see above) can be overcome by surrounding disclosure with secure, predictable and enforceable rules; exposing recipients to liability in the absence of conscious misuse does not advance this goal.

[The limitations of the limited purpose test] The limited purpose for which information was disclosed, once established by evidence, provides the framework of permitted use in normal circumstances. But whose purpose? The two parties may well be at *cross*-purposes; clearly the purpose of the confidor can only be determinative to the extent that it was adequately communicated to the confidee. But even if the purpose of the confidor in providing the information is clear, it may not wholly determine the scope of permitted use. For instance, in *Smith Kline and French v The Secretary to the Department of Community Services and Health* (1991) AIPC 90-821 (Full FC) it was held that the limited purpose SK&F had in contemplation when communicating drug research data for the purpose of evaluation did not wholly circumscribe the legitimate uses the department could make of it. It was legitimate for the department to use the data in the evaluation of an application relating to the same substance by a competing generic manufacturer. Considerations of public policy legitimised a use not just outside the confidor's purpose, but arguably inimical to it; but one indeed desirable from the public interest point of view, since generic competition for drugs out of patent drives down prices. In this context, it should be kept in mind that the action for breach of confidence exists in equity, and in determining a remedy the court exercises a *discretion* to which a wide range of factors is relevant.

[Limited purpose, patents and generic competition] *SK&F* (above) is illustrative of a significant relationship between trade secrets and patents law. At the expiry of the patent term (20 years) the invention enters the public domain. Obviously the 20-year term is intended to reflect a careful calibration of an appropriate and effective incentive to engage in innovation. However, for pharmaceuticals, heavily reliant on patent protection as they are, obtaining marketing approval is a time-consuming process, which reduces the *effective* monopoly term; hence the provisions in the *Patents Act 1990* (Cth) concerning pharmaceutical patent term extension (see Chapter 6, Part III, section 77ff). Nonetheless the need to obtain regulatory approval could also *benefit* the patentee, since generic competitors who intend to market drugs after the expiry of the patent also require approval. If they are compelled to revisit all the regulatory requirements that the patentee had already complied with, the *effective* monopoly term will be extended. As long as the generic drug is a genuine equivalent to the previously patented drug, the resulting duplication is an obvious waste of resources. On the other hand, if the generic competitor need not provide its own data, it simply free-rides on the patentee who has had to bear all the costs of regulatory approval (including clinical trials and the like). Whatever the merits of the respective arguments may be, the matter is now governed by the US–Australia Free Trade Agreement (USFTA) which requires that confidential regulatory data be granted a five-year exclusivity period (as prescribed by the *Therapeutic Goods Act 1989* (Cth), section 25A). A related issue concerning all patented inventions is that of 'springboarding'; ie to what extent competitors can prepare for use, production and sale of patented products prior to the expiry date of the patent. If this is entirely prohibited, the effective monopoly term is extended by the time required to bring competing goods to market after expiry; see further below, in Chapter three.

Detriment and remedies in general

[Actual damage or *quia timet*] The remedy of choice in breach of confidence actions, lying at the core of equity, is the injunction: the applicant petitions the court to *intervene* rather than to compensate. Rather than in its inherent merits, the value of a trade secret lies primarily in the fact that it is unique to its possessor – once the cover of secrecy is blown, its commercial value is *ipso facto* destroyed or severely diminished. The injunction is the preventative legal measure *par excellence*. So where the harm takes the form of public disclosure (eg by putting a product embodying the trade secret on the market), the injunction, if granted in a timely fashion, can prevent the destruction of the value of the trade secret. However, although the law will provide a remedy in the absence of proof of actual damage, on the basis of apprehended damage (or '*quia timet*'), in a practical sense this depends on the plaintiff becoming aware of a threatened breach. If the breach has already occurred, then depending on the degree of disclosure, an injunction will serve little purpose, since it will only stop the confidee, and not competitors at large to whom the information has become apparent. *Ex post facto* a different remedy will be appropriate, whether in the form of an account of profits (an equitable remedy by nature) or now also damages (equity now countenancing compensation). Such a compensatory or restitutionary remedy may also be appropriate where the breach takes the form of misuse rather than disclosure – although again if misuse is only threatened an injunction may be effective and appropriate. It is important to realise however, that the courts will not take kindly to a confidor who, knowing of the breach, delays and then seeks an account; this would amount to the imposition of a compulsory licence. One of the discretionary factors to be taken into account in determining whether the grant of the equitable remedy is appropriate is the delay of the applicant in approaching the court once notified of the breach.

[Actual damage?] Whether actual or threatened damage must be proven at all is one of the least settled issues in breach of confidence law; but actions speak louder than words, and it is readily apparent that courts have not allowed doctrinal questions to stand in the way of granting a remedy in an appropriate case. Equity is a byword for flexibility, and the purpose of the discretionary power to grant equitable remedies is not primarily or in origin compensatory. On one approach, the detriment simply lies in allowing a breach of confidence to go unpunished, something that would be contrary to public policy. Therefore courts will not countenance a breach even in the absence of proof of actual or threatened financial or other damage. Alternatively, courts will accept nominal or minimal damage or detriment merely in the form of embarrassment or injury to reputation as a sufficient basis for the grant of an injunction. Thus in cases where disclosure of personal information is at issue, threatened embarrassment or public humiliation may be a sufficient detriment. In terms of commercial trade secrets, the detriment to efficient commercial interaction flowing from a court's refusal to act in the face of an abuse of confidence is readily apparent.

[Permanent and temporary injunctions; the springboard doctrine] An injunction may be granted on an interim basis, ie on an interlocutory application and until the trial of the action. Quite often breach of confidence cases go no further. But if the matter does go to trial, a court can grant a permanent or indefinite injunction. However, this remedy is not appropriate if, due to the breach at issue or for some other reason, for instance because the confidor has proceeded to put a related product on the market, information has by the time of trial or thereafter become available to others. A permanent injunction puts the defendant at a disadvantage not only vis-à-vis the confidor, which is appropriate, but also vis-à-vis other competitors in the market, thus amounting to an unwarranted restraint on the defendant's ability to compete at large. However, neither should defendants be able to benefit from unconscionable conduct to get ahead of the competition.

The Court in *Terrapin Ltd v Builders' Supply Co (Hayes) Ltd* (1967) RPC 375 (see also above) responded to these conflicting concerns by fashioning an intermediate solution, which has since been frequently emulated: an injunction for a definite term only which prevents the confidee from using a trade secret as a 'springboard'. The principal difficulty with the springboard 'doctrine' lies in determining just how long this definite term should be, an unavoidably imprecise exercise. The court must calculate how long a competitor without direct access to the trade secrets would require: to work back from the published source (eg by reverse engineering); to isolate the trade secret; to work it up into a prototype; to establish manufacturing capacity; to make it; and then to market it. Expert evidence will help to determine how long this might all take – but in the end it is all rather abstract and hypothetical, particularly so where some secret is unlikely to be either uncovered or independently invented at all. But again practical issues have not defeated the courts. In general, they show a robust attitude to difficulties in precisely calculating the size or extent of a remedy; even if the method of calculation must amount to a stab in the dark (ie is 'at large') a plaintiff should not be denied their remedy. However, in cases where there is at least a partial disclosure of a trade secret by the time of trial, the court might alternatively treat the relevant information as having become public, the plaintiff failing on the first requirement in consequence. A delicate balance will have to be struck, and the dividing line between these two scenarios carefully drawn.

[Secrets improved upon and mixed secrets] Courts display this 'robust attitude' to remedies for breaches of confidence in other circumstances as well. Because of the interconnected and amorphous nature of knowledge, an injunction in some cases may be a remedy with far-reaching consequences for the defendant. For instance, the confidee (who may not have intended to misuse the information, albeit being found to have done so) may find that the disruption to production processes caused by an injunction is out of all proportion to the significance of the trade secret in the context of the totality of its knowledge base. Or the information concerned may have become inextricably linked with proprietary information of the confidee. The effect of an injunction is then to prohibit the defendant from using his own information as well as the impugned trade secret; or to greatly disrupt investment, R&D, employment and the ordinary operations of the defendant. But courts tend to take an attitude which should inspire vigilance on the part of those dealing with trade secrets. Again, such circumstances as described will not automatically result in the refusal of an injunction: justice to the confidor is the priority, as is the public policy of respect for confidences in general. However, it may in all the circumstances of the case be more appropriate to grant a compensatory remedy; nonetheless, due diligence in the management of trade secrets in a commercial context is strongly advisable.

Remedies against third parties

[When is a remedy against a third party legitimate?] Third parties in receipt of trade secrets are liable to a remedy for breach of confidence in two circumstances: if they have 'knowingly participated' in the breach itself; and if they have been put on notice at some time after the breach. It is legitimate to impose liability on a party who takes advantage of secret information, aware that it was obtained in circumstances that transgressed another party's rights. The third party adopts the unconscionability of conduct of the original confidee, chooses to benefit from it and should suffer the consequences. However, courts have held that not only actual knowledge (eg where the third party has been told of the breach upon its acquisition) but also constructive knowledge is sufficient: that is, where the third party was not actually aware of a breach, but ought in the circumstances to have been so. Constructive knowledge may flow from the nature of the information itself (it may be of a kind participants in a certain industry or R&D would recognise as someone else's property), or the actual circumstances in which it was imparted (eg suspicious actions or demeanour), or because a third party knows that a person bearing trade secrets previously worked for a competitor (as is further considered below). It certainly imposes upon recipients of confidential information an obligation of care and due diligence, in relation to the origins of any know-how or trade secrets they acquire. This point is further reinforced by the fact that actual notice after acquisition will equally expose a third party to a remedy. Courts have not accepted that in such circumstances *bona fide* for value acquisition is an automatic defence!

[*Bona fide* acquisition for value] A difficult issue arises in those circumstances where an innocent third party is put on notice only after acquisition of trade secrets, for instance, by express notification by or on behalf of the confidor (for instance by its legal advisers). Again the courts are faced with a difficult choice if a remedy is sought against a third party in such circumstances. If the third party is innocent ('*bona fide*'; ie justifiably ignorant of the breach) and paid good value for the trade secrets, should it suffer an injunction at the hands of a previously undisclosed confidor? Conversely, should the confidor be without a remedy, ie have to endure the exploitation of its trade secrets by some third party, without any consideration being received and where a breach of confidence sustained this exploitation? The confidor may have good reason not to proceed against the original confidee (who may be absent, indigent or have dissipated the consideration for the transfer of the trade secrets involved). Courts have not been inclined to tie their hands by accepting a *bona fide* for value acquisition defence. Rather they have taken a traditional stance in emphasising that it will depend on all the circumstances of the case whether a remedy is appropriate. Naturally in some cases the third party will have recourse in damages against the confidee who sold it the trade secrets, either in tort or on the basis of a breach of the contract of sale or licence (for instance of the relevant contractual warranties). However, the confidee may be without resources sufficient to compensate the third party for the disruption of his business, or for other reasons an unavailable or undesirable target.

Conclusions concerning trade secrets law

[Competition and trade secrets] Competition thrives on the circulation and diffusion of knowledge and information, as does innovation. Every competitor has the right, as well as the compelling need to obtain knowledge by any legal means available and to apply it to its own ends. This includes knowledge about or within the control of competitors. However, firms' ability to disclose knowledge on a restricted or conditional basis is fundamental to the conduct of business, and essentially required by the conditions of partial unknowability under which the knowledge trade operates. Trade secrets law ensures that where information is imparted for specific purposes, for instance for the sake of evaluation, its use for other purposes, or its disclosure, can be restrained, thus preserving its commercial value. Where the information does not come into the possession of another by the actual imparting of it by a confidor, the law has more difficulty in dealing with the situation. Some criminal remedy may be available if an offence like theft of some physical record or container has occurred in obtaining the information. But there is a penumbra of cases where the courts have shown a willingness to intervene against those who obtain secrets by surreptitious means, even in the absence of criminality – as indicated above, the limits of this willingness are not clear. However, ultimately the onus is on the confidor to look after their secrets properly, and prevent their obtention by surreptitious means. The possessor of secret knowledge who helps themself in that fashion can call the law in aid.

[Relationship with other areas of IPRs] Trade secrets law is in a sense a residual legal mechanism that supports and surrounds those statutory schemes that provide specific rights in carefully documented knowledge items. All are concerned with the management and trade in knowledge, and naturally there are thus close relationships between trade secrets law and other areas of intellectual property law, for instance patents and copyright. Trade secrets law is both an alternative and a general safety net that applies in circumstances where the conditions of other regimes cannot be met, or which for strategic reasons are to be avoided. Some subject matter is not protected in other regimes (eg service inventions are not patentable) but may be able to be appropriated to some degree (ie without protection against independent invention or reverse engineering) by reliance upon trade secrets law. The law of breach of confidence is also something of a default set of rules in relation to contracts. Where a contractual relationship exists the terms of the agreement will frame the parties' obligations as to the treatment of secret information that passes between them. Alternatively, express contractual provisions (such as in a non-disclosure agreement (NDA)) can replace or modify the extent and character of equitable obligations. However, there are limits to what can be achieved by way of contract, as was referred to above. Where there is an employment contract, somewhat particular and different rules will apply, as we shall see below.

[Flexibility of the action] The action for breach of confidence sometimes seems as flexible as the factual circumstances in which it accrues are varied. A clever marshalling of the facts and proof available is essential, as is skill in manipulating the various concepts and doctrines that underlie trade secrets law. This is not always a predictable or certain area of the law, and the action is constantly evolving. One of the most interesting areas of evolution is in industrial espionage-type cases, but the hesitant emergence of an action for breach of privacy also has a significant impact. In this context, *Australian Broadcasting Corporation v Lenah Game Meats Pty Ltd* [2001] HCA 63 is the latest word: the High Court refused either to extend the action for breach of confidence or fashion a new tort so as to remedy invasions of privacy. Some lower courts have not been as coy about 'discovering' a tort of invasion of privacy: see for instance, *Grosse* [2003] Aust Torts Reports ¶81-706, 64 187. However, in cases where there is no actual imparting, but a surreptitious obtaining of information, the line between invasion of privacy and breach of confidence will become progressively harder to draw.

3 The employment context

Introduction

[Mobility of employees] Other than via proprietary channels, knowledge is diffused by knowledgeable individuals as they migrate between firms. They study, they absorb knowledge on the job, and in a dynamic labour market they also migrate between firms and institutions taking their knowledge with them. Leaving aside labour law, the law of trade secrets is the core mechanism regulating knowledge mobility by migration between firms. The separate rules governing how employees should handle knowledge *during employment* do not normally come under the heading of breach of confidence; rather they are determined by the duty of fidelity or good faith attending the employment agreement. But it is the action for breach of confidence which commonly – although not exclusively – determines what knowledge employees are allowed to freely use '*post-term*' (ie after the cessation of the contract of employment); conversely, it determines what 'belongs' to the employer. As indicated at the outset of this chapter, this is a significant area of the law, in which case law concerning both equity and contractual provisions relating to trade secrets is brought to bear on quite frequently occurring disputes. Although most of those cases are arguably centred on know-who (client data) rather than know-how (technical knowledge), the principles adhering to know-who cases are relevant to instances where the confidential information relates to technical information, know-how, new products and processes or unpatented inventions. Below, the nature of the action for breach of confidence in post-termination cases is considered first, and thereafter the enforceability of contractual variations.

[Trade secrets and proprietary rights] But the rights of employees to the fruits of their intellectual endeavours are not solely determined by equity in the context of breach of confidence. Employees may well be entitled to ownership of inventions (and thus patents) that they make during the term of their employment. The rules that apply to such inventions are discussed below (see Chapter three). In the context of the present chapter all that needs to be said is that whether an employee owns an invention made during the term of employment is critically determined by the nature of their duties: did these include a duty to invent, or conduct research in the area of invention? If yes, then the employer is likely to be entitled to an assignment of the right to obtain a patent in the invention, or in the patent if one has already issued. If not, then the employee is likely to be entitled to retain ownership of the invention for the purpose of patenting. It is thus by no means the case that all inventions made 'in the course of employment' are owned by the employer. However, in this chapter we are not dealing only with inventions in the patent sense, but the broader concept of trade secrets, which includes both unpatentable 'know-how', and such knowledge as the firm has preferred to keep secret rather than patent.

The action for breach of confidence post-term

[Little statutory intervention; modification by contract] Parliament has not taken a great interest in this area of the law and it is thus governed largely by the cases. The well-established policy of the law favouring the right of workers to change employment freely is the backdrop against which the treatment of trade secrets or confidential information in the employment context must be viewed. In an attempt to manage the indeterminacy and unpredictable outcomes resulting from the rules of equity, employers often incorporate contractual restraints on the post-term use of knowledge acquired on the job in the contract of employment. However, courts police these clauses with an eye to the broader public interest in competitive labour markets and a mobile workforce.

[Breach of confidence and duty of fidelity] One set of rules applies during the term of the contract of employment, and a different set of rules after termination. During employment the legal framework is the employee's overarching duty of fidelity implicit in the contract of employment. Employees are under a legal obligation to use knowledge relevant to their duties to advance the interests of the firm, not for their own competing purposes. In other words, the employee should not draw on knowledge of the business to compete with their employer during the term of employment. Concepts, ideas and innovations connected to the employee's duties should be disclosed to the employer, and a firm can restrain the employee from using any such knowledge or information, whether secret or not, in a manner that is at odds with its own interests. The employee's obligation to disclose even inchoate ideas and concepts that might be of interest to the employer naturally has practical limitations: it is inherently difficult for the firm to police; and unless it is recorded in material form, it is effectively unknowable. Thus legal recourse against an employee who goes on to exploit a concept post-term is rarely available in practice, and employees may well be motivated to attempt to treat with the employer on a separate basis when they have conceived of something of particular value to the firm.

[The duty of fidelity] The *contractual* duty of fidelity is the legal framework determining the use of information during employment; the duty governs employees' conduct in general and not just in relation to knowledge acquired or generated on the job. Its nature and extent are more a question of labour law than intellectual property law. However, although the principal action relevant to the use of knowledge post-term is breach of confidence (a question of intellectual property law) the duty of fidelity is not wholly irrelevant in an action against an employee after termination. In certain cases the courts trace back to a wrong committed *during* employment; in other words, a remedy granted post-term is attached to a breach of the duty of fidelity during previous employment. Usually the employee can be shown to have deliberately copied, assembled, stolen or obtained confidential information or a trade secret with a view to using them after departure; the particular record – document, disk or whatever – will be in evidence, maybe as the result of the execution of an *Anton Piller* order against the defendant.

[Knowledge protected as a trade secret post-term] But where that is not the case, the matter will proceed on the basis of equity rather than implied contractual duty, ie as a question of breach of confidence. Precisely in the absence of the deliberate acquisition or theft of some record which is in evidence, serious evidentiary issues usually confront the firm. Tacit knowledge allegedly acquired or created during employment, and which must be shown to amount to a trade secret, is often only fully known or available to defendants, and difficult to connect to a firm they no longer work for. In the absence of a defining physical record it is difficult to accurately identify and demarcate the knowledge in dispute, so as to prove it has all the legal characteristics of a trade secret. Firms will also face considerable difficulties in proving that such knowledge was obtained by virtue of the pursuit of the erstwhile duties of the employee. The position of the employees is further strengthened by the pro-competitive principle that they should be free to rely on all their 'tools of trade', both in their individual interest and in the public interest as a whole. In the innovation age, knowledge, wherever acquired (whether from other employees or during a course of study), amounts to a significant if not the only 'tool of trade'.

Courts are therefore alert to a carefully drawn distinction between genuine trade secrets – which the firm should be able to continue to appropriate – and such knowledge, often referred to as know-how, as constitutes the employee's 'tools of trade' which they should not be restrained from drawing on when migrating to another employer or setting up for themselves, even in direct competition with their ex-employer. Drawing this distinction serves to ensure that the action for breach of confidence does not become a blunt instrument with which to confront competition from ex-employees. As Gleeson CJ said in *Wright v Gasweld* (1991) 22 NSWLR 317 (at 400):

> An employer is not entitled to protect himself against mere competition by a former employee, and the corollary of that is that the employee is entitled to use skill, experience and know-how acquired in the service of the former employer in legitimate competition. It is in the public interest that this should be so . . . At the same time the law will protect trade secrets and confidential information, and will intervene to prevent their misuse.

But the seamless and interconnected nature of knowledge makes it difficult to restrain the use of a trade secret without effectively prohibiting the use of connected or associated knowledge that is only 'know-how', and this has inspired courts to be even more guarded in these types of cases, and protective of the rights of ex-employees.

[*Faccenda Chicken v Fowler*] *Faccenda Chicken Ltd v Fowler* [1987] Ch 117 is the leading case in which the threshold test for distinguishing trade secrets from mere know-how was initially drawn. It is now routinely followed by the courts, but in fact the test is broad and of limited guidance in particular cases, certainly where tacit knowledge is at issue. The basic distinction of *Faccenda Chicken* has been further developed and 'refined' in later cases, such as *Wright v Gasweld Pty Ltd* (1991) 22 NSWLR 317, which has arguably achieved little more than adding layers of complexity without much benefit. Although arguably trending towards improving the position of the firm, these 'refinements' have in truth added a further chilling element of uncertainty. Whatever the exact current rules may be, the outcome of cases turning on the distinction in *Faccenda* is certainly unpredictable and indeterminate enough to motivate firms to seek more certainty from contractual prescriptions, as is further discussed below.

[The duty of fidelity and the duty of confidence are not co-extensive] The knowledge an employee may be obliged not to reveal or misuse during employment because of their duty of fidelity does not necessarily or automatically constitute a trade secret subject to an obligation of confidence post-term. Knowledge acquired by normal processes of observation and participation at work are usually just know-how, skill and experience and not trade secrets. According to Bennett J in *United Indigo Chemical Company Ltd v Robinson* [1931] RPC 178 it is almost impossible to restrain a defendant from using 'information he could not help acquiring' (at 187); and in *Printers and Finishers Ltd v Holloway* [1965] RPC 239 at 256, Cross J pointed out that recalling general matters about a plant, processes or machinery of an ex-employer '[. . .] is, to my mind, quite unlike memorising a formula or list of customers or what was said (obviously in confidence) at a particular meeting'. There is nothing wrong with an ex-employee relying on ordinary recall, even in relation to matters particular or unique to the ex-employer observed in the ordinary course of employment, since it 'is not readily separable from his general knowledge [. . .] and his acquired skill [. . .]' (at 256). However, specifically recorded knowledge deliberately protected as a trade secret will be treated differently; certainly if it is recorded, for instance in the form of a list, manual or data file.

[Avoiding the trade secrets/know-how trap] Courts often experience difficulties in distinguishing between a genuine trade secret, and the know-how, skill, knowledge and experience of an employee. This makes reliance on equity alone often unpredictable and an unattractive proposition for employers. In any case, what firms are commonly most concerned about is exactly what the courts refuse to prevent: that ex-employees use all the experience acquired, all they have learnt both about the firm and about its knowledge base, to compete with them post-term. This may occur in the context of employment with a competing firm or, as often happens, where an ex-employee sets up a new business to exploit some concept, inchoate idea, invention or innovative process or product conceived during employment. The risk and expense involved in actions for breach of confidence in such circumstances, combined with strategic concerns, explains why firms prefer to rely on non-competition clauses in the contract of employment to improve their position. However, this is not an easy row to hoe either: contractual autonomy is often displaced by the courts' longstanding aversion to restraints of trade.

Contractual extension of obligations of confidentiality

[Default rules and contract] The default rules of equity apply in the absence of any agreement to the contrary, so a firm might induce a prospective employee to accept limitations on the use post-term of knowledge that falls outside the confines of what equity would view as a trade secret. But courts regard such contractual extension of the equitable limits with disfavour, tending to discount autonomy of contract in favour of broad policy goals favouring the free circulation of knowledge. Contractual clauses that describe the category of 'trade secrets' or 'confidential information' too widely can be held unenforceable as contrary to public policy. In *Triplex Safety Glass Co Ltd v Scorah* [1938] ICR 211 a contractual term providing that all knowledge the employee gleaned or discovered 'shall be the exclusive property of the Company' (at 28) was too wide and unenforceable, as any claim extending to knowledge that can be readily ascertained from public sources would be. However, at a more marginal level firms may be able, by careful drafting, to extend or at least clarify the limits of their exclusive rights over knowledge. At the very least, particularisation in the contract of employment may pre-empt evidentiary difficulties. But it will have to be done either by specific itemisation, or else by reference to genuine and practical identifiers rather than abstract terms and categories. This might be impossible in practice, certainly in an R&D context where the course of future research and discovery is not predictable at the time of hiring. Keeping that in mind, contracts must be neither too specific to be useful (for instance by failing to cover the unpredictable), nor so abstract as to amount to an unenforceable restraint abhorrent to public policy. But even if certain knowledge is expressed to be a trade secret, the courts will still have to distinguish between that and the general know-how, skill and experience of the employee – with all the attendant difficulties of unpredictability and unfavourable policy setting mentioned above.

[Restrictive covenants: the general rule] Faced with these difficulties and uncertainties firms might attempt to extend their control over the knowledge of ex-employees by more indirect means: a temporary restraint on competition post-term, or 'restrictive covenant'. However, ever since the landmark case of *Nordenfelt v Maxim Nordenfelt Guns & Ammunition Co Ltd* [1894] AC 535, and the later decision in *Herbert Morris Ltd v Saxelby* [1916] 1 AC 688, contractual restraints on general competition by an ex-employee are against public policy and unenforceable, even where there is no doubt about the quality of the bargain. The public interest in employees' free participation in competitive labour markets overrides contractual agreements even voluntarily entered into that restrain their freedom to use all their knowledge, skills and experience to advance their own and/or another firm's interests. Private bargains which aim to isolate one party from competition with the market as a whole (so including parties not privy to the contract) are undesirable.

[Valid covenants] However, the courts *will* enforce covenants that impose restraints on post-term competition that do not go beyond what is reasonably required for the protection of genuine trade secrets. In *Herbert Morris Ltd v Saxelby* [1916] AC 688, Lord Atkinson pointed out (at 702) that the employer is:

> [. . .] undoubtedly entitled to have his interest in his trade secrets protected, such as secret processes of manufacture which may be of vast value. And that protection may be secured by restraining the employee from divulging these secrets or putting them to his own use.

Despite the fact that what is a *reasonable* restraint is very much determined on a case by case basis, and it is therefore difficult to determine *a priori* whether a restraint is valid, such covenants are attractive. A firm may calculate that a legal challenge is unlikely; that industry custom will encourage compliance; or that the consideration on offer will be adequate to dissuade breach. No doubt firms will be tempted to include restraints of probably impermissible scope; many restraints that if challenged would fail may in fact be observed, or on the other hand breaches may often be ignored without any resulting court action; these are empirical questions the answer to which cannot be discerned from the cases. Whatever the case may be, if the matter does reach a court a firm must prove that it has trade secrets to protect in this manner; and that the restraint is reasonable in scope for the purpose of protecting them. A restraint must thus be limited in time and/or area of operation, but there is no hard and fast rule as to what limitations are reasonable: it will depend on the circumstances. The cases have also evinced some disagreement relating to the categories of knowledge whose protection justifies a restraint – Gleeson CJ was at odds on this point with Kirby P and Samuels JA in the significant case of *Wright v Gasweld Pty Ltd* (1991) 22

NSWLR 317, for instance – and in terms of the permitted scope of restraints, on the whole the courts have conservatively deployed various limiting mechanisms.

[Innovation and observance of restraints] An enforceable covenant is arguably the most significant restraint the law countenances on the diffusion of knowledge between firms by migration of employees. Because the law, by recognising the validity of some restraints, gives firms an incentive to include restrictive covenants in contracts of employment, it may be that the resulting restraint on mobility is more extensive than is apparent from the cases. Naturally the public interest in encouraging knowledge diffusion by employee mobility must be balanced with the interest of individual firms in reliable planning for future innovation; but it is not clear whether the law as it currently stands is adapted to the conditions of high mobility of employees and of knowledge in the modern economy. The argument, as proffered by Callinan J in *Maggbury* (see above) that employees are now more informed and in a better bargaining position than in the past, and therefore covenants freely entered into should not be displaced, applies *a fortiori* to knowledgeable employees in R&D industries. However, it tends to discount the fact that the restrictive consequences of the private bargain extend to competition with the world at large, not just between the parties involved; it is for this public policy reason that the courts intervene, not because of some deficiency in the bargain itself.

Nevertheless, despite the enforceability of some restraints, the overall effect of the rules and principles underlying this area of the law is that employees are generally free to migrate with what knowledge they have in their minds. They will rarely have to account for it to any previous employer, and an employee can generally join a new firm with little concern about using knowledge obtained previously, except for very specific items that really are 'trade secrets'. And firms can hire safe in the knowledge that any new employee will be free to disclose and employ what they know, without being beholden to a previous employer. This appears to be an eminently sensible approach to adopt, and is certainly one that favours knowledge diffusion.

3

Patents

Introduction

[Relationship with trade secrets law] The previous chapter discussed how the law assists commercial actors to preserve secrets, including innovative products or processes. But relying on trade secrets law leaves the innovative firm exposed to two major risks of subversion: by independent invention and by reverse engineering by competitors. The law of confidence recognises neither property rights nor anything approaching a monopoly in secrets. It has particular drawbacks for a firm investing substantial resources in innovation, where commercial exploitation exposes it to the risk of reverse engineering and subsequent imitation.

Trade secrets law is also beset by problems of demarcation and by uncertainty. Patents law addresses these problems by *ex ante* demarcation of subject matter and grant of exclusive rights, more akin to a real monopoly: neither reverse engineering nor independent invention nor publication gives competitors the right to use a patented invention – even if and when in genuine ignorance of the patentee's invention or the patent. This absolute right to prohibit commercial exploitation has potentially serious implications for competitors, so a patented invention needs to be carefully identified, demarcated and circumscribed, and a system devised to alert others of the existence of legal rights (a public register). Furthermore, some quality assurance is essential to ensure that whatever attracts such extensive rights meets certain standards of innovativeness, so that the system induces dynamic competition and is potentially welfare-enhancing.

[Public policy drawbacks of secrecy] From a public policy perspective, secrecy also has the rather obvious negative effect of restricting the diffusion of knowledge. Furthermore, secrecy disrupts the coordination of research efforts.

As suggested before, as knowledge resources and research capacity are dispersed, efficient organisation and coordination are crucial, but these are hampered by firms' or institutions' ignorance of each other's knowledge inventories, research pathways and results. Considerable resources might also be expended on guarding secrets – an opportunity cost, since they cannot then be invested in more R&D. By contrast, a central tenet of patents grant is 'no monopoly without publicity': grant is dependent upon publication of the details of the invention concerned. This informs others of the state of research and results of the patentee, assisting efficiency in various ways: it prevents duplication (ie blind investment in R&D in ignorance of existing knowledge inventories of competitors); and it encourages coordination of downstream research efforts (ie the patentee will coordinate R&D that falls within the scope of the patent). However, the patent mechanism also experiences detrimental cost effects: the system of demarcation of knowledge, of examination and of administration is expensive; and the potential for wastage from the race to be first to patent is considerable. Much of the administrative expense is wasted in another sense as well: by its nature the system does not guarantee commercial success for an invention, and empirical studies consistently show that a large majority of patents are worthless in commercial terms – apparently a wasted investment in terms of the administrative effort and financial resources expended on obtaining them. Nonetheless, despite this fact, industry continues to spend up big on patents, which has resulted in extensive speculation as to the gap between the apparent public policy goals of patents, and the real and actual advantages that firms strategise to obtain by amassing patent portfolios.

[**Markets and incentives**] But all the above is only significant in a market-based and competitive innovation system. Alternatively, instigating and coordinating innovation can be either partly or wholly governed by direction from the state bureaucracy. The pros and cons of such an approach have already been addressed – see Chapter one above. So the need for patents stems from an underlying systemic choice: that innovation lies within the functions and competencies of consumer-sensitive firms; innovation is endogenous to markets; and, a fundamental presumption, that on balance subjecting innovation to market forces will enhance the efficiency of the innovation effort. Nonetheless much R&D is conducted in the public sector, *traditionally* insensitive to market forces and unconcerned with patents. In recent times there has been a greater meshing between the two systems, because public institutions such as universities have come to see patents as an efficient way of transferring innovations to the public, and of generating additional research funding in the process. Closer integration between public and private sectors in education, research and innovation has seen the barriers between the two become lower and fuzzier.

[**The orthodox account, constant controversy and expanding reach**] The orthodox account of patents, based on incentive theory and 'social contract' theory (monopoly in return for disclosure), has always generated controversy, ranging from heavy criticism of bureaucracy[1] to a healthy strain of 'patent abolitionism'.[2] Partly this is due to the fact that the empirical account of its economic effects is patchy, and that participants' accounts are also variable – some industries and some firms rate patents as far more important than others. The policy goals are constantly being reassessed, underlying theory being reinvented in the process: in relatively minor ways these debates affect the shape of patents law, but for the most part the patenting behemoth lumbers on largely unchanged. If measured by volume, then in recent times the significance of patents has certainly grown: both in number of grants and, because of the impact of WTO/TRIPS (Trade Related Intellectual Property), in geographical reach. This extension into countries that do not have any supporting infrastructure in terms of education, R&D and innovation has generated perhaps the most acute criticism of the system. Voices advocating patents as beneficial in that they should accelerate an innovation dynamic in any economy are opposed by those that decry them as increasing the costs of more fundamental drivers of economic growth, such as healthcare and public education. If an accelerating innovation dynamic really requires increased private spending on R&D, then it is certainly troubling that the growth in patent numbers has not been matched by growth in private sector R&D expenditure.

[Focus on substantive issues not procedure] This text focusses on substantive questions of patents law, in particular on the threshold requirements for subsistence and core questions relating to infringement. It does not give a detailed account of the procedural and administrative aspects of the system, either in relation to applications or issues that arise during the life of the patent. Suffice it to say here that procedural requirements and the prosecution of patent applications can be complex, and the assistance of suitably qualified patent attorneys is key to the proper operation of the system. They represent applicants and patentees, combining knowledge and experience of legal, bureaucratic and administrative matters with scientific and technological training in the area to which a given invention belongs. Arguably their most important skill lies in the drafting of the claims, that part of an application whose precise wording is absolutely critical to the validity and efficacy of any patent. But claims are supported by the rest of the application, which contains a description of the invention, an account of its antecedents, and focusses on inventiveness and novelty in detail. Patent attorneys deal with patent examiners and delegates of the Commissioner of Patents, *inter alia* responding to their directions and requests, often by making appropriate amendments to the application which will save it from final rejection.

For those interested in the detail of the procedural aspects, which are without a doubt of considerable significance to individual applications, more specifically relevant works are available; but despite successive recent governments' attempts to make the system more user-friendly, the assistance of a skilled patent attorney

---

[1] See Charles Dickens' short story: *A Poor Man's Tale of a Patent*.
[2] As traced in Mark D Janis, 'Patent Abolitionism', (2002) 17 *Berkeley Technology Law Journal* 899.

is in virtually every case crucial. The IPAustralia website[3] also provides useful procedural information as well as access to the Australian Patent Office *Manual of Practice and Procedure*.

1 Patent policy context

[The disclosure of inventions] The 'social contract' theory suggests that a temporary monopoly is the necessary reward for beneficial public disclosure of an invention. Various elements of patents law translate this disclosure policy underlying the system into specific rules. The most significant is the requirement of an 'enabling disclosure' (see section 41 of the *Patents Act 1990* (Cth)), ie disclosure in the application sufficient to enable a person familiar with the area of technology to understand the description and implement the invention. The patentee must disclose the best form of the invention known to him, but he is not required to also instruct readers on the best way to turn the invention to account. Therefore applicants usually attempt, with the help of patent attorneys, to disclose no more than is required to meet the legal standard, without unnecessarily giving away surrounding information (often called know-how).

What, however, is the point of compelling disclosure of an invention which nobody else can legally exploit? Two core aspects of the system answer this question: first, others are only restrained from *exploiting* it – any person can *learn* from it, and use knowledge garnered for further research, and development of *different* inventions. The second aspect is the limited term of the monopoly: 20 years maximum for standard patents but only eight for innovation patents. At the expiry of the term the invention is free for everybody to exploit; however, because of the rapid pace of knowledge development and technological change, only rarely will competitors be waiting to adopt the invention at the end of the term (except in relation to some inventions with continuing demand, such as certain drugs).

[The nature of the incentive] The principal incentive offered by patents law is a monopoly in the making, operating and selling of the patented invention, allowing patentees to appropriate a higher return from their investment in innovation by defeating free-riders. However, because imitation is often imperfect and delayed, investment in innovation can be perfectly rational even in the absence of patents, so they are normally only one option or one aspect of a broader strategy. Patent law establishes a prize-system: whoever is first to apply for the patent will obtain the monopoly prize, to the exclusion of all others. Nonetheless, in itself the prize is worthless; in fact significant up-front costs attend obtaining it. The attraction thus lies in the *potential* of exclusive commercial exploitation. In terms of competitive advantage the exclusive rights granted are indeed extensive: all competitors in the race for the prize will have to desist; if they want to use

---

[3] www.ipaustralia.gov.au

the invention they, like any other person, require the licence of the patentee (subject to the exception of prior (secret) use, see below). And the monopoly is also extensive because there are so few exceptions: any making or operating of the invention that has a commercial flavour or intent, even if indirect, will normally be interdicted. The only major structural exception is compulsory licensing for non-use, which in theory prevents extortionate pricing and the 'burying' of patented inventions; in practice such licences are very rarely granted. The so-called experimental use exception is not settled in Australian law – it is certainly not recognised in the statute, so it all depends on whether a court finds that on the facts the experimental use is commercial in character or not.

[**Demarcation and knowledge transactions**] Knowledge is a difficult commodity to trade: a system of demarcation is required if trade in discrete knowledge items is to operate efficiently. Patents law achieves demarcation by requiring from patentees a very precise description of an invention, in the context of its technological or scientific pedigree. Various methods, from verbal description to graphic representations, are apt. Then the law also requires, by virtue of one or more claims, a refined circumscription of what exactly the patentee chooses to claim as falling within their monopoly. All this serves to identify precisely what the invention is, how it operates, what it achieves, and what it is that others cannot do – because the nature of the patentee's right is negative, ie to prohibit others from exploiting the invention. The underlying technique of the law is to adopt the language and practice of property – the *Patents Act* expressly provides that a patented invention is personal property. This 'property' can be turned to account by direct exploitation, by licensing or by assignment during the term of the monopoly (when the term of the patent ceases, so do agreements relating to its exploitation). The mechanism of ownership and formal authorisation allows the patentee to coordinate the use, but also the further development or improvement of the invention. A patented invention may be able to be exploited or applied in many different technological environments and products, for which it may require adaptation or development, and a patent encourages the pursuit of a coordinated and organised strategy for such purposes.

[**Scope**] However, there is a narrow line between a property-rights-based monopoly, which assists the patentee in financing and coordinating downstream research, adaptations and improvements, and one which amounts to a dead hand on competing or related research. Therefore it is important that the scope of the rights, the extent of exclusivity, is properly calibrated. A number of legal requirements inherently limit the scope of the monopoly in any case: the requirement that some practical application, not just theoretical or desired outcomes be disclosed in the application; the requirement of novelty – the broader the level at which an invention is claimed the more likely that it is not novel; the requirement that the specification be free of ambiguity and uncertainty – the description must be precise as to what is claimed, ie what is within or outside the monopoly. But structural factors also mitigate potentially deleterious effects of monopolies on competition: in an environment dense with patents, competitors will often be dependent on obtaining cross-licences, so unilateral actions against competitors may be counterproductive. In fact, in the context of increasingly complex products relying on multiple technologies, cross-licensing becomes the core bargaining mechanism that permits the practical operation of the system. It partly explains the patent proliferation dynamic: firms observing the expansion of rival patent portfolios in an area of innovation will want to arm themselves with more patents, and so on. Another element that restrains the tendency to act monopolistically on the basis of patents is that they are not guaranteed to be valid: they are always liable to be subverted by a competitor applying for revocation. A patentee may prefer not to see the weaknesses of a patent exposed in infringement proceedings, and therefore desist from speculative infringement actions. The law also provides for remedies against unjustified threats of patent proceedings.

[**A benign monopoly?**] These questions of legal scope and practical use of monopolistic rights must be seen in context: although they impact on competition-by-imitation, patents are usually seen as *benign* monopoly rights, promoting dynamic efficiency by substitution. Rights are restricted to a specific invention, so substitute technologies or products can be developed and provided by others without hindrance. If no substitutes are available, then it must be presumed that the invention is exceptional and the monopoly-price benefits to the patentee rational – it is just the kind of invention the patents system provides an incentive for! It would make little sense to impose limits the moment an invention becomes an overwhelming success without apparent substitute choices. More generally, if patent grant brings into being products and processes *that would not otherwise exist*, then a monopoly in those products or processes, once created, can hardly be problematical. Nonetheless patents of excessively broad or uncertain scope *are* a real concern: they might stifle or chill innovation aimed at developing substitutes, because of overlap concerns; or they may generate a disproportionate reward compared to the actual practical contribution made, encouraging rent-seeking behaviour by the patentee aimed at those who *actually* develop workable inventions for which a real demand exists. Broad patents are a particularly troubling issue in highly scientific areas such as biotech, where the line between theoretical breakthrough and practical application has become more blurred and difficult to draw.

[**Patent misuse**] However, patents do expose the economy to the risk of malign anti-competitive conduct, particularly associated with the accumulation of patent portfolios. Acquisition of numbers of related patents can result in the extension of control from an individual invention, to a whole area of technology or innovation, stymieing dynamic competition by substitution. Once major corporations systematically acquire large portfolios, including marginal patents, with which they erect an insuperable barrier around a dominant position, we have moved beyond the positive effects of patent grant envisaged by orthodox theory. The potential of new entrants to subvert the market power of established corporations under the protection of a patent is then potentially destroyed. Kingston contends that the importance of the requirement of inventiveness lies exactly in this context: if investment alone would entitle a firm to a patent, then the established well-resourced market dominators could hem in their areas of technological pursuit with so many patents that the small and inventive firm would be unable to enter the market.[4] However, to some degree such accumulation of patents by larger firms already occurs, which may partly reflect how easy it is to comply with the threshold test of inventiveness.

[Limitations of the system] Notwithstanding Kingston's and other voices raised in support, the requirement of inventiveness in the patent system is seen by some as archaic, reminiscent of the industrial revolution, when the patent system became more significant, developing its modern form. That was the age of the heroic inventors, whose individual genius was a crucial ingredient of both industrial progress and commercial success. Today, however, applications of basic scientific knowledge are often developed by costly but systematic research. In this context the requirement of inventiveness appears like an anomaly: why, if a firm has invested huge resources in systematic R&D, should the reward of a patent be dependent upon establishing some individual human spark of inventiveness? The answers lie both in policy, and in the realities of the law. As mentioned above, Kingston's view is that in the absence of an inventiveness threshold strategic corporate behaviour would deny market access to inventive smaller players – the kind of start-ups and spin-offs that have emerged as a critical part of the innovation system. Posner et al see inventiveness as an indicator of social usefulness: an increased incentive, in the form of stronger rights than for trade secrets, is then warranted by the greater usefulness to society of a patentable invention.[5] Both these arguments crucially turn on the level of inventiveness required by the law. However, although novelty alone is indeed not sufficient, this inventiveness threshold is comparatively low – a step which is not obvious to the normal uninventive researcher in the field. An alternative way of viewing the inventiveness requirement is as a method for creating clear demarcation between inventions and thus property rights, to prevent overlap and demarcation disputes.

[An industrial-era system for a services-era economy?] The patent system is now also often criticised as adhering too stringently to its industrial roots: it remains focussed on technical, practical, technological inventions and innovations. Since a very large proportion of economic activity lies in the services sector, this seems to leave a lot of the economy deprived of the presumed benefits of patents. The system indeed has little effect on some of the mainstays of the modern economy: ie services like information management, financial management, accounting, etc. There have been recent attempts to expand the boundaries and allow patents for service innovations. Indeed it is often argued that in the United States business methods as such can now be patented. In Australia this is not the case, but where a business method is expressed or exercised in practical

---

[4] See Kingston W, 'Why Harmonization is a Trojan Horse', *EIPR* [2004], 26 (10), 2004, 447–60.
[5] See David D Friedman, William M Landes & Richard A Posner, 'Some Economics of Trade Secret Law' (1991), *Journal of Economic Perspectives*, 5, 1, 61–72.

terms as steps performed by a computer, it can potentially be patented in that guise.

However, why *not* expand patenting into business plans, methods of managing business and the like? Part of the answer lies in the limiting effect of the technicality requirement – the scope of a defined technology with physical parameters is more clearly circumscribed than some management plan, financial scheme or business tactic. Also, if patents are to remedy market failure (the sub-optimal supply of innovations), there is little evidence of a recognised shortage of innovation in business methods or ways of competing or management. A further difficulty lies with the requirement of utility: the law requires that a patented invention should work properly and reliably obtain specified results. Many pure business method inventions would struggle to meet this standard.

[Doubtful empirical basis for expansion] But in the final analysis every argument concerning expansion to a radically new level must be based on solid evidence; and the empirical evidence in favour of expansion into non-technological areas of innovation is not strong. As the economist Lamberton argued years ago about the patent system as a whole: since we have the system there is no justification for abolishing it, but if we did not have it there would be no strong reason to establish it.[6] That is not a ringing endorsement upon which to base a major expansion into non-technical areas of innovation. In spite of the considerable volume of research and writing on the topic since Lamberton's report, both in the legal sphere and in the economics and management literature, there is no hard evidence that the patent system advances innovation in every industrial sector. Although some industries are heavily patent dependent, others have evolved rapidly in the absence of patents; and rapid industrial expansion occurred in the presence of very weak patent systems in some countries, such as Japan and South Korea in an earlier era. In truth, patent rationales seem to evolve in a continuous dialogue between theory and practice. The practical uses made of patents are not always consistent with the theoretical rationales said to underpin them, as already illustrated above. That R&D expenditure has not kept pace with patent growth is evidence of a disturbing gulf between theory and practice. It tends to indicate that firms do not, or do not only, see patents as a protection for significant innovations, but as supporting other strategic behaviour. As explained above, it may be that some industry sectors perceive the advantage of patents as lying in the accumulation of portfolios which allow firms to dominate whole areas of innovation or research. Individual inventions may have little commercial application, but more value as part of a closely interwoven net of patents, which allows firms to erect effective barriers to entry.

[Transaction costs] Demarcation of knowledge units around which transactions can be structured lies at the core of the patent system. However, rigorous demarcation and testing are costly and cause delay. Patent examination occurs

---

[6] See Dissenting Statement by Professor D Lamberton, 'Patents, Innovation and Competition in Australia', Industrial Property Advisory Group, Attorney General's Department, 1984.

before exploitation, and thus at a time of uncertainty about commercial potential. Most patents in fact turn out to have little commercial value *per se*, and many simply lapse because no renewal fees are paid. Although the expenditure on examining patents is therefore often wasted, patent grant around the world has remained predominantly conditional upon *ex ante* substantive examination. Patent and attorney fees can be delayed because of flexibilities in the system, but are nonetheless incurred often long before the patentee enjoys financial returns.

An alternative is a system of grant *without* substantive examination, ie on formal compliance alone, as recently adopted in Australia in the form of the 'innovation patent'. This system represents a different trade-off between cost and certainty; it allows innovators to stake a claim to an invention, obtaining priority, etc, but the validity of the granted patent is unknown until the time an examination is requested. To enforce the patent, substantive examination *is* first required. This system is new in Australia and its success is not yet evaluated in depth.

[The limitations of the patent system] The relatively high cost of the patent system is one drawback; but it is important not to lose sight of the fact that patents are only one part of a broader innovation system. In fact patents are only relevant to a limited range of innovations: those for which firms see potentially profitable markets. Thus where some innovation although socially desirable cannot be profitably exploited, patents alone will not encourage sufficient private investment; public grants may be required. A further limitation lies in the manipulability of the market – rather than only being directed at areas of real need, innovation will be skewed towards areas where the desire for the invention in consumers *can* be influenced by firms (eg towards inventions in areas where advertising is permitted; away from heavily regulated commercial sectors). These limitations illustrate the fact that patents are only one weapon in the innovation policy armament, a fact easy to overlook given the overwhelming presence of patent analysis in the innovation policy and economics literature. Other IP regimes are also significant, as is more direct intervention by government; in parliament[7] the patent system was even described as 'in IPAC's words, "a blunt instrument of industrial policy"'. The private investment, market-based system of innovation is at any rate heavily 'subsidised' by the taxpayer, be it by way of free public education, funding of research in public institutions and universities, transfer of R&D results to industry partners or government procurement.

[The conservative reflex] Patents law is also still *law* – and much of it is case law, since the broad provisions of the Act require extensive interpretation. Law in the courts is inherently conservative, based as it is on binding precedent; does this sit well with innovation? The law is typified by continual tension between the conservative reflexes of the law and the progressive and unpredictable dynamic of science and research. Law seeks to establish a status quo which technology constantly subverts. This is reflected in the recurring debates concerning patentability in new areas of invention. When some wholly new

---

[7] 2nd Reading Speech, Patents Bill 1990, 29 May 1990.

scientific development emerges, there are commonly insistent calls for the drawbridge to be raised: to accommodate *this* within patent law would be going just that one step too far. Yet over time most new areas of technology *have* been accommodated and have developed a jurisprudence of their own, including: computer programs, biotech patents, plants, animals, etc. In this, Australian law has been guided by the High Court's insistence in *National Research Development Corporation v Commissioner of Patents* (1959) 102 CLR 252 ('*NRDC*') that in an era of rapid scientific advance the law must be accommodating and flexible. However, this approach has not always been so readily adopted by the lower courts, by other relevant institutions, by the patent community or by the general public.

[Patents: a value-free system?] Which brings us to the position of patents law in the broader regulatory framework – is it, at least in part, an instrument of technology regulation? In Australia patents law is largely value-neutral: ie if an invention meets the objective standards of novelty, inventiveness, etc, it will attract a patent. The requirement of 'utility' or usefulness (see further below) does not mean that the patentee must prove that the invention is socially beneficial – simply that it works as asserted and obtains the results claimed. The applicant need not establish that the invention is environmentally safe, morally acceptable or meets any community standard. Nor need it be established that experiments or tests have been conducted legally, or that material from which an invention is derived (eg plant, animal or human-genetic material) was obtained with the informed consent of donor or custodian (a significant issue in terms of the relationship between patents law and biodiversity conservation). However, the Commissioner can refuse applications for inventions that are contrary to law, a provision which has been narrowly interpreted.

Other countries' patents laws are more accommodating to technology or science regulation issues. For instance, the European Patent Convention (EPC) allows patents to be refused because they would be contrary to '*ordre public*' or morality. On that basis the patenting of modified animal organisms (eg the Oncomouse) has been fought over in the courts. But arguably patents law is not the proper forum for the regulation of technology: the courts are ill-equipped to consider the contrasting arguments and policy considerations, and patent offices even more so. It is parliament's responsibility to regulate science and technology directly. Furthermore, the fact that a patent is not available will not prevent research being carried out.

[Simplicity and complexity] Before examining the law in more detail, it is as well to accept that patents law is a complex, arcane and specialised area. At its core lie the specification and claims, highly technical documents that make up the application for a patent. The patentee cannot simply include one example of their invention as graphically represented (eg by photo or drawing) and claim a monopoly on the basis of that; many inventions are not capable of being so represented in the first place (eg process or chemical compounds). Thus the core skill of patent drafting, expressing the character of an invention in abstract claim language which captures the essential elements of the invention, is inherently complex. It is the preserve of patent attorneys who combine knowledge of science and technology with training in the rules and practices of drafting. Then there are the various threshold tests – some more technical than others, but all encrusted with deep layers of meaning over the years. The government has at times appeared frustrated by the technicality of law and practice, and has ambitiously attempted to simplify it; this was a professed aim of the new 1990 Act, as was stressed in the 2nd Reading Speech (Patents Bill 1990, 29 May 1990):

> In addition, the Bill uses greatly simplified language and structure in comparison with the present *Patents Act*, so that it will be more comprehensible to people who are not patents experts.

But even a cursory inspection of the law will soon reveal that this was a vain hope. Complexity has rather increased, partly because of the increased density of scientific underpinning of modern patents, but also because of misguided attempts at simplification. Ultimately, complexity and refinement are, and must remain, an inherent part of a properly modulated system of patents law.

[No guarantee of validity] A stark reminder of the technical difficulties and risks inherent in patent applications lies in the failure rates of patent suits, often due to the court's finding that the patent in suit is invalid. Normally every defendant in a patent suit counterclaims for invalidity – so the patentee risks not only losing the infringement case but ending up without a patent. The causes of findings of invalidity are varied, but both drafting errors and strategic misconceptions are commonly to blame. As well, technical rules such as those dealing with 'fair basing' often confuse even the most experienced patent practitioners, as does interpretation of the attendant case law. The failure rate of patent suits has recently attracted some adverse comment in Australia, but the reasons are contested, as is the legitimacy of various inferences drawn from it. It is well recognised that there are 'strong' and 'weak' patents, the latter being ones with doubtful novelty and inventiveness. It may be that the patents that are actually litigated tend to be weaker patents; stronger patents may induce early settlement of disputes or ready capitulation by alleged infringers.

2 Patents law: entitlement

[Introduction] This section examines core aspects of the law of patents in Australia: first, the threshold tests of patentability and other relevant conditions for grant; secondly, the two categories, standard and innovation patents; thirdly, the rules relating to ownership of inventions and patents; and finally, infringement of the exclusive right to exploit the invention. Remedies abroad are briefly referred to at the end of this chapter.

[Requirements for the grant of a patent] Patentability requirements fall into two categories: *substantive* conditions, ie the threshold tests found in section 18 of the *Patents Act 1990*; and *formal* conditions, mainly found in section 40 of the Act. The substantive conditions are addressed below in the following order: whether an application claims patentable subject matter, is novel, is inventive, is useful, and has not been used secretly by the applicant before the priority date. The formal conditions, relating to the content of the specification, are fair basing, sufficiency, best method, and clarity and succinctness of claims. The conditions of patentability arise to be considered at different times, some being examined *ex officio* by the Patent Office prior to grant whereas others only arise in opposition or revocation proceedings. The Commissioner also has a discretionary power to reject an application or refuse to grant a patent for an invention the use of which would be contrary to law or which is a mere admixture of food or medicine or a process for making such an admixture: see section 50. By virtue of section 20 the validity of a granted patent is not guaranteed.

Patentable subject matter

[Subject matter suitable for the grant of a patent] The first condition for grant is that the application disclose subject matter 'suitable for the grant of letters patent'. Most significant in Australian patents law is the fact that the Act's own archaic terms (in section 18 and the Dictionary in Schedule 1) give little guidance as to what is and what is not patentable subject matter. In substance it is a matter left to the courts to determine, as a concept that continuously evolves on a principled basis but in tune with changing times. The terminology used in the Act ('any manner of new manufacture') harks back to the *Statute of Monopolies* and has become so encrusted with judicial interpretation, and has evolved so much, that there is no point in precise textual or terminological analysis, as the High Court itself has pointed out. In other words, for all practical purposes the statutory terms themselves can be ignored: instead the focus should be on judicial precedent.

[*National Research and Development Corporation*] And the most significant precedent for modern purposes is the *NRDC* decision of 1959 (see above). The High Court propounded the basic approach to be taken in any doubtful case, recognising that patentability must remain an evolving and flexible concept, adaptable to changes in science and technology. To ensure this flexibility, the previous approach, which relied on determining patentability by categorising inventions as to their essential nature and then attaching consequences to that categorisation, was effectively abandoned. Every invention is examined for compliance with the same broad conditions: it must belong to the practical arts; and if a process, it must result in an 'artificially created state of affairs' of significance to the economy. These requirements are analogous to the 'industrial application' test in the European Patent Convention, but unlike the EPC the Australian Act does not also comprise a list of excluded subject matter, except for human beings and biological processes for their generation. This means that Australian law remains comparatively permissive and flexible in relation to new or controversial areas of invention. It is not as bedevilled by boundary disputes as are laws with more express exclusions (such as of computer programs), or with vague categories of prohibited subject matter (such as inventions contrary to *ordre public* and morality).

[Is inventiveness part of the suitability test?] Section 18 provides that 'an invention is a patentable invention [. . .] if the invention is [. . .] a. a manner of manufacture within the meaning of section 6 of the Statute of Monopolies; [. . .]'. The Act in the Dictionary (Schedule 1) defines an invention as follows: '"invention" means any manner of new manufacture the subject of letters patent and grant of privilege within section 6 of the Statute of Monopolies, and includes an alleged invention'. This complex statutory drafting was unravelled by the High Court in *NV Philips Gloeilampenfabrieken v Mirabella International Pty Ltd* (1995) 183 CLR 655: to be an invention suitable for patenting, what is claimed must on the face of it have some element of inventiveness; or at the very least, it must not be apparent from the application itself that it totally lacks inventiveness. This is inherent in the term 'invention'. This requirement of inventiveness stands apart from the threshold test of inventiveness, considered below, which requires comparison with prior art (the test of section 18 (1) (b) (ii)). Such inventions as the one at issue in *Philips*, which consisted, according to the Court, of no more than a known use of a known subject matter for a purpose for which its suitability was recognised, can be rejected at the earliest stage, without embarking upon the searches of prior art required to determine novelty and inventiveness. A further example of an alleged invention that will fail the *Philips* test is a mere collocation of existing machinery which does not create a new product: there is no invention in reconfiguring machines in a new order. However, combination patents are different: if the invention consists of known elements, but creates a new effect elevating it beyond the sum of its parts then there is a potentially novel invention (see *Minnesota Mining and Manufacturing Co v Beiersdorf* (1980) 144 CLR 253).

[The Statute of Monopolies] *The Statute of Monopolies 1609* abolished the right of the Crown in the United Kingdom to grant monopolies, with one exception: '[the abolition of monopolies shall not extend to letters patent and grants of privilege for] the working or making of any manner of new manufactures within this realm'. These terms should arguably be read as 'any *kind* of new manufactures', rather than requiring that an invention be a 'manner of manufacture'. No doubt in those days what was contemplated was any manufacturing process or manufactured thing. The aim of the Statute was to encourage the establishment of new manufacturing in Britain. Correctly understood, the terms signify that manufactures *of any and all kinds* were excluded from the general prohibition of monopolies – in other words, the terms were meant to be permissive, open and flexible. *NRDC* reconnected with this original intention, and broke loose from the restrictions that had come to flow from reading the terms not as 'any manner' of manufacture, but as if a 'manner of manufacture' was a concept in itself.

[Product and process patents] The Act envisages that inventions will consist of either process or product claims, or a combination of both, eg relating to a new product as well as the method in which the product is to be used or operated. In truth it is claims, not inventions, which are either suitable subject matter or not – thus in the sleep apnea case,[8] the invention consisted of both product (relating to an inhalation mask) and process claims (relating to application of oxygen mixtures): it was the patentability of the process claims alone, as being methods of medical treatment, which was at issue (see further below).

Process or method claims present the greatest challenge in terms of deciding whether an application concerns suitable subject matter or not. Prior to *NRDC*, processes were patentable only if they resulted in the production of a 'vendible product', but by virtue of *NRDC* it is sufficient that a process results in an artificial state: a state of affairs created or modified by human intervention. The agricultural process (application of a selective herbicide) at issue in the case did not result in the production of a new thing as such (a 'vendible product'), but did generate an outcome differing from the natural state of affairs: it reduced naturally occurring weed loads in a field. That was sufficient for it to be patentable subject matter. Given the practical nature and economic significance of the process, this is not a surprising decision, yet in the process an established legal restriction was overturned: that horticultural and agricultural processes were not suitable for patenting. This illustrates the fundamental nature of the shift that occurred in *NRDC*. Previously the process of determining whether some new process or method was patentable was innately conservative – categorisation of the invention and consequential inclusion or exclusion. The odds did not favour something radically new being recognised as included in a known category of patentable invention.

The Court in *NRDC* rejected this approach: in 1959, on the cusp of great scientific and technological developments, a more flexible test based on common elements was developed: as indicated above, a process should result in 'an artificially created state of affairs', which was actually physically discernible, resulting from the application of the process, and this result was 'economic', in the sense that it offered advantages to the economic activity of the country. But what if the artificial state of affairs is not visible or discernible? In more recent times the requirement has been said to limit patentability to a process that *applies science or technology* to achieve the artificial state of affairs.

[An application of science or technology?] This question was at issue in two recent cases that considered processes that, as claimed, have no apparent technical or practical element, *Grant* and *Szabo*. The Federal Court's decision in *Grant v Commissioner of Patents* [2005] FCA 1100 (12 August 2005) illustrates the multiple difficulties a claim extending to a process consisting only of a series of financial transactions or legal steps as such faces. The legal process in Grant's application was held to be outside the concept of invention. *Peter Szabo and Associates Pty Ltd* [2005] APO 24 concerned a 'reverse mortgage', legal steps whose aim was to provide liquidity to older persons who were asset rich (owning a house) but

---

[8] *Anaesthetic Supplies Pty Ltd v Rescare Ltd* (1994) 122 ALR 141 (1994) AIPC 91-076.

cash poor. The Deputy Commissioner decided that the requirement in *NRDC* of an artificially created state of affairs called for some application of science or technology in what was claimed. Theoretically an artificially created state of affairs could include anything that did not exist without man's intervention, for instance, a contractual relationship. But read in the context of *NRDC* the terms were more restrictive, referring not merely to something that was not 'natural', but something that resulted from new applications of science or technology. A flowchart of legal steps, for instance, to be taken to protect certain assets from legal liability, as in *Grant*, thus had no technological element sufficient to bring it within the concept of invention.

[Different from computer-implemented processes] Contemporary applications may claim a series of steps to be performed on a computer. Such processes are clearly technological in cases such as *CCOM Pty Ltd v Jiejing Pty Ltd* (1994) 122 ALR 417: the process was held to be patentable because it claimed a practical way of producing Chinese characters on a VDU, a practical solution to a practical problem. But what if the invention involves performing a business method, or a method like in *Grant* and *Szabo*, on a computer? *Welcome Real-Time SA v Catuity Inc* (2001) 51 IPR 327 held that a method used within a business is potentially patentable subject matter (if it involves some technical process), but a scheme for carrying on a business *per se* is not. In that case the method to be used within or by a business involved the storage and manipulation of information relevant to customer loyalty programs used by unrelated businesses – it involved computers and steps performed in a technical environment. It was clearly patentable subject matter. In the same way, computer programs are patentable subject matter, where the process or method claimed as a computer program is a novel or inventive one (see further below, Chapter five). Had Szabo claimed the process as a computer program performing the steps described, then it may have been patentable subject matter, if the invention lay in the method whereby the program performed the steps, rather than in the sequence of legal transactions itself. The monopoly would then be limited to the performance of steps on a computer in the manner claimed, not the legal method *per se* – any different way of performing the legal transactions would escape liability.

[Other requirements may present more difficulties] The *NRDC* threshold is low; the requirement, as summed up in the IPAC Report of 1984,[9] '[. . .] involves little more than that an invention must belong to the useful arts rather than the fine arts'. But an invention must pass the other threshold tests as well, of novelty, inventiveness and utility, which may present greater difficulties. In particular, it may prevent alleged inventions that consist of the conversion of known methods to a computing environment from proceeding to grant. They may lack inventiveness if the applicant has not claimed a particular application which itself contains

---

[9] Industrial Property Advisory Committee (IPAC), *Patents, Innovation and Competition in Australia* (August 1984), see p 40.

some non-obvious step or element. The notion of converting known processes to the digital or internet environment has agitated the imagination of many technologists for quite a while now and is neither novel nor inventive. It is in this context that such controversies as for instance engulfed the eBay reverse auction patent should be seen. Conducting reverse auctions via the internet is obviously patentable subject matter: but whether it has sufficient novelty and inventiveness depends on the particular technical method claimed to conduct the process online.

[**Process or method of significance to the economy**] A further issue that can arise in relation to processes or methods claimed is whether they are relevant to the economy, an economic pursuit. *NRDC* required this in so many words, and it is also inherent in the distinction made in that case between the practical and fine arts. Is a painting technique, a technique for performing steps or movements in sport (jumping higher, swimming faster) or dance, a training schedule, etc patentable subject matter? The question whether some process or method is an economic pursuit has been explored in relation to medical treatment methods in particular. In *Bristol-Myers Squibb Co v F H Faulding & Co Ltd* [2000] FCA 316 the Full Court held that medicine was an economic pursuit, and that is where the law now stands; but judges have sometimes expressed doubt that relieving suffering is an economic pursuit rather than a merciful vocation. The prevailing view is consistent with the undisputed position in relation to pharmaceutical substances: if sufficiently novel and inventive they are patentable. As to the examples relating to sport and the arts, there is little doubt that they are not patentable subject matter – although 'there is money in sport', this is only the case for some small fraction of participants. Sport is not inherently an economic pursuit, nor is artistic expression.

[**Generally inconvenient**] The issue of medical treatment methods draws attention to another aspect of the language of section 6 of the *Statute of Monopolies*, which provides that although monopolies could continue to be granted for inventions, where they would be 'generally inconvenient' they should be refused. Patents are, of course, always inconvenient, in the sense that they restrict competition, and also in the sense that an uneasy contradiction lies at the heart of patents law. To take medical treatment methods as an example: to encourage useful developments, a patentee is given the legal right to withhold such care as falls within the monopoly, even in the theoretical case where this results in the patient's death. This dilemma is most starkly exemplified by the struggle over patenting of HIV/AIDS drugs in developing countries, and lies at the basis of WTO/TRIPS permitting member states to exclude medical treatment methods from patentability. In the absence of an express exclusion, is a patent over a medical treatment method perhaps 'generally inconvenient'? The status of this and the other limiting parts of section 6 (hurt of trade, or raising the price of commodities at home) is somewhat uncertain. The *Patent Office Manual* goes so far as to say the following (at [2.9.3]): 'There is really no clear guidance as to when an invention may or may not be regarded as "generally inconvenient". Hence, examiners should refrain from taking this objection.' Finkelstein J, conceiving of it as a potential public policy exception, such as exists in Europe (see eg section 1 (3), (4) of the *Patents Act 1977* (UK)), said the following in *Bristol-Myers* (above, at FCA 141):

> I do not believe that in a controversial issue such as is raised by the present argument, I would be abandoning my responsibility as a judge to follow this approach and to hold that if public policy demands that a medical or surgical process should be excluded from patentability, then that is a matter that should be resolved by the Parliament.

So 'general inconvenience', far from amounting to a general public policy exception, in fact seems to be restricted in its application to situations where the granting of a monopoly would be impractical, or dangerous, or interfere with ordinary rights of possession;[10] but even in that guise the issue rarely forms the basis for any exclusion *as such*, the objection commonly relating to some other area of patents law.

In the past the royal prerogative to refuse to grant a patent could be exercised where an invention was contrary to law 'or morality'. In the UK such a provision last appeared in the *Patents Act 1949* (UK), and arose occasionally where personal morality was at stake: eg in relation to personal contraceptive devices.[11] The present UK Act excludes inventions contrary to public policy or morality from patenting.[12] In Australia, there is no equivalent provision.

[Inventions contrary to law, etc] Hence, notwithstanding speculation about the scope of the 'generally inconvenient' exclusion, community standards and patents law only *clearly* intersect in two ways in Australia. First, by way of the power afforded the Commissioner by section 50 (1) (a) of the Act, to refuse to accept a patent request or a patent grant 'for an invention the use of which would be contrary to law'. And secondly, by way of the statutory exclusion in section 18 (2) of human beings and biological processes for their generation. A recent patent office decision considered both issues: *Re Whang* (2004) AIPC 92-031. The Deputy Commissioner pointed out (at 38,182) that section 50 (1) (a) was rarely invoked: if the main purpose or use of the invention amounted to a criminal act, it should be, but only in the clearest of cases. The invention concerned a method that 'creates an embryo where the nuclear DNA is human, and the mitochondrial DNA is bovine' (see 38,181). This was a hybrid or chimeric embryo, and the creation of such embryos was punishable at law by virtue of section 20 of the *Prohibition of Human Cloning Act 2002* (Cth). It fell into the category of case where the application had to be refused. It could also, however, be refused on the basis of section 18 (2).

[Human beings] In another decision, *Re Luminis Pty Ltd & Fertilitescentrum AB* (2004) AIPC 92-011, the same Deputy considered in more detail the exclusion

---

[10] See eg *Rolls Royce Ltd's Application* (1963) RPC 251.
[11] See eg *In the matter of an Application for a Patent by A. and M.* (1927) 44 RPC 298; and *In the matter of an Application for a patent by Rufus Riddlesbarger* (1935) 53 RPC 57.
[12] See above, section 1 (3), (4) *Patents Act 1977* (UK).

of human beings which was also relevant to *Re Whang* (above). The Deputy's account of the history of the exclusion draws attention to the fact that it did not appear in the Bill as originally introduced by the government. It emerged at the Senate Committee stage, first as part of a wider exclusion proposed by the Democrats and then in its present form, as suggested by Senator Harradine. The Deputy pointed out (at 37,915) that '[F]rom this history, it might be inferred that s. 18(2) owes its existence more to political process than to detailed policy deliberation'. Nonetheless, from what limited material that was available concerning the amendment, the Deputy arrived at various intermediate conclusions, which then led him to two significant determinations relevant to the invention at issue, which concerned ensuring that a substance present in the natural environment of the fallopian tubes, and which assisted embryos in their development, could be present in an IVF environment (see 37,910). First, he stated that a human being is in the process of generation from the moment of fertilisation to the moment of birth; and second (at 37,917), the prohibition of human beings 'in my view is a prohibition of patenting of any entity that might reasonably claim the status of a human being'. In the result the method claims related to biological processes for the generation of human beings, and were thus excluded under section 18 (2). Many potential issues (such as the status of human organs) are not addressed in the decision, but nonetheless it is a worthwhile first exploration of the exclusion. It will significantly affect R&D in relation to methods for the enhancement of fertility and evokes challenging questions concerning the interaction of patents law with other areas of law and public policy, such as the regulation of abortion.

[Living organisms are patentable subject matter] The broader exclusions proposed by the Democrats, referred to above, would have barred all genetically altered life forms, whether animal or plant, lower or higher, from patentability, as well as 'a gene or genes, whether derived from cells or chemically synthesised' (see *Luminis* at 37,913). But ultimately parliament did not choose to modify the established practice of granting patents in living organisms, other than humans. The US landmark decision in *Diamond v Chakrabarty* (1980) 447 US 303 expressly held that living organisms can constitute patentable inventions, but in fact patents relating to living organisms had been granted in Australia at least as far back as 1921.[13] For plant varieties, registration of a Plant Breeder's Right (see further below, in Chapter five) is an alternative, certainly where the new plant results from conventional cross-breeding. In some other jurisdictions this is the only option for plants, because they are excluded from patentability in conformity with the WTO/TRIPS provision permitting this. In other jurisdictions, such as Canada, a distinction is made between higher and lower life forms. But even where all living organisms are considered patentable in theory, significant other issues arise. One is related to the nature of novelty and inventions in this context, as further considered below; another again results from considerations of ethics and public policy.

[13] A tuberculosis vaccine containing a tuberculosis bacterium – see second reading speech by Hon Crean, Patents Bill 1990, per *Luminis* (at 37, 915).

[Living organisms: public policy] Ethical concerns are at their most acute when the patentability of living organisms is under consideration, and particularly so in the case of higher life forms. Arguably other legislation should – and does, if rather unsystematically – regulate technology that is dangerous or ethically reprehensible. Prohibiting patenting of certain technologies, as well as being an ineffective regulatory tool, may be counterproductive from that perspective: patents tend to alert public opinion to issues relating to technology regulation. At a more systemic level, it undermines the logic of the patents system to exclude *ex ante* certain technologies. Mills (2005)[14] favours the isolation theory, ie keeping patents law and technology regulation apart. Patents law is an instrument of economic policy, and not of 'moral policy': 'As far as regulating biotechnological inventions is concerned, denying patentability on the basis of morality is misguided as such a solution does not match the nature of the problem'. Nonetheless the patenting of human beings or processes for producing human beings, certainly cloning or in vitro genetic modification, does generate strong adverse reaction, as well as being illegal. The perception that it is morally reprehensible to 'own' human beings is understandable, and is analogous to our revulsion at slavery; but otherwise most ethical concerns are really with the *technology itself* rather than with patenting. Animals and other higher life forms are a different case: they are already 'owned', and whatever concerns there may be about genetically modifying animals (as in the Oncomouse case) are related to the nature of the technology itself: in such cases direct regulation is the proper response.

[Genetic information] Apart from ethical concerns about owning life, the commercial control of genetic information also elicits adverse reactions, not so much about methods or processes for the discovery or manipulation or transfer of genes, but about ownership of genetic information *as such*. The amendment proposed by the Democrats in the Senate (see above) was aimed at preventing the accumulation of ownership of genetic information in corporate hands; in other jurisdictions, above all those with rich biodiversity, express exclusions in similar terms are indeed to be found.[15] But concerns about owning genes are adequately addressed if the rules of patents law are properly applied, in particular those concerning the need for some *application* of science or technology rather than patents over information or discoveries as such, and concerning novelty and inventiveness. Discovering the presence of genetic information in nature is one thing; devising a use or application of such knowledge to a practical purpose is quite another. Between the stages of identification and of use in actual therapy or a therapeutic substance lies a challenging process of isolation, synthetic production and practical application. It remains essential that patents law prevent the risk that a patentee obtains a monopoly over knowledge for which he has not specified some specific, useful application. Hence isolation

---

[14] Mills O, *Biotechnological inventions: Moral Restraints and Patent Law*, Ashgate, 2005, p 11.
[15] See eg Decision 486 – Common Intellectual Property Regime, Andean Pact Countries, excluding the genome or germ plasm of any living thing.

and synthetic production of gene sequences may not be enough, if the patentee does not specify some application of the synthesised material to a particular practical purpose or result. Many of these issues are considered in useful detail in ALRC Report 99.[16]

[The proper scope of a patent] The distinction between knowledge as such and some practical application of knowledge is relevant to many other areas in which theoretical understanding or scientific discovery lie at the heart of an invention. Thus an algorithm *per se* is not patentable, but a practical process to generate a curved line on a VDU, which includes an algorithm, is (see *International Business Machines v Smith, Commissioner of Patents* (1992) AIPC 90–853; a business plan or scheme *per se* is not patentable but a practical way of implementing a method in business by way of computers is (see *Catuity*, above), and so on. Insistence on disclosure of a concrete application of knowledge, rather than knowledge as such, limits the scope of patents, and permits the law to actively police the borderline between enlightened incentive and stifling monopoly. The patentee should be made to specify very clearly what it is that others cannot do – too much uncertainty at the edges has a chilling effect on competitors. The formal conditions of clarity, fair basing and enabling disclosure all tend towards the same goal. The ability of a property structure to minimise demarcation disputes, ease transaction costs and provide certainty by clear demarcation is undermined by claims of uncertain scope, such as ones extending to whose practical application is knowledge not adequately revealed in the application.

[Language and monopoly] The claims form the core of a patent application – they stake out the scope of the monopoly; the rest of the application, although sometimes relevant to the interpretation of the claims, merely serves to describe the invention and its background. Claims are expressed in language, not in pictures, nor by reference to representations or examples (as is by contrast the case in designs law; see below, Chapter four). This has resulted in the development of a special language combining terminology common to all patent claims, with terms of art specific to the area of science or technology of the invention. Obviously, as pointed out by Garde:

> [C]larity in the scope of protection is essential to promote progress and innovation. However, it is also accepted that the limitations of language make it impossible to capture the fundamental nature of an invention. Further, because a patent requires publication of the invention, the patentee runs the risk that competitors will make every effort to define narrowly the outer limits of the patent scope.[17]

Therefore the patentee engages in a careful balancing act when drafting claims, aiming to capture the essence of the invention in a manner quite different from a simple description of one or another specific embodiment, but without being so abstract as to go too far beyond actual manifestations. In the process, the

---

[16] Australian Law Reform Commission (ALRC), Report No 99, *Genes and Ingenuity: Gene Patenting and Human Health* (2004).
[17] See Garde T V, 'Legal certainty, *stare decisis* and the doctrine of equivalents' [2005] *EIPR* 365, at 366.

patentee must remain conscious of the potential for very critical scrutiny from competitors.

Novelty and inventiveness

Novelty

[Novelty and inventiveness] The tests of novelty and inventiveness ensure that no monopoly is granted in something that was already known – something the patent applicant should not benefit from *allegedly* first disclosing to the public. The two tests are distinct and very different in character: whereas the test of anticipation (novelty) is comparative in nature and objective in style, the test of inventiveness requires a judgment to be made through the eyes of a person familiar with the area of invention (the person skilled in the art) and thus has a subjective element. The test of anticipation or novelty requires a comparison between the invention concerned and the 'prior art' published before the priority date, ie the date of filing of an application revealing the invention. The prior art includes publications by the applicant, and by others, either in other patent applications or elsewhere. Any publication after the priority date is irrelevant to the question of novelty: the applicant can publish his invention in journals or books, by pictures or description, or can work the invention in public or sell it, without affecting the validity of the patent. Thus exploitation can start immediately after the filing of an application for the invention. However, caution is required: if it should become apparent that the essence of some invention was not included in the application, then its public exploitation or exposure may amount to anticipation. This is not uncommon: inventions may be complex or multifaceted; something may work, or work well, for a reason that was not fully understood, and therefore not disclosed, at the time of filing for a patent.

[Significance of the priority date] So why not delay and only file for a patent in good time? Because the system is 'first to file', winner takes all, and because of the potential dire consequences of public disclosure, delay exposes the applicant to risk. First, another party may independently invent the same product or process, and publish it: this would constitute anticipation and destroy the applicant's opportunity to obtain a patent. Secondly, another party may file first for a patent on the same invention: then not only is the opportunity of obtaining a legal monopoly lost, so may be the right to use the invention at all. The expenditures on R&D already incurred will then not be recoupable from exploitation of the resulting invention. The perceived risk of independent invention will thus influence the timing of lodgment – intelligence about competitors' research progress, if available, may inform this judgment, as will the inherent character of the breakthrough at issue. As we saw above, if the risk of independent invention is very small (an exceptional breakthrough) then the inventor may choose not to patent at all but to rely (potentially for ever) on secrecy, as long as the invention can be exploited in confidence. However, if he does choose to exploit the invention in secret, a patent can no longer be obtained at some future date: section 18 (1) (d) prohibits secret use by the applicant before the priority date. The existence and extent of an actual opportunity to exploit the invention may also influence timing: if it can be rapidly brought to market, then there may be an advantage in not delaying the application; if actual exploitation will be delayed (eg because of regulatory issues) then there may be less urgency in filing for a patent.

[**Provisional applications possible**] A complete application, consisting of specification and claims, is a complex document, certainly where scientific inventions are at issue. The drafting of a complete application, with the precision required for claims, may be time-consuming and delay the moment of actual filing, even accepting that amendments are allowed under certain conditions. Under Australian law the applicant has the option of filing a provisional application, which allows the securing of an early priority date (see sections 19 (2); 40 (1)). A provisional need only describe the invention – claims, etc are not required, nor a particular form or detail of description. However, an early priority date can only be secured for the actual invention disclosed in the provisional, if the complete application deriving priority from it discloses the same invention – the complete application must be 'fairly based' on the provisional application. This aspect of the requirement of fair basing is further analysed below (see the Fair Basing sections below; the other aspect is that the claims should be fairly based on the matter described in the specification). Furthermore, a complete application based on the provisional must be filed within one year. Even when a complete application has been filed, the patentee can further defer costs by delaying substantive examination as permitted by the Act and Regulations (Patent Regulations 1991). To obtain an early priority date in multiple jurisdictions a Patent Cooperation Treaty (PCT) application can be filed in Australia, nominating a number of other countries in which the applicant wishes to file. The Australian filing date will serve as the priority date abroad (and vice versa if the initial filing occurs in another jurisdiction). But the prosecution of each application must then be pursued with the domestic patent office of each jurisdiction nominated, and the substantive requirements of the patents law of each jurisdiction will determine the outcome; they may differ from those of Australian law (eg certain subject matter may be patentable here but not in Europe or the USA).

[**The basic test of novelty**] The basic test of novelty is whether the invention is disclosed in an alleged anticipation, ie some public disclosure by doing (an act), or in documentary form before the priority date. Anticipatory disclosure can be by the applicant, or by another party, and it can occur either by means of a previous patent application for the same invention, by publication in journals, books, online publications, etc, or by oral disclosure in open conversation or public address. Confidential disclosure of an invention, either in documentary form or by working the invention secretly within the confines of a business and its employees, does not constitute anticipation. The rule of thumb is to disclose the invention only on a 'need to know' basis before the filing of an application, and then only in circumstances that make it clear that an obligation of confidence attaches to the disclosure. Further, so as not to waste time and expense on patent applications, an applicant should conduct preliminary searches, either personally or through a patent attorney, to ascertain whether some invention is not already in the public domain. Although preliminary searches may quickly reveal anticipations, ultimately searches need to be thorough, because even obscure publication in some distant country can constitute anticipation.

[What is the 'prior art base'?] In terms of the Act, the novelty test requires a comparison between the claims in the application, and the 'prior art base': see section 7. The prior art base consists of prior art information, as defined in the Dictionary (Schedule 1). In the past, publications by doing an act in some other jurisdiction were not taken into account, but now anything published anywhere in the world, either by an act or in documentary form, is relevant prior art and can constitute anticipation. The prior art relevant to anticipation is far more extensive than the prior art that can be taken into account to determine whether an invention is non-obvious – only a limited fraction of the prior art can be relied on to support an argument of obviousness, as will be seen below. Secret use and prior user rights are also dealt with below.

[No guarantee of validity] Given many disparate sources of potential public disclosure, a foolproof search is basically impossible, whether conducted by the applicant or his advisers, or by the patent office during examination. This is one reason why the validity of a granted patent cannot be guaranteed – even after grant some anticipating publication may be easily discovered, for instance during infringement proceedings where the defendant counterclaims for invalidity. Results of prior or preliminary searches (eg conducted by a foreign patent office) may have to be revealed to the patent office when an application is filed. To have anticipation, there must be publication, ie the information must have been made *available* to the public; but whether members of the public actually accessed the information is irrelevant. In this sense the standard is higher than applies in trade secrets cases – there the theoretical availability in some place those in the know would not normally access may not be enough to put the information 'in the public domain'. Conversely, if exploitation occurred in secret, then there will be no anticipation, although secret use by the patentee is a separate ground of invalidity – see further below.

[The reverse infringement test] What if there is some difference between an alleged anticipation and the invention disclosed in an application? Either a difference will be irrelevant, and the prior disclosure is anticipatory, or it is significant enough to treat the disclosure as concerning a different invention. Judging non-identical disclosures is not an inventiveness test in different guise – it should not focus on the qualitative difference with the alleged anticipation. Rather, the relevant approach is the 'reverse infringement test': would the alleged anticipation constitute an infringement if a patent were granted over the invention in the application being considered? Infringement only occurs if each and every essential feature of a claim is taken, so the prior disclosure must be clear enough and complete (for instance, publication of a photograph which does not clearly show all the elements of the invention as claimed is not anticipation). However, a prior publication which gives direction or instruction sufficient for a person skilled in the art to make the invention does constitute anticipation. The disclosure must also be in a single source: it is not permissible to undermine a patent or reject an application by claiming that each element or integer is disclosed in different documents, and it would be obvious to put those elements together (some exceptions apply). Some anticipations may come to light during the 'prosecution' stage, either as a result of the examiner's searches or during opposition. In that case it may be permissible to amend the application by narrowing or varying the scope of the claims to avoid including the anticipation.

Claims are commonly multiple, and tend to go from the more general to the more specific, with some claims being 'dependent' on others. Combination patents provide a useful example of the interaction between novelty and scope: to preserve novelty it may be necessary to limit the claimed area by including more combined parts. For instance in *Grove Hill Pty Ltd v Great Western Corporation Pty Ltd* [2002] FCAFC 183 patenting only the cutting blades was problematical if they already existed as used in other machines. But a cutting blade combined with a row cultivator could amount to a new combination; although the resulting patent would have a narrower scope of monopoly, it would also be at less risk of anticipation.

[Naturally occurring substances] When does an invention derived from a naturally occurring organism or substance constitute something new? The answer is partly related to the issue of patentable subject matter, partly to novelty. Facts, discoveries, things existing in nature cannot be patented as such: some application to a practical end must be disclosed. In terms of novelty, a constituent part of a living organism or natural substance in its natural state is not new. But if a component of a living organism, such as a gene sequence, is identified as having a useful effect in nature, is isolated, and then artificially reproduced, and the fact *and* mode of its utility are identified, then something new has been created, something artificial that did not exist in the form claimed at the priority date. Does it matter that the organism from which the therapeutic compound or gene sequence was isolated and claimed as integral to a practical invention was well known to have those therapeutic effects, or was publicly used for that purpose, for instance by traditional healers? Generally speaking the answer is no – something new has been brought to light by the patentee, ie the nature of the underlying genes or compounds and associated processes that generate the previously observed useful effect. Furthermore, the clinical effect is generated and delivered in a manner which is artificial, in the sense that it did not exist in nature in the form claimed, and therefore the invention is indeed novel.

[Grace periods] On 1 April 2002 Australia introduced a so-called 'grace period'. As a result, publication of the invention by the applicant within a period of 12 months before the filing of the application does not now constitute anticipation. This protects patent applicants against the harsh consequences of their own disclosures (eg resulting from perhaps understandable ignorance of the law) prior to filing an application. IPAustralia has recently conducted a review of grace periods.[18] The main drawback of the grace period provisions is that they have

---

[18] See IPAustralia, *Review of Patent Grace Period*, August 2005.

no effect in relation to applications in other jurisdictions where no or different grace periods exist. Most European countries do not provide for a grace period, whereas the United States, Japan and Canada, amongst others, do but for varying periods. Another significant drawback of reliance on grace periods is that others who use the invention as disclosed but before the application is filed, will retain prior user rights in relation to it. Close rivals who monitor disclosures carefully may enjoy the right to use the invention in competition with the patentee. Further disclosures before the priority date are also a complicating factor: if they can be connected to the patentee's primary disclosure during the grace period they do not amount to prior art anticipating the invention. However, if they can *not* be so connected, they may well be treated as anticipations coming from a different source: see eg *Stephen John Grant* [2004] APO 11; (2004) AIPC 91-994.

Inventiveness

[The basic test of inventiveness] Novelty alone is not enough: inventiveness is in addition required: see section 18 (1) (b) (ii). The invention must have a quality that sets it apart, clearly demarcating it from other inventions and ensuring that it is more than a trivial step not meriting a monopoly. In terms of the Act, an invention will only pass this threshold test if it represents an advance over the relevant prior art information which is not obvious to a 'person skilled in the art' (PSA). That person's qualities and characteristics will have to be construed in light of the nature of the invention, as will the content and demarcation of the relevant field of technology. The PSA must be imputed with certain knowledge: either the common general knowledge of all such persons in the relevant field, or alternatively the common general knowledge together with knowledge of specific publications which such a person can be expected to have read and understood. Thus the prior art information relevant to the test of inventiveness is much narrower than the information relevant to novelty; in other words, some publication revealing something that is not commonly known to a PSA, and that would not normally be consulted by them, cannot be relied on to undermine inventiveness. The mental exercise required can be fairly described as surreal: a person, not in fact a person skilled in the art, such as a judge or examiner, must first construe what the relevant field is; who would be a PSA; what such a PSA would know; then, having donned the mantle of the PSA, ask whether in their eyes, the invention disclosed an inventive step or not. In answering this question, they will pretend to have the abilities of an ordinary worker in the field not endowed with any special inventive skills. Although the person deciding the matter must make the judgment, they may be assisted by expert evidence where such evidence is available. In reality, therefore, if a number of experts presented by both sides can be considered persons skilled in the particular art, the outcome will depend on which expert opinion the court prefers.

[Different prior art: more limited than for novelty] Section 7 of the Act and the Dictionary (Schedule 1) delineate the prior art for the purpose of inventiveness.

The significant differences with relevant prior art for novelty purposes are as follows. First, common general knowledge is taken into account. This is a concept with no equivalent in the novelty context, and consists of the background knowledge that every PSA would have because of study and experience in their art. An important preliminary issue therefore is to determine what the relevant art is, and who might fit the bill of being a person skilled in that art. In practical terms, at least in the context of court proceedings, this will boil down to the parties presenting and/or contesting that certain experts who might give evidence as to obviousness are persons skilled in the art. However, each expert may not perfectly fit the bill, so the decision-maker will construe a composite PSA on the basis of the expert evidence (in areas where team investigation is the norm the PSA may in fact be a team). That expert evidence will most significantly be directed at the nature and extent of the common general knowledge of a PSA at the priority date. Once the nominal PSA is armed with the common stock of knowledge in the trade, they can also be imputed with knowledge of specific publications, eg articles in journals, that the typical PSA in Australia would be expected to have 'ascertained, understood, [and] regarded as relevant' (see section 7 (3)). These sources are far more limited in number than the prior art relevant to novelty, since they are filtered by reference to the normal reading and study patterns of the PSA.

However, while in the context of novelty 'mosaicing', ie piecing together an invention from unrelated sources, is not allowed, for inventiveness purposes it is: by virtue of section 7 obviousness can be established by showing that, in the light of a number of the 'ascertained, understood, [and] regarded as relevant' pieces of information *taken together*, the invention is obvious. Due to a perception that Australia's inventiveness level was out of synch with other jurisdictions, the level of inventiveness required has effectively been increased by recent legislative changes, which allow for more prior art to be taken into account, and to allow for mosaicing to a greater extent than previously.

[A mere scintilla of inventiveness] With the relevant prior art in mind, how big must the step to the invention be? The answer to this question is firstly determined by the level of ability imputed to the typical PSA. The cases provide that the proper approach requires the PSA to be shorn of any special inventive capacity: he is a typical *uninventive* worker in the field. This again is rather surreal, certainly in a field where inventiveness is a common attribute of every typical worker, as for instance at the higher end of scientific research. Then all that is required is that the invention, as a step onwards from the prior art, is not obvious. No ingenuity, revolutionary insight, creativity or major step forward need be shown; some small inventive spark is enough, and it matters not whether that inventive step resulted from a sudden insight, or from careful study, reflection and research. Evidence of secondary indicators of inventiveness may be admissible, including of a long-felt want (eg well-known limitations of existing technology), of a lengthy course of experimentation and trial, or of resounding commercial success (in marketing after the priority date). Nonetheless the primary test of inventiveness is whether the decision-maker, donning the mantle of the PSA, armed with the relevant knowledge, knowing what the problem addressed by the invention is, considers its resolution obvious or not. All these issues will, given that defendants normally counterclaim for invalidity, normally be addressed by expert evidence in litigation, a major source of expense. Arguably the gravamen of the test of inventiveness lies, rather than in the assessment of the quality of the step forward, in construing the knowledge base of the PSA (common general knowledge and specific pieces of information), a matter on which experts can easily be at odds. Since the ultimate judgment required is often both complex and fine, there is an inescapable level of uncertainty and unpredictability in most litigated matters.

[*Philips v Mirabella*, **patentable subject matter and inventive step**] As indicated above, the concept of invention, as considered in the context of suitability for the grant of letters patent, requires that the invention is not lacking in inventiveness on the face of the application, ie without necessary reference to the prior art. This is a threshold test which stands entirely separate from the test, which takes into account certain prior art, that we are considering here (the test of section 18 (1) (b) (ii)). Therefore questions of inventiveness may arise at two points, but are addressed differently at each. For instance, a combination patent may consist of a combination of elements each of which taken individually was publicly known before the priority date. If the combination does not generate a new effect, ie if it is apparent from the application that the invention adds up to no more than the sum of its individual elements, the alleged invention can be treated as a mere collocation, failing the *Philips* test. On the other hand, if the sum apparently amounts to more than its parts, a question may still arise whether, combining together various elements published in *certain* individual sources prior to filing, as is permitted in the context of the inventiveness test, the combination would be an obvious invention to a PSA.

[**New use for an old substance**] So also a new use for a known substance can be a patentable invention, if the use is not simply analogous to its prior known uses. Naturally, such patents do not then extend exclusivity to the substance itself, only to its new use. Where the alleged invention amounts to no more than additional directions for use of a known substance for its known purpose, there is also no patentable invention – the application will fail at the *Philips* hurdle. This is significant in the context of pharmaceutical patents. On one side of the divide lie valid patents, such as claimed in *Bristol-Myers* (see above) where a significant problem in the administration of a known drug (taxol), in line with its known purpose for combating refractory cancer, was overcome by a new administration regime considered inventive. On the other side lie inventions considered no more than additional instructions to use a known drug for its known purpose in a manner analogous to the dosage regime already employed before the priority date: see for instance *Arrow Pharmaceuticals Ltd v Merck & Co., Inc.* [2004] FCA 1282, per Gyles J, concerning an attempt at so-called 'evergreening' of an invention.

[Australia and the world] The higher level of inventiveness and novelty introduced initially with the 1990 Act, and then further increased with the recent amendments already mentioned above, is in line with the intention of the 1990 Act to foster Australia's export performance. A novelty standard which permits us to ignore inventions disclosed abroad would hardly foster indigenous innovation; rather it might encourage imitation of foreign inventions that have not as yet been published or entered the common general knowledge in Australia. Only genuine invention at home will result in additional exports in the R&D sector. The standard of inventiveness in particular is now in line with that of Australia's major trading partners; however, it should be noted that the standard discussed here applies only to *standard* patents. While the novelty test is the same, innovation patents have a lower standard of inventiveness, requiring only an innovative step, ie a substantial contribution to the working of the invention, rather than an inventive step. The standards applicable to innovation patents are considered further below.

Utility, secret use and section 40 requirements

Section 40 requirements

[Certainty and full disclosure] Clarity of demarcation and adequacy of disclosure go to the heart of the policy goals of the patent system. The application must afford others both clear instruction concerning the invention, and clear circumscription of the scope of the monopoly. A competitor must be able to ascertain what they can and cannot do. Section 40 sets out mandatory guidelines concerning patent applications which encapsulate these goals. They are designed around three themes: adequate disclosure ('sufficiency'); clarity; and a monopoly whose scope does not exceed the confines of the disclosed invention. Ambiguous language is anathema in patents and thus the claims must be as clear and succinct as possible (see section 40 (3)) – overly general, abstract or vague terminology is to be avoided. The claims must also be 'fairly based' on the specification, which in turn must fully describe the invention, 'including the best method known to the applicant of performing the invention' (see section 40 (2) (a)); a monopoly should not be granted to the patentee who keeps the optimal application or use hidden, nor should the patentee disclose one thing and obtain a monopoly on another.

On the other hand, the patentee is under no compulsion to disclose *more* than is required by section 40. Drafting will thus attempt to balance legal standards with the strategic goals of the patentee, which are to disclose no more than absolutely necessary, and not to limit the monopoly any more than is required to meet the standards of novelty and inventiveness, and of section 40. This tension is apparent in applications, and patentees sometimes stray across the line, which can result in a finding of invalidity. Non-compliance with the requirements of section 40 is a ground of opposition (section 59), which can result in refusal to grant a patent; and a ground of revocation (most commonly on the basis of a counterclaim in infringement proceedings, see section 121).

[Fair basing and the risks of pedantry] The requirements of section 40 will not be analysed in any detail here; they are the preserve of patent attorneys who must translate the decisions in the not infrequent cases in this area into practical prescriptions for the drafting of applications. However, fair basing merits some further mention, since its status and role have been controversial in recent times. 'Fair basing' takes two forms: first, the complete application must be fairly based on any provisional application (if one was filed; a provisional application is not mandatory). Here the underlying concern is to ensure that the priority date obtained by filing a provisional early is fairly accorded to the actual invention as disclosed in the complete application allegedly based on the provisional. Secondly, the claims must be fairly based on the specification: here the concern is that the monopoly (delineated by the claims) should be based on what is disclosed – that it is not wider or different from the invention as described elsewhere in the application.

In the *Grove Hill* case on appeal[19] the Court points out that the public interest is served by not allowing the patent to claim more than what is 'the true subject matter of the invention'.

There is a perception that fair basing, and other section 40 requirements, have caused the revocation of patents on the basis of an overly technical and narrow interpretation of the rules, which has worked unfairly against patentees.[20] Patents law, being rule-dense, is always at risk of becoming so impenetrable that it operates unfairly against patentees and causes inefficiencies because of low predictability. Nonetheless, such technical rules as fair basing also go to the heart of the policy goals underlying the system, and therefore attentive policing of the statutory standards is arguably critical. Notwithstanding this, as some courts have appropriately stressed recently, fair basing should be approached in an ordinary way and not become overly technical and contrived. In *Lockwood*,[21] the High Court reinforced this message.

[*Lockwood*: the latest word on fair basing] The Lockwood invention overcame a known problem with security locks. It combined five known integers with a sixth, which, in the claims, was expressed not in specific but general terms: means whereby the internal locking mechanism would be undone by unlocking the door from the outside so that a person once inside the house would not be dangerously locked in. The preferred embodiment then described a specific mechanism whereby this result could be achieved, but the claims were not restricted to such specifics, being expressed in terms of the broader principle that unlocking the door from the outside enabled the deactivation of the internal locking mechanism. The lower courts' decisions suffered from two main failings: the conflation or elision of distinct issues of obviousness and section 40; and a narrow and overly detailed approach which flew in the face of the warning in *CCOM*[22] that no 'over meticulous verbal analysis' should be undertaken (see McBratney at 222). The

---

[19] See *Grove Hill Pty Ltd v Great Western Corporation Pty Ltd* [2002] FCAFC 183, at [170].
[20] As discussed in McBratney A, 'The Problem Child in Australian Patent Law: "Fair" Basing' (2001) 12 *AIPJ* 211, 212.
[21] *Lockwood Security Products Pty Ltd v Doric Products Pty Ltd* [2004] HCA 28 (18 November 2004).
[22] *CCOM Pty Ltd v Jiejing Pty Ltd* (1994) 122 ALR 417 (1994) AIPC 91-079 (1994) 51 FCR 260 at [69].

case is nicely analysed by McBratney,[23] and in the earlier article by the same author mentioned in the previous paragraph. If a broad principle that is new is referred to in the specification, then the claims can extend to any embodiment of that principle even if only one specific embodiment is given in the specification. But if the specification does not reveal a new principle but, for instance, a new combination of existing integers which is non-obvious, the claims would more normally be restricted to the actual embodiment given.

Utility

[Section 18 (1) (c)] The requirement of utility (or 'usefulness') is not concerned with any assessment of the moral worth, commercial value or social utility of the invention. Rather, at least one of the embodiments of the invention as claimed must work or achieve the result promised. This requirement is not examined prior to grant – it can only be a ground for revocation after grant. Nonetheless, usefulness is also implicit in the 'manner of manufacture' requirement, since an invention must offer a material advantage of economic significance. Utility questions can also arise in the context of the sufficiency requirement of section 40, in the sense that the applicant may supply insufficient information to enable a person skilled in the art to make it work. It is usual to read section 18 (1) (c) as requiring that the invention works as claimed, rather than that the invention should have 'specific, substantial and credible utility'. However, this terminology, derived from US patents law and also found in the US–Australia Free Trade Agreement (USFTA), is particularly relevant to patents that identify and isolate gene sequences, and which describe a particular application but also claim multiple potential or hypothetical analogous uses, but without disclosing how to obtain them. Such claims might fail under section 18 (1) (c); might amount to little more than a discovery; and could also offend against the fair basing requirement.[24]

Secret use; prior user rights

[Prohibition of secret use by the patentee] One of the starting premises of this chapter was that secrecy and patenting are *mutually exclusive* strategies. The provisions of section 18 (1) (d) legally compel innovative firms to make this choice. Public working of the invention by the patentee will constitute anticipation and therefore, unless the grace period applies, an application concerning an invention publicly exploited by the applicant will fail. But secret use evidently does not constitute anticipation. However, if the patentee were allowed to derive commercial benefit by working the invention in secret, thus enjoying monopoly use of it, and still obtain the advantage of a patent at a moment of his own choosing, the effective monopoly term would be extended beyond the 20 years of a patent – the patentee would be double-dipping. But this is ruled out by virtue of the

---

[23] McBratney A, 'Does the fair basing "problem child" escape Lockwood?' 16 (2005) 4 *AIPJ* 210.
[24] On this question, see further ALRC, Report No 99, *Genes and Ingenuity: Gene Patenting and Human Health*, (2004): Chapter 6, Patentability of Genetic Materials and Technologies.

terms of section 18 (1) (d), which makes secret use by a patentee a ground for revocation.

[Secret commercial use] Only secret use by the patentee that falls within the concept of 'exploitation' is a ground for revocation. But use with any commercial flavour at all will put validity at risk: see for instance *Azuko Pty Ltd v Old Digger Pty Ltd* (2001) 52 IPR 75. Secret use may be the actual commercial working of the invention by the patentee, or alternatively the exploitation by licensing or offering to license (under the cover of confidence) an invention before the filing of an application; see for instance *Wheatley's Patent Application* (1984) 2 IPR 450. Even a single instance of offering to license an invention may amount to secret use; in other words, the choice for the inventor is stark: either exploit the invention in secret, and rely on breach of confidence in equity to appropriate returns from the innovation, or file for a patent. Any attempt to benefit in both ways is fraught with risk. However, experimentation for the purpose of ascertaining whether an invention works, or as part of the R&D process, will not constitute the kind of secret use that can result in revocation.

[Prior user rights] By contrast, prior use by a third party, if not conducted publicly, will not undermine a patent application, since there is only anticipation by publication. Furthermore, by virtue of section 119, a person exploiting an invention at the time of filing by an unrelated patent applicant may continue to do so if a patent is granted.

3 Standard patents and innovation patents

[Two patents] The Australian patents system offers a choice between a standard patent and an innovation patent. By virtue of the *Patents Amendment (Innovation Patents) Act 2000* the latter superseded the petty patent, considered ineffective because virtually the same novelty and inventiveness threshold resulted in a shorter monopoly term than a standard patent. The main advantage of a petty patent was strategic because of the accelerated grant process, although lodging a provisional application for a standard patent was a potentially useful alternative. The innovation patent addresses these concerns by adopting a lower standard of inventiveness, and simultaneously reducing the cost, delay and administrative burden of prosecuting the initial application, by granting the innovation patent without substantive examination. Limited subject matter restrictions apply, no innovation patent being available for plant or animal inventions, and the maximum term is eight years. Innovation patents also have a maximum of five claims: they are not intended to cater for complex inventions but, like their European equivalent the 'utility model', are for relatively simple mechanical inventions made by sole inventors or small and medium enterprises (SMEs).

[Sealing without examination] The goal of low cost and minimal opportunity for delay is achieved by providing that the innovation patent is granted on the basis of a formalities check only; after grant but prior to substantive examination, it has limited value. To enforce the innovation patent it must first be *certified* – which means to pass a substantive examination of the various requirements for patentability. Although not formally required, one suspects that certification would be a standard condition of any commercial transaction involving an innovation patent as well. However, the innovation patent application procedure can also simply be used as a means of publishing the innovation, allowing the inventor to prevent others from obtaining a patent in it. The deferral of substantive examination prevents the wastage that flows from examination of all standard patents, many of which are never enforced or exploited, or are simply allowed to lapse.

[The innovative step] The core of the substantive distinction between standard and innovation patents lies in differing levels of inventiveness. Section 7 (4) provides that an invention does not involve an innovative step if it only varies from the prior art 'in ways that make no substantial contribution to the working of the invention'. According to the Australian Patent Office *Manual of Practice and Procedure* (September 2003 at [30.4.5.4]), this requires that the variation be of practical significance and not trivial or superficial or peripheral. This is a markedly different requirement compared to inventiveness for standard patents; it draws attention to the working of the invention rather than to a subjective assessment of the mental step that has brought it about. Whether the provisions actually achieve the legislative object of providing a lower threshold level has been doubted. A 'substantial contribution' appears to set a reasonably high bar, keeping in mind that the level of inventiveness required for a standard patent is very low anyway.[25]

To date there have been very few published innovation patent decisions: see *Datadot Technology Ltd v Alpha Microtech Pty Ltd* [2003] FCA 962; *Masport Ltd v Bartlem Pty Ltd* [2004] FCA 591; and *Aus Fence Hire Pty Ltd v Thomas* [2004] FCA 557, and none has considered this core issue, so we must await a judicial analysis of the provisions to clarify matters. The prior art information that can be taken into account for the purpose of the innovative step requirement also differs from that for inventiveness: see section 7 (5). The provisions in this regard are very complex; a decent analysis is presented in the article by Blows and Clark (above). Inventiveness levels can be modified by tinkering with the extent of the relevant prior art; but Blows and Clark cast doubt on whether the statutory provisions have actually given effect to the policy goal of introducing a lower threshold in this way as well.

Whatever the case may be, the origins of the innovative step requirement position lie somewhere between novelty and inventiveness. It is said to be based on or be an 'extended' version of the test in *Griffin v Isaacs* (1938) 12 AOJP 739. That case expounded a test to be applied in the context of novelty where there was some difference between an alleged anticipation and the relevant invention. The latter

---

[25] See discussion above; see Blows J and D Clark, 'Is an innovative step so easy that "any fool could do it"?' (2006), *Australian Intellectual Property Law Bulletin*, 18, 8, 129ff.

was not to be considered new if it varied only in ways that made no substantial contribution to the working of the invention. So unlike the inventiveness test, being rather 'novelty like' the 'innovativeness test' does not focus on whether or not the modification would occur to an average person active in the field, but on the characteristics of the invention itself – have the changes had a material functional effect that is more than trivial? Thus the test is in spirit closer to a novelty test than an inventiveness test as applicable to standard patents. The statutory language is obviously more consistent with incremental advances than major breakthroughs, as it refers only to improvements to existing devices, rather than to entirely new ones.

[An accelerated process] An innovation patent is expeditiously granted and sealed; in the absence of problems with the formalities check, no more than three months passes between filing and grant. This is much faster than for the grant of a standard patent, which involves substantive examination, often the making of amendments, and also potentially opposition proceedings. Generally an application for an innovation patent is said to take only three weeks from filing to grant; nonetheless the formalities check does include verification that no excluded subject matter or scandalous matter is included in the application, and that the applicant is an eligible person (ie a person entitled to the innovation patent). In substance, no more is required than information that appears to amount to a description, which can be a verbal description, claims, drawings or no more than some diagrams. However, a complete application for the purpose of certification (ie substantive examination) must end with a maximum of five claims. Standard and innovation patents cannot be cumulated. Conversion is permitted prior to grant, but not post-grant. A person, including the patentee and the Commissioner but also any third party, can request the Commissioner to undertake substantive examination of the innovation patent at any time after grant and prior to certification. After certification (ie in relation to a 'certified innovation patent') a third party can file an opposition with the Commissioner, or apply to a prescribed court for revocation.

[The utility of innovation patents] The pressing question flowing from this structure is: what use is a granted but uncertified innovation patent, which possibly contains only a vague and uncertain description of something potentially devoid of either novelty or innovation? An early priority date staking a claim to an invention is advantageous, and delaying substantive examination may save otherwise wasted expenditure on examination. Flexibility is certainly increased: some granted innovation patents can be ignored or forgotten, no great expense having been incurred in obtaining grant, while others can be certified and enforced if and when necessary or desirable. On the other hand, at worst an uncertified innovation patent could be misleading to the uninitiated; at best it tells third parties very little. Potentially it imposes on them the onus of requesting examination and giving the Commissioner notice of matters affecting validity. This reverses the normal situation which requires patentees to back up their belief in an invention with material supporting validity. The innovation patent may well be aimed at sole inventors and SMEs who cannot afford the up-front costs of standard patents, but such businesses require certainty too. Whereas the patentee may enjoy some guarantees of priority, patents of uncertain stature create additional insecurity for their rivals, who may also be small businesses in the same sector.

[The subject matter of innovation patents] The majority of innovation patents granted between 2001 and 2003 were for: consumer goods and equipment; civil engineering, building, mining; transport; information technology; and handling and printing.[26] ACIP has recommended that the exclusion of certain subject matter (plant and animal matter) should be maintained.[27] One reason for the exclusion was that regulatory approval requirements would make the shorter term unsuitable. If plants *were* included, there would be obvious overlap concerns with the Plant Breeder's Right system: in the absence of a true inventiveness requirement, a plant that had different characteristics which were of a useful kind would possibly attract an innovation patent even if those characteristics were obtained by traditional techniques, such as cross-breeding. As to Plant Breeder's Rights, see Chapter five.

4 Ownership of patents

The inventor's entitlement to a patent

[The inventor is entitled to the patent] The Act does not limit who can *apply* for a patent; but only the inventor or a person entitled to take an assignment of the invention from the inventor can be *granted* a patent. Two significant questions therefore confront the courts: who is a 'True and first inventor' (an expression used in section 6 of the *Statute of Monopolies*); and who is entitled to an assignment of somebody else's invention or patent? The second issue most commonly arises in the employment context, and is addressed in more detail below.

[Who is an inventor?] An inventor is he who 'performs the intellectual and practical work involved in the development of the invention'.[28] Practical work alone will not be enough – some inventive spark must come from the alleged inventor. A person who merely learns about the invention from another cannot claim as an inventor; in *Stack* the Court pointed out that:

> *Marsden* establishes that in the absence of express statutory provision, a personal representative could not obtain a grant on behalf of the estate of a deceased inventor because the representative would not be the true inventor. Obviously, the decision also excludes any claim by a person who, not being the true inventor, bases his claim upon knowledge derived from that inventor.[29]

Furthermore, first publishing an invention communicated by another does not amount to invention.

---

[26] See IPAustralia, Issues Paper, September 2005, *Review of the Innovation Patent*, p 6.
[27] See Advisory Council on Intellectual Property (ACIP), *Should plant and animal subject matter be excluded from protection by the innovation patent?* (November 2004).
[28] See *Stack v Davies Shephard* [2001] FCA 501 (4 May 2001) at FCA [12].
[29] At FCA [18]; referring to *Marsden v The Saville Street Foundry and Engineering Co Ltd* (1878) 3 ExD 203.

[Co-inventors] Two or more individuals who contribute to the making of the invention in the relevant manner are co-inventors and thus co-owners. The Court in *Stack* pointed out (at [21]) that:

> [. . .] one of two inventors each responsible for a part of the invention cannot claim a patent over the total invention. That is because such a patent would confer upon him or her the benefit of that part of the invention for which he or she was not responsible.

Therefore the position where there are co-inventors is (at [28]):

> Each may have been entitled to a patent over his part (if it was otherwise patentable), while they both may have been entitled to a joint patent over the whole. Neither was solely entitled to a patent over the total invention. It follows that they could not, by arrangement between them, create in [one of the inventors] an entitlement to a patent, save to the extent that they created a relationship pursuant to which he satisfied either par 15(1)(b) or par 15(1)(c).

Section 15 (1) (b) & (c) contemplates a situation not of joint inventorship, but where an inventor either passes on title to another person, or where another is entitled to the benefit of an invention due to the circumstances in which it was made (usually employment). The other person is not treated as an inventor but as an assignee.

[Individual invention in industry] Invention today has two features that are somewhat at odds with the notion of the individual who is entitled to property in an invention resulting from their personal mental endeavour. First, most invention is the result of teamwork and collaboration; and secondly, most inventions are made during employment. Nonetheless it is not possible to obtain a patent without nominating an individual person or persons as inventor(s). Where a number of people have made an intellectual and practical contribution to a single invention, each will be considered by the law to be an inventor and a patent will be jointly owned. By virtue of section 16 of the Act co-owners have an equal and undivided share of a patent. They are each entitled to exploit the patent without having to account to others, but require the consent of all other patentees to license its exploitation. In those circumstances, assigning the patent to a single entity, most commonly the employer or a company established for the purpose of retaining intellectual property, will reduce complexity and limit transaction costs. Perhaps unsurprisingly, the law in Australia provides that if the invention is made in the performance of employees' duties, whether individually or by a team of co-inventors, the employer will be entitled to take the benefit of the invention (either by obtaining a patent or by an assignment of the patent from the inventor(s)).

Employer entitlement to inventions and patents: some policy issues

[Inventions in the course of employment] Firms (the term includes any economic unit with legal personality) are the institutional vehicles in which complementary material, intellectual and financial resources are collected and organised to manage the risks inherent in innovative activity. From that perspective firms are the logical repositories of legal rights over inventions, or any other relevant IPRs. However, for the purpose of patents law, only individual employees can be inventors, so the law must moderate the relationship between the firm and individuals employed to invent. In Australia the applicable default rules, although variable by contract, are found entirely in the common law and not in the Act. The IPAC Report of 1984 (at p 53) reveals that the Industrial Property Advisory Committee could not agree on an approach giving rights to employees additional to those recognised by the common law. It recommended that 'a scheme giving rights or opportunities to employee inventors, including the right in some circumstances to take out a patent, be further studied'. That never eventuated, although there are many examples of legislative intervention in other jurisdictions, with provisions usually ensuring additional employee benefits or entitlements. This is an area of IP law that is not harmonised around the world nor governed by mandatory provisions in international instruments. In some jurisdictions, such as the Federal Republic of Germany, the rights and financial entitlements of employees are comprehensively regulated, employer ownership being combined with a statutory right to royalties for employed inventors. In the United Kingdom, a more modest statutory modification of the common law has granted employees a statutory entitlement to a return from their inventions in cases of windfall profits. Statutory provisions may or may not be mandatory, ie they can be varied by contract in some jurisdictions but not or not wholly in others.

[Incentives and efficiency] It may be most efficient for firms to control inventions that conform to their technological and commercial profile, since they can most efficiently gather the complementary skills and resources required to exploit them. This may require firms to *own* inventions, or alternatively to be able to obtain the benefit of an invention by way of a licence from an employee-owner. Australian law favours employer ownership: if an employee is paid consideration to research and invent, the employer is entitled to the fruits of his intellectual work, as he would be entitled to the fruits of paid physical labour. As consideration the employee obtains a salary, which partly insulates him from the risk and uncertainty inherent in inventive activity. However, salary as an incentive to invent is a blunt instrument; efficiency gains may result from offering (by means of contract) additional rewards more closely targeted at the making of inventions, or the obtaining of patents. Employee ownership of a patent is one such incentive, but with exclusive user rights for the employer. But it has the drawback of cost, both financial and administrative, and loss of complementarity by encouraging researchers to direct their efforts at *any* patentable invention rather than inventions the firm can efficiently exploit. It also risks encouraging employee defections (in favour of owned start-ups and spin-offs, or competing champions) to take advantage of patent ownership. Premiums attached to inventions or patents are an alternative, but they may encourage employees to undervalue other duties, and are difficult to target at inventions useful to the employer. For these reasons, allowing employers to own work-related inventions but giving employees an additional return above salary from internal or licensed exploitation may strike an efficient balance. The main drawback of such an approach is administrative cost, as experienced with the statutory system that operates in Germany. Where the invention is not complementary with the firm's activities, employee ownership of course makes more sense; an employee who owns the invention can also be a more effective champion, and in terms of innovation levels, employee defections for the purpose of exploiting a patent may not be a bad thing.

[Patent focus in industry and academe] As institutional barriers to patent grant diminish and the innovation imperative permeates industry, inventorship has arguably become more commonplace. Employees are more conscious of the existence and potential value of patents. At the same time, firms are tempted to cast their net as wide as possible to obtain ownership of employees' inventions – an ambition upon which the law places certain restraints. Transition to a more patent-sensitive environment has particular implications for the academic sector, but also for industrial sectors that traditionally rely on free and open exchange within industry and with academe, and for those dependent upon low-cost access to knowledge (eg in developing countries). Because patent law inspires a race to file first, and secrecy is critical pre-filing, the sharing of knowledge to gain peer-recognition is threatened in a patent environment: knowledgeable persons risk becoming secretive actors in a competitive race. But the free exchange of knowledge, not only within the academic sector, remains a crucial dynamic in a knowledge-based society. The patenting-impetus in public sector institutions must therefore continue to be balanced with a peer-recognition dynamic which encourages publication. The discussion concerning patenting in universities, and in particular about ownership and licensing of inventions made by academic employees, is therefore crucial; but it remains controversial and difficult to resolve, as recent debate at Cambridge and Oxford universities demonstrates. Monotti and Ricketson's work[30] demonstrates how in Australia institutional approaches have also been very varied. How the balance between free, peer-recognition-based knowledge sharing and the proprietary, profit-driven exchanges is to be struck is not resolved.

The law of ownership of employee inventions in Australia

[The default rules] The common law default rules concerning ownership of employee inventions allow only two outcomes: either the employee or the employer takes the full benefit of the invention. In other words, only by virtue of contract can more limited and specific rights such as a non-exclusive, royalty-free licence be allocated to either party. In the absence of such contractual variation, the employer or the employee will own the invention, be able to patent it, and license or assign the patent without regard to the other party. The critical factor

---

[30] Monotti A and S Ricketson, *Universities and Intellectual Property, Ownership and Exploitation*, Oxford University Press, UK, 2003.

determining ownership of inventions made by an ordinary employee in Australian law is whether their duties include the making of inventions; however, somewhat different rules apply to some managerial employees under a duty to advance the interests of the firm overall. Use of an employer's resources therefore does not automatically result in the latter being entitled to an assignment of an invention. *Victoria University of Technology v Wilson* [2004] VSC 33 (18 February 2004) rejected a constructive trust over an invention, with the employer as beneficiary, as the appropriate remedy where the dispute revolved around the use of employer resources in the making of an invention. Instead the Court suggested that an action for breach of contract may be the correct remedy if the employee made unauthorised use of university resources for purposes of personal gain, such as working on a personal invention.

[The Australian position in more detail] In the unusual *Kwan* case, relating to an invention made by prisoners,[31] the common law rules in Australia were held to be equivalent to the relevant statutory provision in the United Kingdom, which itself:

> sets outs the broad principles of ownership of inventions made by employees, and confirms the position which existed according to common law before 1 June 1978 [...]. It is reasonable to assume that this section also reflects the position in Australia. [...].

The decision then sets out section 39 of the UK Act, which is as follows:

> 39. – (1) Notwithstanding anything in any rule of law, an invention made by an employee shall, as between him and his employer, be taken to belong to his employer for the purposes of this Act and all other purposes if (a) it was made in the course of the normal duties of the employee or in the course of duties falling outside his normal duties, but specifically assigned to him, and the circumstances in either case were such that an invention might reasonably be expected to result from the carrying out of his duties; or (b) the invention was made in the course of the duties of the employee and, at the time of making the invention, because of the nature of his duties and the particular responsibilities arising from the nature of his duties he had a special obligation to further the interests of the employer's undertaking. (2) Any other invention made by an employee shall, as between him and his employer, be taken for those purposes to belong to the employee.

[Does the law only superficially favour employers?] Superficially the law thus favours the employer. However, in *VUT v Wilson* the court explained the position as follows (at FCA 104), sounding a valuable warning against a liberal interpretation of the rule:

> But the mere existence of the employer/employee relationship will not give the employer ownership of inventions made by the employee during the term of the relationship. And that is so even if the invention is germane to and useful for the employer's business, and even though the employee may have made use of the employer's time

---

[31] *Kwan et al v The Queensland Corrective Services Commission* [1994] APO 53; (1994) AIPC 91-113; 31 IPR 25.

and resources in bringing the invention to completion. Certainly, all the circumstances must be considered in each case, but unless the contract of employment expressly so provides, or an invention is the product of work which the employee was paid to perform, it is unlikely that any invention made by the employee will be held to belong to the employer.

The Court made reference to recent English decisions as being consistent with its narrow approach to employer-ownership: see *Greater Glasgow Health Board's Application* [1996] RPC 207; but a strong line of similar authority goes back to *Worthington Pumping Engine Co v Moore (1902)* 20 RPC 41; *British Reinforced Concrete Co v Lind* (1917) 34 RPC 101; *Triplex Safety Glass Co Ltd v Scorah* [1938] 1 Ch 211; and *Fine Industrial Commodities Ltd v Powling* (1954) 71 RPC 253.[32]

[Determining the nature of the employee's duties] Furthermore, in *Wilson* it was held not to be sufficient that the employee was employed to *research*: 'It is not enough that the process of invention can be characterized as one of research. It all depends upon the nature of the research that the employee is retained to perform' (at FCA 108). Ordinarily the research of the professor concerned, falling within a social sciences discipline, was not of a kind that would likely result in the production of patentable inventions. The inquiry should be whether there was a duty to do research with an eye to producing patentable inventions. The relevant duties are those *at the time the invention is made*, rather than exclusively what is contained in the initial contract of employment. The duties of an employee may evolve over time, and variations to the initial terms need not necessarily be in writing. Acceptance of certain tasks may vary the nature of the employment, and hence the scope of an employer's possible legal claims. But it is a duty to make inventions that must exist: neither a duty to modify or redesign, nor a duty to advance business opportunities amounts to that. A suggestion that an employer add a product to their range or modify a product, coming from a sales agent or manager, does not amount to the exercise of a putative duty to invent, because the input required or expected from the employee must be creative rather than in the nature of suggesting standard modifications or alternative settings.

It is also not enough that the employer's resources are used nor that the invention made is in line with the employer's business. As the Delegate put it in *Spencer Industries*:

> It is true that the patentee's business was at the time of his employment concerned with the manufacture of the same class of products to which the present invention is directed (cf. *Harris' Patent* [1985] RPC 19). However, as I see it Mr Collins had only an obligation to effect sales of those products and to ensure after-sales service. Although in fulfilling his primary duty Mr Collins may have alerted the patentee to problems experienced by their customers, there is no satisfactory evidence to support the contention that it was incumbent upon him to provide solutions to such problems.[33]

[Very senior employees] There is an second strand of cases that focusses on inventions made by employees so senior that they owe the employer a fiduciary

---

[32] See also Loughlan P, 'Of patents and professors: IP, Research Workers and Universities' [1996] 6 *EIPR* 345.
[33] See *Spencer Industries Pty Ltd v Anthony Collins and B & J Manufacturing Company* [2002] APO 4 (18 January 2002).

duty (as opposed to merely an implied contractual duty of good faith; cf section 39 (1) (b) of the UK Act, above). Very few employees fall into this category. Actual authority and control over the business concerned will have to be found to be so extensive that retaining the benefit of the invention would be incompatible with that managerial employee's broad duty to advance the interests of the firm. In such cases the relationship between employer and employee would normally be of a very close and confidential character. The issue was considered in *Eastland Technology Australia Pty Ltd v Whisson* [2005] WASCA 144 (Malcolm, Steytler, McClure JJ), in which the older case of *Fine Industrial Commodities Ltd v Powling* (1954) 71 RPC 253 was called in aid. The key issue in these kind of cases is to identify the nature of the relationship – is it fiduciary or not – rather than the precise content of the employee's duties – what the employee is paid to do.

[Contractual expansion of entitlement] The employer may seek to remedy his limited residual entitlement to beneficial ownership of an invention by contractual means. But the law subjects provisions that extend employer ownership beyond inventions made in the course of duty or upon specific direction to careful scrutiny. They may be treated as inequitable restraints or as so uncertain as to be unenforceable (see *Electrolux Ltd v Hudson* [1977] FSR 312). The judicial approach is analogous to that taken in relation to confidential information (see above, Chapter two): if an employee makes an invention he himself should have the benefit of it, unless he was paid to pursue such inventions; if he misused the time or resources of the employer, the remedy against him may lie in damages, but not in a constructive trust favouring the employer (see above). It is certainly unfair that an employee should be compelled to hand over beneficial ownership of inventions that they were under no obligation to pursue, or could expect no consideration for. However, striking down contractual provisions on the basis of broad standards such as uncertainty or abhorrence to public policy engenders uncertainty.

By comparison, the statutorily mandated rules preferred in many other jurisdictions provide more clarity and predictability. The effect of the UK provision (section 40) is only limited, because it goes no further than guaranteeing a return to the inventor in all cases where an invention results in windfall profits. However, the very comprehensive German approach guarantees a return to employees from every patented invention. Under the Japanese model the employee owns the invention but the employer obtains a royalty-free but non-exclusive licence, so the employee can grant licences to others. According to the law, the employer can negotiate with the employee to obtain an assignment or an exclusive licence, subject to the payment of a reasonable amount (terms not however further specified in the Act).

5 Rights and infringement

[Literal and non-literal interpretation of claims] The scope and extent of the patentee's monopoly is determined by the claims; anything that falls outside what is expressly claimed is permitted. It is therefore to the precise claim language that regard must be had to determine whether some impugned invention falls within the exclusive rights of the patentee or not. Quite often it is not immediately clear whether that is the case or not – claim 'construction' is required. A literal interpretation of the claims would mean that any small, functionally irrelevant variation would defeat the patentee's rights. Nonetheless the words deliberately chosen by the patentee are the anchor to which interpretation or 'claim construction' must remain firmly attached; courts should not be invited to make good the failings of the language the patentee has had ample opportunity to choose with care. Courts have struggled to find an interpretive device which holds the patentee to the language he consciously chose, but does not permit the patent to be too readily circumvented. They have settled upon two strategies: the pith and marrow approach, and the purposive approach. The latter has substantially but not wholly supplanted the former in more recent times in Australia.

[The pith and marrow approach] The pith and marrow doctrine allowed a decision-maker to stray somewhat from the literal words of the claims, to ask whether an impugned invention adopted the pith and marrow of the patented invention – were all the elements of the invention reproduced in substance? However, this approach has a tendency to encourage courts to recast the scope of the monopoly rather than interpret the claim language. In other words, the fact that the patentee had the opportunity to choose the claim language with care and deliberation may be unjustly discounted in the process of claim construction. The approach is also inherently uncertain and unpredictable, in that it introduces an indeterminate question rather than a clear framework for interpretation of the claim language. It may therefore have a chilling effect on competition. In the US non-literal infringement was to some extent approached by reference to an analogous device, extending claims to 'equivalents' (the 'doctrine of equivalents') – but this approach is justifiably criticised both within the US and elsewhere as allowing indeterminate extension of the claims beyond their actual terms. The problem with extending the monopoly to equivalents is that it is not easy to know where to draw the limits, as pointed out by Lord Hoffman in *Kirin-Amgen Inc v Hoechst Marion Roussel Ltd* [2004] UKHL 46; [2005] 1 All ER 667 ('*Kirin-Amgen*'). The same could be said about the pith and marrow approach. In any case, the door has been firmly shut on the doctrine of equivalents in Europe, because article 69 of the European Patent Convention prohibits this approach; and it has never gained much support in Australia.

[The purposive approach] The purposive approach is intended to provide a clearer interpretive framework. It differs fundamentally from the pith and marrow approach in that it undertakes interpretation of the claim language through the eyes of a person skilled in the art. In the course of his very useful analysis of the various approaches to claim construction in *Kirin-Amgen*, Lord Hoffman indicates that, rather than sticking to literalism and then supplementing the claims with equivalents, the purposive approach *abandons* literalism, and instead '[a]dopt[s] a principle of construction which actually gave effect to what the person skilled in the art would have understood the patentee to be claiming' (at [43]). Applying the purposive approach, a variant falls outside the scope of the patent if, in relation to the wording at issue, a person skilled in the art would take it that strict compliance with terms or phrases of a claim was intended by the patentee. Conversely, if it is apparent to a person skilled in the art that strict adherence to the terms or phrases of the claim cannot have been intended, with the effect that minor variants, which persons skilled in the art know could not have 'a material effect on the way the invention worked', should be ignored, then an apparent limitation in the terms of the claim can be ignored. But the issue will only ever arise if the variant is one that does not introduce a functional advantage, or a 'material effect upon the way the invention worked'.[34] Notably also, in the case of a combination patent, the plaintiff must establish that 'each and every one of the essential integers' is replicated.[35]

[The background of the purposive approach] The traditional English approach to textual interpretation focussed almost exclusively on the actual words present, ascribing them their 'natural and ordinary meaning' (ie what dictionary and syntax reveal). However, then:

> [I]t came to be recognized that the author of a document such as a contract or patent specification is using language to make a communication for a practical purpose and that a rule of construction which gives his language a meaning different from the way it would have been understood by the people to whom it was actually addressed is liable to defeat his intentions.[36]

This general change in attitude then gave rise to the adoption in *Catnic* of a purposive approach to construction of patent specifications. As a result, the construction of claims does not centre upon a 'detailed semantic and syntactical analysis'[37] but rather on context: ie the 'identity of the audience he is taken to have been addressing and the knowledge and assumptions which one attributes to that audience'.[38] The notional addressee of a patent specification is the person skilled in the art armed with common general knowledge, who:

> [R]eads the specification on the assumption that its purpose is both to describe and to demarcate an invention – a practical idea which the patentee has had for a new product or process – and not to be a textbook in mathematics or chemistry or a shopping list of chemicals or hardware. It is this insight that lies at the heart of 'purposive construction'.[39]

[But the words count most] However, Lord Hoffman emphasises that the words chosen still have primary significance:

> The question is always what the person skilled in the art would have understood the patentee to be using the language of the claim to mean. And for this purpose, the

---

[34] See Lord Diplock in *Catnic Components Ltd v Hill & Smith Ltd* [1982] RPC 183 (1982) RPC 183 at 242–243.
[35] *Populin v H. B. Nominees Pty Ltd* (1982) 41 ALR 471 at 475.
[36] *Kirin-Amgen* per Lord Hoffman at [30].
[37] See Lord Diplock in *The Antaios* [1985] AC 191 (as quoted by Lord Hoffman in *Kirin-Amgen*, at [31]).
[38] *Kirin-Amgen*, at [32].
[39] *Kirin-Amgen*, at [33].

language he has chosen is usually of critical importance. The conventions of word meaning and syntax enable us to express our meanings with great accuracy and subtlety and the skilled man will ordinarily assume that the patentee has chosen his language accordingly.[40]

The specification is a document of the patentee's own choosing, often upon skilled advice; it is not a document *inter rusticos*, Lord Hoffman goes on to point out. The purpose or intention of the patentee can only be deduced from that document – there is no other evidence of it, so interpreting those actual words remains critical, and giving them their ordinary meaning remains the norm. It would be rare for the interpretation to depart from the actual wording of the claims, ie:

> for the notional skilled man to conclude, after construing the claim purposively in the context of the specification and drawings, that the patentee must nevertheless have meant something different from what he appears to have meant.[41]

[The *Improver* questions] The purposive approach was further elaborated upon in the *Improver* case, *Improver Corporation v Remington Consumer Products Ltd* [1990] FSR 181, a UK decision which has, like *Catnic* (see above), been very influential in Australian courts. The '*Improver* Questions', also referred to as the 'Protocol Questions',[42] are as follows:

> If the issue was whether a feature embodied in an alleged infringement which fell outside the primary, literal or acontextual meaning of a descriptive word or phrase in the claim ('a variant') was nevertheless within its language as properly interpreted, the court should ask itself the following three questions:
> (1) Does the variant have a material effect upon the way the invention works? If yes, the variant is outside the claim. If no?
> (2) Would this (ie that the variant had no material effect) have been obvious at the date of publication of the patent to a reader skilled in the art? If no, the variant is outside the claim. If yes?
> (3) Would the reader skilled in the art nevertheless have understood from the language of the claim that the patentee intended that strict compliance with the primary meaning was an essential requirement of the invention? If yes, the variant is outside the claim.

> On the other hand, a negative answer to the last question would lead to the conclusion that the patentee was intending the word or phrase to have not a literal but a figurative meaning (the figure being a form of synecdoche or metonymy) denoting a class of things which include the variant and the literal meaning, the latter being perhaps the most perfect, best-known or striking example of the class.[43]

[*Catnic*, *Improver* and the present state of the law in Australia] The *Improver* approach is not a new departure, but an application of *Catnic*, or what Finkelstein J in *Root Quality Pty Ltd v Root Control Technologies Pty Ltd* (2000) 177 ALR 231;

---

[40] *Kirin-Amgen*, at [34].
[41] *Kirin-Amgen*, at [35].
[42] As for instance in *Wheatly v Drillsafe Ltd* [2001] RPC 133.
[43] As quoted in *Kirin-Amgen*, at [51].

[2000] FCA 980 referred to as an *elaboration* of the purposive approach. In the same case at [44]–[45] Finkelstein J said:

> In Australia the so-called 'purposive approach' to construction has been adopted (see *Populin v HB Nominees Pty Ltd* (1982) 41 ALR 471; *Nesbit Evans Group Australia Pty Ltd v Impro Ltd* (1997) 39 IPR 56) although some cases imply that the former approach [ie the pith and marrow approach] can still have application: see *Populin* at 475–477; see also J W Dwyer and A Dufty (eds), *Lahore on Patents Trademarks and Related Rights*, 1996 paras 18,135 and 18,140. On the other hand, when the *Improver* questions are posed and answered, it is difficult to see what can be achieved by recourse to the 'pith and marrow' approach.

Merkel J in *PhotoCure ASA v Queen's University at Kingston* [2005] FCA 344, at [168]–[175] and [195]–[208], carried out a comprehensive review of the authorities, at the conclusion of which his Honour decided to consider the case on the basis of the *Improver* questions within the framework outlined by Lord Hoffman in *Kirin-Amgen*. In *Root Quality* (see above, at [27]ff) the matter was also considered on the basis of the *Improver* questions. However, judges have taken on board the warning of Lord Hoffman that the *Improver* questions will not be appropriate to all inventions; they have also held that the *Improver* questions are not necessary if the terms of the claims are clear and unambiguous, such as the terms 'concrete spacer' in *Baygol Pty Ltd v Foamex Polystyrene Pty Ltd* [2005] FCA 624 (18 May 2005). In *Baygol* Tamberlin J considered that *Catnic* was accepted into Australian law but that the 'pith and marrow' approach had continued application as well; in such cases the *Improver* questions will inevitably not be applicable either. Merkel J in *PhotoCure* (see above) accepted that:

> Since *Improver* a number of decisions of the Court have considered the question of 'infringement in substance' without reference to *Improver* or the *Improver* questions: see for example *Doric Products Pty Ltd v Lockwood Security Products Pty Ltd* (2001) 192 ALR 306; *Leonardis*; *Azuko* and most recently *Gambro*. However, in at least three instances the Court has applied *Improver*. In *Nesbit Evans Group Australia Pty Ltd v Impro Ltd* (1997) 39 IPR 56 the Full Court referred to the *Improver* questions as relevant, although there was no dispute in that case as to their applicability under Australian law: per Lindgren J (with whom Hill J agreed) at 80–81, and per Wilcox J at 58. The *Improver* questions were also applied by Finkelstein J in *Root Quality* at [55] and [69]–[74], and more recently by Kiefel J in *Neurizon Pty Ltd v Jupiters Ltd* (2004) 62 IPR 569 at [139]. See also *Sydney Cellulose Pty Ltd v Ceil Comfort Home Insulation Pty Ltd* (2001) 53 IPR 359 ('*Sydney Cellulose*') at [43].

In the end his Honour accepted that the *Improver* questions were not in substance different from the *Catnic* approach but, as seen above, an application of them. In the final analysis, as observed by Lord Hoffman (with whom the other members of the House of Lords agreed) in *Kirin-Amgen* (at [48]) the purposive approach attempts to achieve something relatively straightforward: '. . . to give the patentee the full extent, but not more than the full extent, of the monopoly which a reasonable person skilled in the art, reading the claims in context, would think he was intending to claim'. That leaves the question of the status of the purposive approach (rather than of *Improver*) as the key issue. And although Tamberlin J rightly pointed out that it will not always be the appropriate approach, this does not mean that the purposive approach is not fundamentally accepted in Australia.

[**Claims and specification**] Often, when attempting to determine whether some impugned invention falls within the claims, they will have to be interpreted to determine *what exactly the patented invention is*. A logical way of developing an accurate verbal description of the invention would be to have recourse to the specification as a whole: use the other parts of the application to interpret the claims. But the *claims* are what the patentee uses to stake out his monopoly; and the old English approach therefore only allowed recourse to the rest of the specification if there was some inherent ambiguity or uncertainty in the claim language. However, section 69 of the EPC now specifically prohibits this approach: it provides that '[T]he extent of protection conferred [...] shall be determined by the terms of the claims. Nevertheless, the description and drawings shall be used to interpret the claims.' But Australian cases still reiterate that if a term of a claim is not a term of art and is used in a plain, clear and unambiguous way, there should be no resort to the body of the specification.[44]

However, although this may be possible as an isolated theoretical exercise, it is rather artificial in the context of a case where the claims have to be measured against a concrete and specific invention, allegedly infringing. It may be that a court is perfectly able to understand what exactly comprises the invention; the terms of the claim may be so clear and ordinary (as opposed to terms of art and/or ambiguous) that expert evidence is not admissible as to their interpretation. However, if the purposive approach is to be taken to determine whether a variant falls within or without the scope of the invention as claimed, it will almost always be necessary to have recourse to expert evidence, since this approach requires that the question of the intention of the patentee in choosing certain terminology be assessed through the eyes of the person skilled in the art. It will be a rare case where both the construction of the claims in terms of their meaning, and the comparison with an impugned invention before a court, intermingled as they naturally are, will be able to be resolved without appropriate reference to expert evidence.

6 The nature and extent of the exploitation right

[**Exploitation of products and processes**] The patentee enjoys a true monopoly right: with the exception of some prior users (see below), nobody can exploit the patented invention. Whether or not they arrived at it independently, or were ignorant of the existence of a patent is irrelevant, although knowing of a patent may be significant in terms of remedies, as is explained below. On the other hand, exploitation may have been authorised by the patentee, either in express

---

[44] See eg *Pharmacia Italia S.P.A v Mayne Pharma Pty Ltd* [2005] FCA 1078 at [56].

terms or by implication; for instance, the sale of a patented product may imply that the purchaser has a right to use it (see further below). As we saw above, a patented invention consists either of process claims, or product claims, or a combination of both. The statutory definition of the term 'exploitation' recognises this. What was previously the right to 'make, exercise and vend' the invention is circumscribed in more detail in the 1990 Act (see the Dictionary, Schedule 1), although in theory not exhaustively. In relation to a product patent, the patentee has the right to make it, to work it (to use a machine to do what it is claimed to be useful for) and to deal (sell, rent, etc) with it commercially. A process claim has, in a sense, a more extensive scope, since the patentee not only has the exclusive right to work or operate the process, but also the same exclusive rights in the product that results from the process as he would enjoy if that product itself was patented. The rights of the patentee are also extended by virtue of section 117: the *supply* of products other than the invention as such can in some circumstances constitute an infringement (sometimes referred to as 'contributory infringement').

[When and where?] An Australian patent only gives exclusive rights in Australia (the 'patent area'), but this includes the right to prohibit importation of a legitimate patented product from abroad. The rights of the patentee only take full effect when the patent is granted (at least as far as standard patents are concerned; innovation patents must be 'certified' before they can be enforced). However, although infringement proceedings can only be *initiated* after grant, damages can be obtained for any infringement that occurs after the date on which the complete specification became public; from then on, others are on notice. The term of the patent is 20 years, after which the invention enters the public domain and can be freely exploited; any contractual terms to the contrary becoming unenforceable. The term is generally calculated from the priority date. For pharmaceutical patents, in recognition of the fact that obtaining regulatory (ie marketing) approval reduces the effective monopoly term, the patent term can be further extended for a maximum of five years. Thus, lodging a specific application for extension is one option for the pharmaceutical patentee; but in recent times there has been some concern about another tactic used to *de facto* extend the monopoly term: that of 'evergreening'.[45] This is the practice of reformulating an expiring product patent in process terms, for instance focussing on a new dosage regime, for which a new patent is then sought. But it may also take the form of claiming inventiveness in a new and different application of a previously patented substance, for instance for its therapeutic effect for different indications. However, the novelty and inventiveness requirements will often stand in the way of such applications – as is discussed above. Another tactic relies instead on trade mark protection of pharmaceutical names; however, the *Trade Marks Act* contains specific provisions preventing the patentee from monopolising certain terms used to refer to patented drugs by way of their registration as a mark: see section 25, *Trade Marks Act 1995* (Cth).

---

[45] See for instance *Arrow Pharmaceuticals v Merck & Co, Inc* [2004] FCA 1282.

[Exploitation] The exclusive rights are formulated so as to ensure that only the patentee obtains any commercial benefit from the patented invention. That leaves certain uses of patented inventions in a grey area, where it is unclear whether they fall within the realm of commerce or not. On the one hand, certain actions will clearly be performed with an ultimate commercial goal, although they do not have the character of commercial exploitation in themselves. Thus the importation of a sample of a patented drug into New Zealand by a generic competitor, for the purpose of submitting it to the relevant Ministry to obtain marketing approval, was considered to be an action conducted for a commercial advantage and therefore an infringement of the rights of the patentee (the purpose being to obtain a 'springboard' for the introduction onto the market of the drug the moment the patent ran out). This issue of 'springboarding', ie generic competitors obtaining all necessary approvals, or gearing up for production of pharmaceuticals prior to the end of the patent term, is controversial. Questions also surround so-called experimental use, terms that in themselves are imprecise.[46] Experimenting in the sense of testing of a patented invention may well be legitimate without the approval of the patentee – how else will it be determined whether an invention has the required utility, or whether the description is adequate? But a patent being *used in experiments* is a different matter; if the experimental context is purely academic, the use may fall outside the patent monopoly; but if the context has any commercial overtones, then the situation may be different. The ACIP Report examines whether greater clarity is required in relation to experimental use, certainly in today's innovation environment, where patented inventions more frequently extend to processes used purely in conducting research rather than in commercial exploitation in the more traditional sense.

[Strict approach] But the courts are jealous guardians of patent monopolies; they do not allow them to be whittled away at the edges. No clear exceptions have been judicially devised, and the statutory exceptions are narrowly circumscribed (see section 118: Use on foreign vessels, etc; see also further below, Prior user rights). However, one critical limitation, fashioned by reliance on the general principles of the common law, relates to the property rights of the purchaser of a patented product. These are usually construed as comprising the right to use the product for the purpose for which it was intended (a separate exploitation right) and to sell the product on (the so-called theory of non-derogation from rights). However, they do not extend to the right to reconstruct the product should it be damaged, although the owner does have the right to make repairs, properly so-called. Furthermore, even if a patented product is made only as a passing stage in a larger construction process, unless the making is trifling or insignificant there will be an infringement in the absence of a proper licence; and supplying parts that are easy to assemble will be treated as supplying the patented *product* itself.

[Compulsory licences] A third party wishing to use a patented invention should obtain a licence, but if frustrated in attempting to do so, the Act provides for an

---

[46] See ACIP, Final Report, *Patents and Experimental Use* (October 2005).

application to be made to a court which can grant a compulsory licence on terms it determines (see Chapter 12 of the *Patents Act*, section 133ff). However, in reality these provisions are rarely activated and the grant of compulsory licences is not common in most jurisdictions, partly due to the fact that the evidentiary burden on the applicant is quite onerous. For instance, the applicant needs to establish that proffered licence terms were unreasonable, that the requirements of the Australian public are not met, etc; see sections 133 &135. Another reason is that where an invention is commercially viable, usually it will either be fully exploited by the patentee, or be made available on commercial terms. Given that so many patented inventions are in fact never exploited, empirical evidence revealing the incidence of refusal to license for the purpose of 'burying' a competing technology is anecdotal at best.

[Prior user rights; Crown user rights] A rather more significant statutory derogation from the rights of the patentee applies to others who were exploiting the invention immediately prior to the priority date of a claim (rather than adopting it after that date). By virtue of section 119, they will be entitled to continue to exploit the invention even after a patent is granted. Obviously the prior use has to have been conducted in secret, or else the invention will not be novel. The prior use must have been continuous and in existence just prior to the date of filing, and the patentee himself must not be concerned with the exploitation. As seen above, if the patentee *is* himself involved with the secret exploitation of the invention before the priority date, this constitutes a separate ground of invalidity which can result in the revocation of the patent (see section 18 (1) (d)). The Crown also has extensive rights to use a patented invention for the services of the Commonwealth or a State (as broadly interpreted, including some city councils). However, this right (unlike the prior user right) is subject to the payment of a royalty (see Chapter 17 of the *Patents Act*; section 165). The Crown is not compelled to seek approval from the patentee prior to initiating exploitation, but is liable to pay compensation as agreed between the parties, or failing agreement, as determined by a court. The right of exploitation is not restricted to the Crown and its departments itself, but extends to parties authorised by the Crown to work an invention. The right of the Crown to exploit inventions without prior agreement is considered in detail in a recent ACIP report.[47]

[Infringement by supply] In circumstances where the patent claims a *process*, section 117 allows a patentee to bring an action against persons who supply products for use in the process, but only in circumstances where it can properly be said that they contribute to the infringement of the patent. By virtue of section 117 (2) that will occur: where the product is only capable of one reasonable infringing use; where the product is not a staple, and the supplier had reason to believe that the recipient would put it to an infringing use; or where the product is supplied with instructions or inducements to use it in an infringing manner. Section 117 was an innovation introduced with the *Patents Act 1990*, only general law

---

[47] ACIP, *Review of crown use provisions for patents and designs*, November 2005.

principles applying to such circumstances previously. Early decisions (notably *Rescare*, see above) read down the provision to the extent of stripping it of any capacity to fulfil the legislative intent, which had been mainly aimed at reinforcing process patents in the farm sector (supply of chemicals to be applied to crops by way of a patented method). However, more recently the section has been restored to its full force and intent (see *Bristol-Myers* above). The provision enables patentees to sue suppliers, rather than multiple end-users who apply or use a product individually by way of a method that falls within patent claims.

[Strengthening of the patentee's position] It has become more difficult to obtain a patent due to the extension of the relevant prior art, and the greater allowance for *mosaicing* in the context of inventiveness, as indicated above (see the Inventiveness section). However, the position of the patentee has also been strengthened in recent times, in two ways in particular: one, the introduction of contributory infringement with the 1990 Act (as discussed above), which helps the patentee overcome the restrictive effect of general law rules relating to vicarious liability, etc; and secondly, the more recently introduced aids to proof in relation to process patents. The concern addressed by these new provisions (see section 121A) is that the owner of a process patent is in a difficult position if he must prove that some product being dealt with commercially has been produced by the application of a patented process. Proof of that fact may be uniquely within the knowledge of the defendant, and be otherwise hard to obtain; to remedy this, the Act now reverses the onus of proof subject to certain restrictions. By virtue of section 121A, if the defendant alleges that he or she has used a process different from the patented process to obtain a product identical to the product obtained by the patented process; and (b) the court is satisfied that: (i) it is very likely that the defendant's product was made by the patented process; and (ii) the patentee or exclusive licensee has taken reasonable steps to find out the process actually used by the defendant but has not been able to do so; then, in the absence of proof to the contrary the onus of which is on the defendant, the defendant's product is to be taken to have been obtained by the patented process.

[Knowledge and remedies, counterclaims and unjustified threats] Knowledge of a patent is not relevant to liability: a person may genuinely believe they were the first to arrive at some invention and are entirely within their rights to exploit it, but still be liable for infringement. Even though the patent Register is a public document readily available to be consulted by any commercial actor, there is a risk that the law operates unfairly against an 'innocent' defendant. It may thus be inappropriate to award damages in such cases, and by virtue of section 123 (1):

> a court may refuse to award damages, or to make an order for an account of profits, in respect of an infringement of a patent if the defendant satisfies the court that, at the date of the infringement, the defendant was not aware, and had no reason to believe, that a patent for the invention existed.

However, by virtue of section 123 (2):

if patented products, marked so as to indicate that they are patented in Australia, were sold or used in the patent area to a substantial extent before the date of the infringement, the defendant is to be taken to have been aware of the existence of the patent unless the contrary is established.

Naturally, an injunction will in all instances still lie. The natural reaction of a defendant in a patent infringement suit, is to counterclaim for revocation of the patent – as we saw above, it is not uncommon for patent litigation to result in the exposure of the weaknesses inherent in the plaintiff's patent. But before proceedings are even formally initiated, a 'defendant' can also attempt to forestall a patentee's attack by bringing an action for unjustified threats, if the cause being made out by a patentee seems particularly unmeritorious: see section 128ff. If successful, this will enable the plaintiff to recover damages that might have resulted from some patentee airing threats to litigate; such threats can indeed have a very adverse impact on any innovative firm's operations. To some extent these provisions mitigate the potential chilling effect of unmeritorious patent actions.

[Remedies abroad] Although the Patent Cooperation Treaty, WTO/TRIPS and other international instruments have simplified foreign applications and partially harmonised the law, patents remain national awards. That means both patent applications and remedies for infringement must be pursued through foreign domestic patent offices and courts. In this context, the considerable remaining differences between domestic patent laws can be very significant, both in terms of patentability (eg human treatment methods are excluded in Europe) and in terms of the relief sought. In devising a global patent strategy, regard must be had to these differences, as well as to the varying costs and benefits of patenting in different countries.

4

Copyright and designs

Introduction

Policy context

[Form and function] Intellectual property law makes a significant if imperfect distinction between monopolisation of *form* and of *function*. Patents law bestows rights related to the functionality of inventions; by contrast, copyright and designs legislation grants exclusive rights in form or visual appearance only. Copyright and design rights, with their narrower scope, are therefore relevant only if a firm sees commercial value in the specific appearance of its product. As an illustration, take an original technical drawing (a copyrightable 'artistic work') of an automotive spare part incorporating improved functionality compared to the prior art. Such a drawing may serve the purpose of describing the invention as claimed in a patent application. If a patent is granted, others will not be able to make a product with the same improved functionality even if it looks different. Contrast that with copyright or design rights in the same drawings: they prevent competitors from copying the drawing as such, or from making a three-dimensional (3D) article reproducing the drawing, but not from making a product that looks different but incorporates the same improved functionality. Nonetheless copyright or designs registration may go some way to monopolising function, if the shape or appearance of the product is integral to its functionality – in other words, if an article must have the same form to achieve the same functionality.

[An exception to the form and function distinction?] Copyright's principal purpose is to provide some legal protection for authors against the copying of artistic or written expressions conveying information and/or enjoyment. Copyright attaches to communicative works rather than to functional products, and is thus not well adapted to legal appropriation of product functionality. However, copyright's wide remit includes computer programs (classified as literary works), which *are* functional tools. It is true that computer programs, certainly in source code, afford information, although only information about the program itself (underlying structure, concepts, etc), which is quite different from other forms of copyright (the information derived from a book is not just about how the book was written). But nonetheless software fits uneasily into copyright, since it is essentially produced for the functional purpose of controlling the operation of a computer.

Two things flow from this: first, copyright is not adapted to the monopolisation of novel *functionality* of computer programs; and secondly, the wider principles of copyright law are sometimes difficult to apply to computer programs. These issues are further considered below in Chapter five; because computer program copyright has both peculiar features and unique statutory provisions within the *Copyright Act*, it is somewhat removed from the common realm of copyright protection. It also makes sense to consider copyright for programs in conjunction with the alternative and increasingly common form of protection, software patents.

[Product appearance and innovation] Innovation in product appearance *per se*, ie irrespective of any resulting functional advantages, is often a significant component of a firm's competitive strategies. Firms invest in product design innovation because they expect (and can influence) consumers to prefer new-look designs over existing ones, and to pay a premium for them, whether or not they also work better. However, the free-rider problem acts as a particular disincentive for investment in product design innovation. New product appearance, most significant for consumer goods, can only be protected by secrecy in the development stage. Product innovation usually consists of incremental changes within predetermined parameters, so competitors face very low barriers to reverse engineering and copying. Because imitation will be quick, cheap and usually effective, and secret exploitation is not an option, there is a *stronger* case for some form of legal intervention than in relation to inventions. But from the public policy perspective there is arguably a *weaker* case; whereas patent protection will provide a shield for investment in inventions that at least in some cases are genuinely useful to mankind, it is difficult to contend the same in relation to new product appearance as such. However, form and function are not always readily separated – in other words, innovation in appearance will often present functional advantages, and vice versa. The search for new appearance and for improved functionality tend to coincide; in fact, that is arguably what 'designing' is all about. Also, increased aesthetic enjoyment enhances public welfare, and improved appearance more efficiently communicates information about the product itself. Conversely, imitation of consumer goods' appearance is potentially misleading to consumers, since appearance and commercial origin are often intimately linked in their minds. Finally, exclusive protection for new appearance is an historical fact, and forms the bedrock now supporting a number of established industries.

[Not just consumer goods] All this amounts to an arguable case in favour of exclusive rights of some kind in the new appearance of consumer goods that enhances their attractiveness to consumers. The difficulty with this approach lies in the judgment that it requires – whether the appearance is new can be readily established; but whether it enhances consumer attractiveness is more difficult to determine. In the absence of information concerning the comparative success of a new design in the marketplace, the question whether a new design is more attractive to consumers inevitably requires some subjective judgment by the decision-maker. Subjective judgment tends to distort decision-making, and the resulting idiosyncrasy and unpredictability reduce legal certainty which tends to dissuade investment. It can be avoided by simply granting some form of protection for *any* new appearance, whether it is an aesthetic enhancement, attractive or not. This properly addresses the first point made above (that appearance and function are often inextricably linked) and, arguably, if the system is adequately calibrated, does little harm since competitors will still be free to adopt underlying functionality, except in the relatively uncommon case where function and appearance are so closely linked that exclusive rights over appearance have an overflow effect into functionality. This is the approach taken in Australian designs law, where the appearance of a product can be registered if new, whether it delivers enhanced consumer attraction or not; in other words, even new product appearance entirely determined by function can be protected by law as a registered design.

[Copyright and designs] If some form of legal protection for the look or appearance of products is appropriate, then copyright would seem to fit the bill. However, instead the designs registration regime lies at the heart of protection for product innovation in Australia, because the policy of the law is to constrain reliance on copyright and compel innovators to apply for registration of new designs, as is further examined below. This is a longstanding policy which has not been significantly disturbed in the recent overhaul of designs law (the introduction of the *Designs Act 2003* (Cth), replacing the *Designs Act 1906* (Cth)). Therefore the designs registration system has overwhelming importance in the area of product innovation, certainly where the innovation of appearance lies in shape and not merely in decoration: in other words, is three-dimensional rather than two-dimensional (as further explained below, see the Copyright–designs overlap section). It is certainly the case that product design is different from most other subject matter protected by copyright: it is concerned with the appearance of functional items, within the context of industrial production and distribution, rather than with entertainment and the arts; and also, it concerns design choices rather than creative choices – in other words, innovation in design almost always occurs within defined functional parameters inherent in the product. The policy reasons underlying the restrictions on access to copyright remedies in relation to industrial designs are further discussed below (see the Copyright–designs overlap section).

[The structure of exclusive rights: copyright vs designs] Copyright subsists automatically, without any registration requirement; it subsists in original (ie non-copied) subject matter rather than new (ie never published) subject matter; it is of relatively long duration; it extends only to copying, so is not a true monopoly system; and 'copying' covers both direct facsimile derivation but also some degree of non-literal and transformative reproduction. Are these traits well adapted to legal protection of product innovation in industry? Where only anti-copying protection exists, so in the absence of monopolies, investment in design innovation and in the production and commercialisation of articles with new designs is subject to the risk of independent development by rivals, although reverse engineering can be restrained. From the point of view of the innovator, monopolistic protection provides a more secure commercial and industrial environment. As to the threshold conditions for subsistence, copyright requires originality, ie that the work is not in substance copied. If design development is mostly about *derivation with modification*, and about incremental advance rather than original departures, then copyright may present problems in terms of subsistence. Further, because copyright subsists without registration, it is not easy to assess the risk of infringing upon another party's rights when producing and marketing a new product. However, the risk of unintended infringement is mitigated by the requirement of actual copying: the need for notification by way of a public register, to protect against the risk of unintended infringement is inherent only in a monopoly system. Despite these arguments, the case against reliance on copyright is not overwhelming and in some industries with rapid product innovation cycles the informality of copyright presents distinct advantages, eg in clothing design. Hence the fact that in other jurisdictions coexistence, cumulation or alternative protection by copyright for industrial designs is tolerated (see eg the unregistered design right in the EU), and the fact that the general prohibition on copyright protection for industrially produced articles is not universally applied in Australia (see further below).

[Relationship with other areas of law] Although central to the approach to legal protection of product design innovations, the Copyright–designs overlap is not the only significant relationship. The interaction, first, with patent monopolisation of new functionality and, secondly, with protection of reputation by trade marks also deserves consideration. The first relationship is close because protection of form and of function cannot always be strictly segregated. The design registration regime in Australia does attempt such segregation: it does not exclude new designs whose appearance is determined by function from registration, and there is also no prohibition in theory on dual protection for designs and inventions.[1] However, this does not mean that the method of making or using a new design or its functionality can be monopolised by design registration. Although some incidental appropriation of functionality may be the inescapable consequence of the registration of a design whose shape is determined by function, if a new design presents significant new functional advantages, a patent is always

---

[1] See for instance *Fisher & Paykel Healthcare Pty Ltd v Avion Engineering Pty Ltd* 103 ALR 239; 22 IPR 1 (1992) AIPC 90-850, where the new construction of a wheelchair was the subject of a registered design and a petty patent.

more advantageous. It is broader in scope and longer in term – unless only an innovation patent is considered, which may be appropriate for the kind of modification of existing articles which may also qualify for designs protection. At the other end of the spectrum lies trade mark protection: if in the mind of consumers the appearance of a product evokes its commercial origins, such protection may also be appropriate. Normally trade mark protection will be secondary to designs protection, however, since new designs may not be distinctive enough to be registrable as trade marks – such distinctiveness may however develop with actual sales in the marketplace, when consumers come to see the shape of the article as a badge of origin. This issue is further considered in Chapter five.

[Patent and design innovation standards] The relationship between designs and patents in Australia deserves further attention, particularly since in this country purely functional products *can* be registered as designs if their appearance is new. However, designs registration has sometimes disappointed litigants who expected that registration of purely functional designs would deliver control over underlying functionality. For a product design innovation with functional advantages, a patent may be preferable, because a monopoly over function is potentially broader than a monopoly over singular appearance. However, the threshold tests for patenting are more demanding, as well as being directed at different considerations (function rather than appearance). The two systems are not simple alternatives. A design application sets a novelty standard only (a new and distinctive appearance, concepts further explored below); a patent application requires both novelty *and* a functional advantage that is *non-obvious to a person skilled in the art*. Even in the case of an innovation patent, the innovation standard, as well as being directed to function rather than appearance, may be higher (a 'substantial contribution to the working of the invention') than in relation to a designs registration (a '(new and) distinctive' design). Where singular appearance and function are intimately linked, a design registration may inevitably go some way towards monopolising function; where that is not the case – and it should be remembered that designs registration is narrow in scope – an innovation patent may offer a useful alternative, even accepting existing doubts whether the innovative step standard *is* actually as low as was intended by the legislator (see above, Chapter three).

[The segregation of function, appearance and reputation] That the segregation of appearance, function and reputation in intellectual property law is to some degree both artificial and difficult to maintain is illustrated by reported cases. Litigation concerning product imitation is often based on multiple or closely interlinked actions. Cases concerning very functional registered designs struggle with the appropriate relationship and choice between designs registration and patents.[2] *Koninklijke Philips Electronics NV v Remington Products Australia Pty Ltd* [2000] FCA 876 (30 June 2000), a case concerning triple-headed rotary

---

[2] See for instance *Firmagroup Australia Pty Ltd v Byrne & Davidson Doors (Vic) Pty Ltd* (1987) 180 CLR 483; or *Fisher & Paykel* (above).

shavers, illustrates the intimacy of the relationship between design registration of appearance and protection of reputation, whether through passing off, or by way of trade mark registration of the shape of the product (as is discussed further in Chapter five). It also illustrates the inherent limitation on cumulation of various protection regimes, due to their divergent functions and principles. For instance, adopting a striking and visually attractive new design to enhance the appearance of a product may preclude attempting to monopolise the resulting shape as a registered trade mark: in consumers' eyes, the shape does not act as a badge of origin, but as an aesthetic enhancement.

The legal regimes covered in this chapter

[Copyright] Copyright operates to provide exclusive rights in relation to the appearance of manufactured products in two basic ways. First, original drawings are protected by copyright as artistic works. 'Originality' requires no artistic merit or creativity, only that the works are not copied and thus originate with the alleged author. Drawings produced during every stage of the conception and production process of a new product will attract copyright, including: initial artistic impressions and concept drawings; engineering drawings; drawings related to various stages of the production processes, such as ones depicting moulds, etc. Since these are usually produced by employees, copyright normally vests in firms. No formalities such as registration exist, and copyright subsists automatically when the work is made. Copyright does not only comprehend the right to copy drawings as drawings (so-called 'plan to plan' copying), but also to reproduce the depicted items in three-dimensional form (and vice versa; see section 21 (3) of the *Copyright Act*). Secondly, certain three-dimensional works, in particular 'sculptures' and 'engravings', are also protected as artistic works. These categories of statutory subject matter have been liberally interpreted, so that objects forming an integral part of the production process, such as moulds, plugs and patterns have all been included as artistic works. The actual product manufactured then constitutes a reproduction of the underlying mould, plug or pattern and therefore the manufacture of such items falls within the exclusive rights of the copyright owner. Thus if it were not for the designs–copyright overlap provisions, manufacturers could usually rely on copyright to prevent free-riding. However, the *Copyright Act* only grants anti-copying rights, so actual access as well as substantial similarity must be established; independent developers or designers who do not derive their designs from the copyright works are not at risk.

[Designs] Designs registration, on the other hand, *does* result in the registered owner obtaining monopoly rights. In other words, a registered design owner is protected against competition from an independently developed but similar or identical design, as well as from free-riders. However, the design must be novel, not merely original in the copyright sense; ie not just independently developed (not copied), but also not the same or virtually identical to any published design predating the application. The scope of protection of a registered design is relatively narrow, reflecting the fact that designs innovation tends to be incremental and constrained. A registered design is only infringed if an impugned design is very similar in overall appearance, and the monopoly resides in the particular appearance of a design as represented in the application, not in some underlying concept, general idea or special feature, however revolutionary in form or function it may be. The maximum term of protection of a registered design is 10 years from filing under the 2003 Act; the copyright term of artistic works is determined by the lifespan of the author, plus 70 years. The purpose of the Register of Designs, as maintained by the Registrar, is to enable easy searching of pre-existing design registrations, whether it be for the purpose of checking the novelty of another design, avoiding infringement or ascertaining ownership.

[Overlap issues] The legislative policy of limiting cumulation of copyright and designs protection, and prohibiting access to copyright remedies for industrial reproduction of manufactured goods, is effected by section 74ff of the *Copyright Act*. These sections establish a defence to a copyright infringement action: if a product design is the subject of a designs registration, or the product concerned has been industrially manufactured, reliance on infringement of the reproduction right in an artistic work, whether two- or three-dimensional, is foreclosed. If the design is indeed registered, then the registered owner can of course bring an action for infringement under the *Designs Act 2003* (Cth); if it is not registered, the injured party may be left without a remedy. The overlap provisions, however, do not operate in relation to buildings or works of artistic craftsmanship, nor do they operate fully where the reproduction complained of consists only of the application of a two-dimensional artistic work to the surface of a product (or 'article'; so 2D to 2D rather than to 3D). Further details are provided below; the provisions are quite significant, and the various exceptions and complicated permutations give rise to litigation in which the boundaries of copyright categories are often pushed, because one party is seeking to avoid the radical effect of the defence of section 74ff of the *Copyright Act*.

1 Copyright

Introduction

[Copyright in computer programs elsewhere] This book considers two topics in the law of copyright: first, protection against imitation of original product appearance derived from artistic work copyright; and secondly, the protection of computer programs as literary copyright works. However, the latter topic will not be dealt with here but in Chapter five. This may appear unusual, as there is no *sui generis* statute dealing only with computer programs; rather they are either treated as literary works or as patentable inventions. However, as explained above, the classification of computer programs as literary works is somewhat anomalous. Although they may, in source code, afford information to programmers, this cannot be said to be their essential purpose; rather, as the statutory definition reveals, they are to be 'used directly or indirectly in a computer in order to bring about a certain result' (see section 10 *Copyright Act 1968* (Cth)). So in that sense they stand quite apart from other copyright subject matter; that they provide some information or meaning to computer programmers is purely incidental. The 'fit' of computer programs into copyright is, as a consequence, fundamentally uneasy: as a result, fundamental copyright principles have been modified or adapted in their application to computer program copyright; and special provisions that deal only with specific issues pertaining to computer programs have been inserted into the Act. All this virtually amounts to the creation of a *sui generis* regime *within copyright* – and it is on that basis that the issue is dealt with in Chapter five. This also allows a comparison to be made with patenting of computer programs.

[Copyright issues considered here] The general topic considered here is the extent to which copyright protection for two- and three-dimensional artistic works can operate to inhibit product imitation; ie how copyright might be used to appropriate better returns from investment in the development of innovations in product appearance. In that context, the critical issues addressed in more detail are: first, the interpretation of the statutory terminology relating to the relevant categories of artistic works; secondly, the nature of the test for infringement of artistic works; and thirdly, the relationship between copyright and designs protection, in particular the overlap provisions (section 74ff of the *Copyright Act 1968* (Cth)). The presence of copyright in the technical, functional and industrial areas of product development and manufacturing is controversial; the narrower scope and shorter term of protection afforded by designs registration may be more appropriate for industrial rather than artistic pursuits, given the derivative and incremental nature of advances in industrial design. A published Register as exists for designs may also be advantageous because it provides some measure of certainty about the existence, extent and ownership of competitors' rights, which may be difficult to ascertain in relation to unregistered copyright works. The statutory provisions regulating overlap between copyright and designs are dealt with below in section 3.

Subsistence of copyright

[Artistic works in which copyright subsists] The *Copyright Act* exhaustively defines the term 'artistic' work by including in that category a number of more specific sub-categories of artistic expression (see section 10 of the Act). 'Artistic' in this context refers to the artistic techniques or processes employed to create such works, rather than to artistic merit, except where 'works of artistic craftsmanship' are concerned. Artistic works thus basically fall into two categories: artistic works requiring no artistic quality; and works of artistic craftsmanship, which, by virtue of section 10, do require 'artistic quality'. For present purposes the relevant works, *other* than works of artistic craftsmanship, are drawings, engravings and sculptures. Works of artistic craftsmanship are considered below: the real significance of this categorisation follows well-nigh exclusively from its role as an exception to the operation of the designs–copyright overlap provisions. In other words, in the absence of those provisions little would be gained by seeking to rely on artistic craftsmanship copyright. Many artistic products that could be classed as works of artistic craftsmanship may also constitute other artistic works, such as sculptures or engravings, or may be based on underlying two-dimensional drawings, copyright in which would be more readily obtained (no artistic quality or craft skill being required) and equally effective to prevent imitation. Buildings and models of buildings are also treated as artistic works, but this is of little consequence when it comes to manufactured product innovation (impermanent structures are not considered buildings under the Act).

[Two-dimensional artistic works] If drawings are in existence, the copyright owner will be able to rely on them to further a claim in copyright infringement against a free-riding manufacturer or vendor. If a drawing is reproduced without authority, either as a drawing or, by virtue of section 21, as a three-dimensional version of what the drawing depicts, the copyright owner will be entitled to a remedy. Naturally, the claimant will have to establish both substantial reproduction *and* access to the drawing, because copyright is only an anti-copying right and not a monopoly right. But courts have accepted that such access can be indirect, ie via the intermedium of a three-dimensional version of the drawings. In other words, sufficient access to drawings may be established by proving that the imitator saw and copied the manufactured article based on those drawings. If there is a very close resemblance between the two articles concerned, or directly between an impugned product and a 2D artistic work, then access can sometimes be inferred without any independent proof of it being necessary. Reliance on copyright is only possible if the two-dimensional artistic work qualifies as a 'drawing' in the sense of the Act. Technical drawings, engineering drawings, artistic and concept drawings will all readily qualify as such. The fact that the subject matter is technical, and provides technical instruction rather than aesthetic satisfaction, does not matter. As mentioned above, artistic quality is not required; if a mode of expression properly characterised as artistic has been used (drawing, drafting, etc) copyright will subsist, as long as the work is original. In this context this requires no more than that the work originates with its author and is not copied. As an example of the kind of prosaic and technical subject matter that amounts to an artistic work, in *SW Hart Co Pty Ltd v Edwards Hot Water Systems* (1985) 159 CLR 466 the works were:

> drawings of parts of the solar energy hot water systems which it manufactures on a large scale. Two of the drawings [. . .] together depict the absorber panels and header pipe connection nuts which go to form one of the important parts of a solar energy hot water system, to which I shall refer as the absorber unit. The third drawing [. . .] depicts another important part of the system, a storage tank.

There was no doubt that these drawings amounted to artistic works under the Act.

[Sculptures] In the absence of drawings on which a claim might be based (eg because they have been lost and their existence cannot be proved; or none were ever produced), reliance might be had on copyright in three-dimensional artistic works, ie sculptures or engravings. It will normally be too far-fetched to classify manufactured items, whether made of plastic, metal, wood or some other material, as either of those, since they have not been made employing a process or technique that can be described as 'artistic', but rather by a process of industrial manufacture. As was held in the New Zealand case of *Wham-O Manufacturing Co v Lincoln Industries Ltd* [1984] 1 NZLR 641, they are 'utilitarian objects' which it was 'inappropriate' to regard as sculptures for the purpose of copyright (at 662).

However, it may be different for various moulds, models, plugs and other three-dimensional objects used in the industrial production process, of which the finished article is then a reproduction. For instance, in *Wham-O* (above) the question was whether a wooden model of a Frisbee amounted to a *sculpture*, under the terms of the relevantly similar New Zealand copyright legislation. Working drawings were given to a model-maker who produced the wooden model – this *was* held to be a sculpture, having regard to ordinary understanding of the term, the fact that no artistic quality was required and that it had expressive form which conveyed the idea of the author. The work had to be original to attract copyright – that does not require it or the underlying concept (eg the concept of a plastic flying disc) to be novel, only that the work, here the sculpture, was created by the independent work and skill of its 'author', and not simply copied from an existing article. The Australian position is discussed below.

[Engravings] Although the wooden model was held to be a sculpture, the finished product (a plastic flying disc) was not, but by an odd quirk of the statutory provisions it did amount to an engraving (the New Zealand provision being in terms relevantly similar to section 10 of the Australian Act, which provides that '"engraving" includes an etching, lithograph, product of photogravure, woodcut, print or similar work, not being a photograph'). The mould or die for the making of the final product was an engraved plate, and thus an 'engraving'. The actions used to make the die, cast or mould were ones that corresponded to the dictionary meaning of the word 'engrave', which included both the making of prints from a plate and the engraving of the plate itself. Since no artistic quality is required it did not matter that the die or mould was only to be used in making an article and not intended to appeal. As to whether the finished product was an engraving, this would depend on it being a print, presumably made from an engraving, as the term 'print' is one of the items included in the category of 'engravings' in the statutory definition. Because each disc was an image created from an engraved plate, it did amount to a print and thus an engraving itself, and hence an artistic work (engravings being different from a situation where an article is made by any other manufacturing process, which would not amount to a mode of artistic production). The mould, die or cast was held to be an 'engraving', since it was a metal item whose surface had indented striations which were reproduced as elevated features on the finished product.

If some item created during the production process is classified as an artistic work in this manner, any article produced by an imitator may then amount to a reproduction (in the copyright sense) of the sculpture or engraving and if unauthorised may be impeached on that basis. The selling or offering to trade such items may also amount to a breach of section 38 ('Infringement by sale and other dealings'), where the person so engaged knows, or at least ought to know 'that the making of the article constituted an infringement of the copyright' (see section 38 (1) (b)).

[The Australian law] In the Australian case of *Greenfield Products Pty Ltd v Rover-Scott Bonnar Ltd* (1990) 95 ALR 275; (1990) 17 IPR 417 Pincus J closely scrutinised the perhaps surprising outcome of the *Wham-O* case (above). The claim was for copyright in certain moulds and in a driving mechanism. The latter was made up of components which themselves were alleged to be artistic works. His Honour said (at [43]):

> It appears to me clear that neither the moulds nor the drive mechanism, nor the parts of the latter, are sculptures in the ordinary sense. It is true, as was pointed out in the course of argument, that some modern sculptures consist of or include parts of machines, but that does not warrant the conclusion that all machines and parts thereof are properly called sculptures, and similar reasoning applies to moulds. I respectfully agree with the conclusion arrived at in the New Zealand Court of Appeal, in *Lincoln Industries Ltd v Wham-O Manufacturing Co* (1984) 3 IPR 115 at 131 that frisbies are not sculptures under the *Copyright Act 1962* (NZ); that conclusion is consistent with mine.

Pincus J doubted the interpretation given of a mould being an engraving, as was accepted in *Wham-O* (at [47]):

> It is true that dictionary definitions of engraving refer to cutting, but it is not all cutting which is engraving; for example, to cut a piece of steel rod into lengths is not to engrave it. Nor, in my opinion, is the process of cutting metal from a block spinning on a lathe a process of engraving the block, in the ordinary sense of the word. The term does not cover shaping a piece of metal or wood on a lathe, but has to do with marking, cutting or working the surface – typically, a flat surface – of an object.

Thus his Honour focussed on whether the method or technique used in producing the object was properly categorised as artistic in nature, with respect to the particular sub-category of artistic works at issue. It should be kept in mind that no originality of idea or underlying concept is required, just skill and labour in the expression of some idea in material form.[3]

[Artistic works in manufacturing] The following cases further illustrate the usual approach to copyright subsistence in 3D works: *L.B. (Plastics) Ltd v Swish Products Ltd* (1979) RPC 551 (drawers); *Interlego AG v Croner Trading Pty Ltd* (1992) 111 ALR 597 (1992) 25 IPR 65 (plastic building blocks); *Swarbrick v Burge* [2003] FCA 1176 (plug and mould for yacht); *Darwin Fibreglass Pty Ltd v Kruhse Enterprises Pty Ltd* [1998] NTSC 44 (fibreglass pool). The generally

---

[3] See *L.B. (Plastics) Ltd v Swish Products Ltd* (1979) RPC 551, at p 567 per Whitford J.

permissive approach taken by the courts means that as long as a creator has employed a method or technique characteristic of some statutory sub-category of artistic work (eg sculpture, engraving, etc), and the work is not simply copied (hence is original), a resulting three-dimensional article should attract copyright protection. This flexible approach, and the fact that underlying original drawings of any kind are copyright protected, gives rise to significant demarcation issues between copyright and designs protection. The most fundamental choice is whether to restrict access to copyright remedies where works are reproduced by way of an industrial manufacturing process. This can be achieved by excluding certain works from copyright protection, or by in certain circumstances limiting the exclusive rights that copyright owners normally enjoy. That in turn can be done by restricting the exercise of the reproduction and adaptation rights, or by providing a specific defence to infringement of such rights by way of reproduction in the course of manufacturing. The latter option forms the backbone of the Australian approach, as is further examined below (see Copyright–designs overlap). The reasons underlying this approach are there further considered, but one influential factor is the scope of protection afforded by copyright: a broad scope of protection may not be suitable to a manufacturing environment if industrial designs variation over time is incremental and within constrained functional parameters. The following investigation of copyright infringement in relation to three-dimensional reproductions is relevant from that perspective. It is also relevant to those cases where copyright does continue to apply without limitation due to the peculiar operation of the overlap provisions.

Infringement of copyright: reproduction of works

[Copyright infringement] By virtue of the *Copyright Act*, section 21 (3) a three-dimensional version of a two-dimensional work is deemed to be a reproduction, and vice versa. Thus if an article is derived from a drawing to the point that it constitutes a three-dimensional 'version' of it, in the absence of authorisation it infringes copyright. Alternatively, a three-dimensional article derived from a three-dimensional copyright work such as a sculpture (see above) may also amount to a reproduction, as will a two-dimensional version of a 3D artistic work, for instance, a drawing or a photograph of a sculpture (note that an exception applies to sculptures and buildings in public places: see section 65). If the three-dimensional article from which an allegedly infringing reproduction is derived cannot itself be classed as an artistic work (see eg the clutch assembly which was found not to be a sculpture in *Greenfield*, above), the impugned article might still amount to a reproduction of an underlying two-dimensional copyrightable work (eg technical drawings used in the manufacture of the clutch assembly). This is because the courts accept the concept of indirect copying, ie that a work – here the underlying plans or drawings – can be reproduced even where the copyist has not viewed that work itself, but only some version, copy or representation of it (here a 3D article manufactured on the basis of the underlying plans or drawings).

By these methods copyright enters the arena of product manufacturing and designs.

[Plix Products v Frank M Winstone] *Plix Products Ltd v Frank M Winstone (Merchants) Ltd* (1983–1985) 3 IPR 390, a New Zealand case, is a famous example of copyright in operation in the manufacturing sphere. The defendants had set out to produce a range of pocket packs for kiwifruit on the basis of the New Zealand Kiwifruit Exporters Association Inc's *Packing Specifications for Export Kiwifruit*. These specifications were in their turn based on the export packaging developed by the plaintiffs Plix. The defendants only had access to the packaging instructions, the Association's specifications, and the weighing and measuring of kiwifruit, as pointed out by Pritchard J at first instance (*Plix Products* at 400). Many of the parameters involved in packaging kiwifruit were in fact commonplace even before Plix arrived at its set of pocket packs. The main originality of the Plix range lay in the chosen numbers of kiwifruit pockets per pack, each of which would in total accommodate the same approximate weight of fruit. Plix devised, with some effort, a range of packs with 25, 27, 30, 33, 36, 39, 42 and 46 pockets of different sizes. The 'count' was included in the *Packaging Specifications* mentioned above, and it was to these specifications that the defendants' designer worked. Pritchard J concluded that the resulting pocket pack of the defendants infringed copyright in the underlying drawings, etc of Plix, sight unseen. The defendants had reproduced original parts of the Plix packs, in particular the counts. They had not had to work out these counts for themselves, nor obtained a licence from Plix. Upon the appeal, the Court stressed that rejecting the possibility that copyright can be infringed by way of a verbal description, indirectly, would be an illegal copyist's or infringer's charter: see *Frank Winstone (Merchants) Ltd v Plix Products Ltd* (1983–1985) 5 IPR 156 at 160. The Court said (at 161): 'If words alone enable a drawing to be reproduced, it seems to us that copyright in the drawing is infringed'.

[Copyright, function and independent sources] But *Plix* draws attention to a critical distinction drawn in copyright law between form and function: copyright does not extend to the function, concept or idea embodied in a certain artistic work, but only to a particular form of expression. To prove infringement, *actual* copying of expression must be established. This requires either such similarity as will enable an inference of access to be drawn, or, in a more marginal case, direct evidence of access (eg that the designer of the impugned article saw the source work, maybe during previous employment). Where similarity is relied upon to support an inference of copying, one should be alive to the possibility that it may result *not* from copying, but from external constraining factors common to a certain branch of industry, technology or product development. An industrially manufactured article may be designed to a certain shape because that form is required for it to perform a desired function – rather than because of copying (as was raised by the defendant in *Edwards Hot Water* (above, at AUSTLII [7])) or communality of source (such as the need to comply with regulations as in *Plix*, above).

In the *Swish* case (see above) the defendant's drawers were alleged to infringe copyright works, being drawings of the plaintiff's drawers. Buckley LJ in the

Court of Appeal made the point that there is a fine line to be drawn, because similarities between industrial designs could be the result of many causes, being (at RPC 607):

> (1) the need for interchangeability; (2) the adoption by the defendants of the concept of the plaintiffs' device without actual copying, (3) coincidental similarity between a feature of [certain drawings of plaintiff and defendant], (4) actual copying from [the plaintiff's drawer].

Buckley LJ further analysed how Whitford J (the trial judge) came to his conclusions, but ultimately disagreed with them (at RPC 608):

> [. . .] we differ from him [. . .] in attributing such similarities as there are to copying rather than adopting the concept, distinguished from the detail, of the plaintiffs' design. In our judgment, the plaintiffs have failed to discharge the onus of establishing that the defendants have copied the Sheerglide drawer, and so indirectly [the relevant drawing], to any substantial extent.

Buckley LJ spoke for the court. The appeal to the House of Lords was unanimously allowed, three of the Lords giving substantial reasons with which the others agreed. Their Lordships' approach is instructive. Lord Wilberforce held that the onus on the defendant, given the *prima facie* similarity between the two works, to show that these similarities occurred by other means or processes than copying, had not been discharged. This the trial judge had found based on the evidence before him, and that judgment should have been respected. In other words, the defendants had the opportunity by their evidence to dispel the inference of copying drawn from the similarities, by showing how the similarities came about other than by copying, but the trial judge had rightly concluded that their evidence failed to do this. The trial judge had not drawn the wrong inference, but correctly assessed the evidence. Lord Hailsham substantially adopted similar reasoning, although he more harshly criticised the weight the Court of Appeal had placed on the constraining factor of interchangeability, which he rather saw as an incitement to copy. Lord Salmon delivered a less substantial judgment. Thus the *prima facie* close resemblance between the articles caused a shifting of the onus of proof, the defendant having the option of showing that the similarities were due to causes other than copying. A note of caution, however: since industrially manufactured items are at issue here, artistic expression is more constrained than in the fine arts, and therefore arguably greater similarity is required to infer copying than in fine arts. Copying of expression not adoption of an underlying idea, function or technical concept must be shown.

[Reproductions do not have to look like source works] It is clear from the statutory extension of the term 'reproduction' to include reproduction in different dimensions, that there need not always be direct resemblance between a source work and the alleged reproduction. A house does not look like a house plan, nor does an article look like a technical drawing or a die or mould used in manufacturing it – but it could still be an infringing copy. It may be that it is only apparent to a person with knowledge and experience of such matters that a certain article is based on certain drawings. In the past the so-called non-expert defence could be invoked in such cases, in the sense that if it was not apparent to a non-expert that a certain article was a version of a two-dimensional work, no reproduction could be found. But this defence has been removed from the Act, so an article can amount to a reproduction as a three-dimensional version of an artistic work even though an uninformed person would not recognise it as such. It may be that the writing on a technical drawing assists the process of recognition, and it is legitimate to have recourse to such markings or writings (eg measurements) for that purpose. However, what is said above must be taken in the context of the requirement that an allegedly infringing article must be a substantial reproduction of a source work.

[General principles concerning infringement] The most common cases considering reproduction of artistic works in three dimensions are architectural copyright matters. Architectural copyright falls outside the scope of product innovation and manufacturing that this book considers; but principles can usefully be extracted from such cases and applied in this context. Other useful cases, such as *Plix*, *Swish* and the other cases mentioned above, *do* specifically address reproductions of works generated in the context of industrial design development and manufacturing. Although such cases frequently revolve around the statutory delineation between designs and copyright law, they still provide some relevant general guidelines (as well as the points already mentioned above). I say 'guidelines' rather than 'rules' because the courts avoid tying themselves down to formulaic approaches or rigid rules, insisting that the question of reproduction is 'a question of fact and degree depending on the circumstances of each case'.[4]

As a matter of general copyright principle though, the question of reproduction in the absence of simple facsimile copying is approached on the basis of assessing what is often, but somewhat misleadingly referred to as 'substantial similarity' (see section 14 of the *Copyright Act*). This assessment actually tends to develop along two distinct paths: first, indeed as an assessment of overall 'substantial similarity', where there are slight differences on certain points which call for a fine judgment; and secondly, an assessment of the importance of some specific part of the source work which is allegedly also found in the impugned work. Thus the court in *Compagnie Industrielle de Precontrainte et D'Equipment des Constructions SA v First Melbourne Securities Pty Ltd* [1999] FCA 660 (20 May 1999) ('*CIPEC*') quoted with apparent approval a passage appearing in Lindgren J's judgment in *Eagle Homes Pty Ltd v Austec Homes Pty Ltd* (1999) 161 ALR 503, which he himself adopted from *Copinger and Skone James on Copyright*.[5] That book indeed makes the distinction between the approach in cases where a discrete part is taken and in cases where the whole is taken but dissimilarities are present. In the latter case the key question is there said to be whether a 'colourable imitation' results, and the court in *CIPEC* agreed with Lindgren J's approach that where deliberate

---

[4] Wilson J in *Edwards*, above, at AUSTLII [7].
[5] (13th edn 1991), Sweet & Maxwell, UK.

copying is established an imitation will more readily be found to be colourable than where there is no clear proof of deliberate copying. *Very* close similarity will be required not only to prove that a substantial part is taken, but also to justify an inference of copying, in the kind of case where it is not impossible that similarities will arise by coincidence, due to the nature of the subject matter – in *CIPEC*, expansion joints for bridges, in *Eagle Homes*, project homes, and in the context of this chapter, manufactured articles in general.

[A substantial part taken?] As to the second path mentioned in the previous paragraph, the relevant question is whether the part copied (which of course implies actual access) is a substantial part of the source work or not – this goes to the heart of section 14, which is less relevant to the first path mentioned above. The well-established principle is that what counts is the quality of the part taken and not the relative quantity. To determine quality then two questions must be answered: one is whether the part taken is an original part of the source work. 'Originality' is not used here in the sense of the low threshold for subsistence of copyright, but rather in the sense of a qualitatively significant authorial contribution. The core question is whether the impugned party in copying a certain part of a source work has taken illegitimate advantage of the real judgment, skill and ability of that work's author. Have they filched exactly that which copyright is meant to protect? The other question is whether the part is a significant part of the source work. And, as was pointed out in *Coogi Australia Pty Ltd v Hysport International Pty Ltd & Ors* [1998] FCA 1059: '[. . .] the answer depends on whether the part taken is a visually important part of the original work, ie, on the significance the part taken plays in creating the work's distinctive appearance'. Or to use the broader terms used by Mason CJ in *Autodesk Inc v Dyason* [No 2] (1993) 176 CLR 300 at [10], it depends on 'the importance which the taken portion bears in relation to the work as a whole . . .'. The part is thus not to be judged in isolation but in the context of the totality of the work. As pointed out by Wilcox & Lindgren JJ in *Tamawood Limited v Henley Arch Pty Ltd* [2004] FCAFC 78 at [39], this means that:

> [T]he notion of 'substantial part' may be found most useful and illuminating where particular, quantitatively small parts of the work in suit are taken: cf *Hawkes* (20 bars of the military march 'Colonel Bogey'); *Kipling v Genatosan Ltd* [1917–1923] MacG CC 203 (four lines from a poem of 32 lines); *G Ricordi & Co (London) Ltd v Clayton & Waller Ltd* [1928–1935] MacG CC 154 ('*Ricordi*') at 162 (eight bars of a particular motif in a well known opera).

It may be possible to conflate the two questions into two aspects of a single test, as is illustrated by Mason CJ's words in *Autodesk*: having indicated that one should ask whether a part was an 'essential or material' part of the work (at 305), he went on to say that: 'the essential or material features of a [copyright] work should be ascertained by considering the originality of the part allegedly taken' (at 308). But on the other hand, in *Edwards Hot Water* Wilson J (at [8]) pointed out the following:

[I]f it is said that a substantial part of it has been reproduced, whether that part can properly be described as substantial may depend upon how important that part is to the recognition and appreciation of the 'artistic work'. If an 'artistic work' is designed to convey information, the importance of some part of it may fall to be judged by how far it contributes to conveying that information, but not, in my opinion, by how important the information may be which it conveys or helps to convey. What is protected is the skill and labour devoted to making the 'artistic work' itself, not the skill and labour devoted to developing some idea or invention communicated or depicted by the 'artistic work'.

However, although quality is the key and therefore a quantitatively small part may indeed be considered substantial for copyright purposes, quantity may still be relevant, as also pointed out in *Tamawood*:

> But quantity may be relevant. Where the same degree of labour, skill and judgment contribute uniformly to all parts of the work, so that no part is distinguishable from any other part in this respect, it will apparently be necessary to demonstrate reproduction of a quantitatively substantial proportion of the work in order to establish reproduction of a substantial part: cf *Accounting Systems 2000 (Developments) Pty Ltd v CCH Australia Ltd* (1993) 42 FCR 470 (reproduction of 25 per cent of computer program).[6]

In an industrial context, there may be an argument that some part of a source work is not original because it merely reflects well-known concepts or forms in the industry – if this is indeed a possibility, close resemblance in the detail will be required.

[Substantial similarity overall] As pointed out above, what may be required is an assessment of substantial similarity *overall* rather than of the 'quality' of some isolated part allegedly taken. '[R]eproduction does not require a complete and accurate correspondence to a substantial part of the work';[7] so the test of reproduction in these types of cases requires the identification of similarities and dissimilarities – it is an assessment of 'objective similarity' in that sense. The court makes a direct visual comparison between the impugned article and the artistic work (drawing or sculpture and the like); it is entitled to have regard to any writing on drawings which assists to explain what they represent. Do the similarities substantially outweigh the dissimilarities; or are there differences that are significant? In the manufacturing context it may again be relevant that an article takes a certain form not because it is a reproduction of the plaintiff's artistic work but because it is derived from a publicly available source of information, or because its form is technically required. In *Edwards Hot Water* this point was raised by the respondent (per Gibbs CJ at [7]):

> Next it was submitted on behalf of the respondent that having regard to the dissimilarities, and notwithstanding the similarities, the respondent's products did not constitute a reproduction of the drawings or a substantial part of them. Brinsden J identified sixteen points of similarity. On behalf of the respondent it was submitted that these similarities could be explained by the fact that both parties had relied on sources of information commonly available in earlier products or publications or by the fact that the function to be performed by the absorber units had determined their nature.

---

[6] *Tamawood*, per Wilcox & Lindgren JJ at 50 (see above).
[7] *Edwards Hot Water*, per Wilson J at [7] (see above).

This is a matter that the court will have to assess – as we saw above, if the plaintiff can show that the similarities are substantial and detailed, this may shift onto the defendant the burden of establishing that they do *not* result from copying.

On the other hand, minor differences may not matter as they exist only because of a deliberate and colourable attempt to dissimulate copying. In *Edwards Hot Water* the similarities greatly exceeded the dissimilarities, which were regarded by the court as trivial; evidence was also available consistent with access to the drawings, so inferences of copying did not have to be drawn from the similarities only. By contrast, in *Mainbridge Industries Pty Ltd v Gordon Whitewood* F 456 of 1984 deliberate copying was not clearly shown on the evidence. As a consequence, the test was simply whether there were sufficient similarities between the two machines involved or between the plaintiff's drawings and the defendant's machine. The number and quality of differences were too great to allow for the relevant inferences, favouring the plaintiff, that actual copying had taken place.

[Copyright, function, ideas and the limits of substantiality] The test of infringement which assesses the significance of some part to the whole runs the risk that it may be resolved by reference to functional rather than visual significance; couple this with the *Plix* approach which admits of indirect copying, and the copyright distinction between protection of concept, function or idea and of expression is under threat. It is striking that the effect of the *Plix* decision was that the copyright owner had a virtual monopoly in the supply of pocket packs for the duration of its copyright. In circumstances where most aspects of the packaging were determined by pre-existing factors such as the size of fruit and the standard weight per pack, it may be questioned whether that result was not based on flimsy grounds, and effectively copyright ended up granting an exclusive right in a practical innovation. In *Coogi*,[8] Drummond J stressed the importance of adhering closely to the requirement of close overall similarity to avoid copyright straying into protection of function or novel underlying ideas which are in fact the realm of other regimes, in particular patents:

> Where, however, A copies only what is said to be a substantial part of the original work, since substantiality depends upon the quality rather than the quantity of what is taken, it does not logically follow that objective similarity need necessarily exist between the two works for infringement to be made out. But it is settled that proof of such similarity is essential. Proof of objective similarity provides an important protection against a finding of copyright infringement being made where substantial reproduction only is alleged, when all that a person has taken is the author's idea rather than any significant part of the author's form of expression of the idea, ie, that which alone attracts copyright. The rule has particular relevance where the question is whether there has been infringement of copyright in a work which possesses a degree of real novelty: there is always a risk that an element of the allegedly infringing article may so evoke the novel idea which is the subject of expression in the original work that that will be treated as the taking of a qualitatively important part of the original, even though the two forms of expression are quite different.[9]

---

[8] *Coogi Australia v Hysport International Pty Ltd*, see above.
[9] *Coogi*, at AIPC 37,712.

Thus whether some section of source drawings or plans is a substantial part is not to be determined by its functional or operational significance, or whether that part was inventive in the patent law sense, or unique. This same point was also at issue in *CIPEC* (see above), where the fact that one functionally significant part was substantially the same did not matter because the overall appearance was significantly different (at [33]). *CIPEC* also considered the submission that where the shape of a work is constrained by functional requirements, an exceptionally close resemblance only will result in a finding of infringement. The court agreed with the reservations expressed by Lindgren J in *Eagle Homes Pty Ltd v Austec Homes Pty Ltd* (1999) 161 ALR 503 about that approach, in relation to cases where independent evidence of copying is also available. Part of the relevant passage quoted in *CIPEC*, which appears at [92] in *Eagle Homes*, was as follows:

> I do not accept, however, that where, as here, actual copying is found to have occurred, 'reproduction', and therefore infringement, cannot be proved in the absence of such a specially close similarity as might be required in a particular case to support an inference of subjective copying. To insist that a copyright owner can satisfy the 'sufficient objective similarity' limb of reproduction only by establishing such a close similarity, is a hurdle too high to be placed before a copyright owner who is found to have proved subjective copying.

[Copyright and designs infringement compared] Comparison between copyright and designs infringement is dealt with further below, but a few points deserve mention here. With the introduction of the new *Designs Act 2003* (Cth), the tests of infringement in designs law and in copyright may well have drawn closer – the legislator did after all intend to increase the scope of protection of registered designs. The nature of the two systems is of course fundamentally different – designs registration results in a monopoly, but copyright is a mere anti-copying right. In other words, independent development of some article is no defence to designs infringement whereas it is to copyright infringement, as was mentioned above. However, under the old *Designs Act 1906* (which still applies to many older designs; see below) the scope of protection is broader if the plaintiff *can* establish access, by recourse to the statutory device of 'fraudulent imitation': where a copyist makes changes deliberately to disguise copying, certain differences may be ignored and infringement still found. This concept has not been retained in the present Act (2003) but instead the scope of protection has been further extended in a number of ways.

The new test of infringement is whether an impugned design is 'substantially similar in overall impression', which is intended to result in fewer infringement actions being defeated by excessive judicial attention to enumerated differences in detail. Significantly, now also under the 2003 Act, similarities must be given more weight than differences. Furthermore, by way of a 'Statement of Newness and Distinctiveness' a design applicant can draw attention to a certain part of the overall design, to which particular regard is then due in the overall assessment of similarity in an infringement action. These changes (as well as some others discussed below) extend the scope of the monopoly of the design owner and bring it more into line with the scope of copyright protection: one of the main differences between copyright and the 1906 Act may well lie in the fact that there is no design infringement if the copying of only part of a registered design does not result in overall similarity, whereas if the part copied was 'substantial' there might well be copyright infringement. Those provisions of the 2003 Act which allow more regard to be had to certain parts of a registered design in an infringement action potentially reduce this distinction between the two regimes (see section 19; and as analysed further below in this regard).

2 Registered designs

Introduction and policy context

[The old Act and the present Act] For many years the design registration system established under the 1906 Act remained substantially unaltered, not because of general satisfaction with its operation, but because no consensus could be reached concerning the shape of appropriate reforms. Finally introduced in 2003, the present Act represents a major overhaul of the system, with a higher threshold for registration resulting in a broader scope of protection, but at the expense of a shortened term of validity (from maximum 16 years to maximum 10 years). The reforms were substantially based on the ALRC Report No 74, *Designs*, a very valuable resource in this area of the law. The major reform stumbling block, design registration of spare parts, an issue in which car manufacturers, insurers and generic spare parts suppliers had a paramount stake, was finally overcome with a compromise: whereas spare (or 'component') parts remain registrable, a repair exception was introduced. By this device, the potential impact of design registrations on the downstream market for compatible component parts was reduced. The test for infringement has also substantially changed, with the previous two-tier approach (obvious/fraudulent imitation) being replaced with a single test of 'substantial similarity in overall impression'. But in some significant ways the designs registration system remains unaltered. No short-term unregistered designs protection was introduced, which presents a problem for industries such as fashion with very rapid design turnover, for which a registration system is unattractive. No substantial changes have been made to the rules concerning overlap between designs registration and copyright in artistic works, the latter remaining excluded where a design is registered or an article is industrially manufactured (with some rather complex exceptions continuing to apply, as considered below). Functionally determined product shapes remain registrable, if they are new and distinctive, a continuing point of distinction with other jurisdictions, in particular the EU, where designs law places express limitations on the registration of designs if appearance is determined by function. Although functionally determined designs remain registrable, even if their *appearance* is actually of no significance to potential purchasers of the article concerned, it is still only appearance and not function which is monopolised by registration. In this context it is worth remembering that those who might in the past have turned to the designs registration system for some measure of protection in relation to minor but visible innovations in technical design, now also have the option of applying for an innovation patent (as discussed above in Chapter three), which has somewhat altered the overall protection landscape.

[What constitutes a design?] Some of the apparent confusion in industry concerning the object of registration stems from the varied meaning of the term 'design' in ordinary language. As a noun the term 'design' can be used in an engineering sense as in the design of a refinery, for instance; or in a more artistic sense, as in the design of a Mies van der Rohe chair. Both uses have in common that the term 'design' concerns the configuration of useful or functional articles, and is in that sense distinct from art which is created for its own sake. Furthermore, 'a design' refers to a useful article whose appearance results from applying *a design process*, ie a process of considering various conceptual options constrained by functionality and choosing a final novel shape for a useful article (thus arguably if what results is not novel, or no real design choices are exercised in creating it, there is no 'design'). In the same way that a copyright artistic work is defined by reference to the artistic process of authorial creation, an industrial design is what results from a process of designing, properly so-called.

The process of designing may be influenced in varying degrees by multiple objectives and constraints, whether or not including aesthetic ones – it will always result in a 'design' properly so-called if choice exercised within functional constraints has determined the novel appearance of a useful article. At least, that is the Australian view of industrial designs fit for registration – in other jurisdictions a design can only be registered if it is attractive in some way: design there implies a process resulting in an article whose novel appearance will positively influence consumer choice. Thus where in Australia a part of a slurry pump used in the mining industry can be registered as a design if its appearance is new, in other jurisdictions this may not be possible because *appearance per se* is irrelevant to any purchaser of mining equipment.

[Monopoly over appearance, not function] But irrespective of the objective, whether aesthetic or purely functional, or both, the monopoly resulting from design registration resides *only* in shape, configuration or appearance, not in functionality. Any appropriation of function that flows from exclusive rights in the design is therefore purely incidental. An article with a new design shape that has functional advantages and is not an obvious step forward from the prior art may alternatively attract the grant of a patent. In that case the precise appearance of the design is relevant to the legal right, not *per se* but to the extent that it has an impact on the product's function. But where the new design does not represent a functional advance, or is not inventive, a patent is not available. Naturally, if there were no design registration system, copyright in underlying artistic works (drawings, etc) would automatically apply. But although copyright in artistic works has a relatively broad scope of exclusivity, just as with designs registration this does not amount to an exclusive right over an underlying functional concept or idea, rather than its expression in a specific form. However, again as with designs registration, it may incidentally go some way towards it – quite a bit more than literal or facsimile copying is restrained by copyright, as explained above.

[**Salient features of the design registration scheme**] Two salient facts about industrial design influence the nature of the registration regime: first, since it is concerned with useful articles, designing occurs within strict constraints, with limited rather than infinite options for variation. In the main, design innovation is evolutionary rather than revolutionary, so a new design is commonly, although not always, a derivation or re-working of existing designs. The prior art builds up incrementally over time. Under the old Act, the design process was conceived of as one of adding features to a standard or 'ideal' form of a certain article. The present Act abandons this conceptually challenging approach, recognising that designers mostly innovate by adapting, modifying and combining existing designs, rather than by applying features to a standard form. Secondly, design lies in the realm of industrial production, mass-manufacturing; it is not concerned with the production of one-off or unique items, as the fine arts usually are. In other words, considerable financial and manufacturing investment is at stake in the development of new designs and the production and commercialisation of complex articles embodying them. Such investment is less likely to occur in the private sector in conditions of uncertainty engendered by the risk of independent development as well as copying. A registration system which allows producers to ascertain other persons' rights, and bestows monopoly rights, protecting investment against the risk of independent invention as well as free-riding by competitors, reduces uncertainty and should encourage investment in design innovation.

[**Incremental change and legal rights in designs**] The first point – that change in industrial designs is incremental and constrained – is highlighted by reflection on the difference between artistic liberty and design liberty. Artistic creation is theoretically unconstrained other than by inspiration and by the medium of expression, because artistic works need not serve other than aesthetic purposes. But the designer producing a new chair design, for instance, can only work within the constraints of the configuration of an article that functions as a chair. These constraints will mean that the requirements imposed by the scheme of legal rights in designs, in terms of threshold difference with existing designs (or 'novelty'), and in terms of scope of infringement (what amounts to an actionable copy), must inevitably be relatively narrow. As Lockhart J put it in *Conrol Pty Ltd v Meco McCallum Pty Ltd* (1996) 34 IPR 517, at 527:

> The [1906] Act thus requires that a design must be new or original to qualify for registration. This requirement manifests the parliament's intention to balance or reconcile two competing elements of public policy: first, the encouragement and protection of the intellectual activity which is put into the production of industrial designs; secondly, the concern not to impede or oppress the natural development of industry.

[Why have design protection at all] But why have legal protection for new industrial designs at all? On the one hand, the rationale is akin to that of copyright protection: to enhance general welfare by the diffusion of more pleasing designs. Monopoly rights encourage the development of multiple variations of shapes and decorations of omnipresent articles, so that design innovation is more closely aligned with evolving consumer tastes or aesthetic sensibilities. But new designs also function to signal the underlying or invisible qualities of the goods – visibly good design signals a product of higher quality in all its aspects, aesthetic and functional, visible and invisible. In that sense a cutting-edge design performs a function analogous to search cost reduction by reference to trade marks, a shorthand message informing consumers about untested characteristics of a product. Designs or design styles can also be distinctive, in the sense that they become associated with a certain manufacturer in consumers' minds. Imitation may then result in consumer deception as to the source of a certain article – a cost that may be avoided by appropriate regulatory structures. However, this only applies to new designs that have visual consumer appeal, not to designs whose novel features are determined purely by function. Naturally such purely functional designs can be excluded from legal protection, as is done in some jurisdictions (see above). The policy arguments in favour of granting it are less compelling, and in any case functional protection can be obtained by patent grant.

So why allow design registration as well for purely functional designs? Partly the answer lies in the artificiality of distinguishing strictly between functional and attractive designs, keeping in mind that the essence of design is the production of new functional articles in any case; as well, purely functional articles often become aesthetically striking with the effluxion of time, or in a particular place. It may be that there is in any case little harm in allowing purely functional designs to be registered, given the difficulty and potential cost of policing their exclusion from registration. In any case, the scope of protection of such designs will tend to be very limited so as to avoid straying across the line of demarcation with patents law and avoid monopolisation of function.

[Design and reputation] There is a close and circular relationship between aesthetics and reputation: the more attractive a product the stronger its reputation, and the better reputed it is the more it appears attractive; whether or not something is attractive is a subjective question of taste – beauty is in the eye of the beholder. The power of a good reputation or 'goodwill' differs from the immediate attraction flowing from pleasing appearance. It is an acquired taste resulting from familiarity or, from a different perspective, a secondary meaning, indicating source, which may develop over time around a recognisable and distinct feature of a product. But nonetheless reputation is inherently connected to the aesthetic qualities and inherent distinctiveness of a design: the more distinctive, unusual, striking or different a design is, the more it can become the point of recognition or distinction for a consumer (note that under the present Act, a design must be 'new and distinctive' to be registered). It is thus tempting to rely on legal protection of reputation to indirectly monopolise design shapes that have become recognised and distinctive to consumers. But there are two difficulties with this approach – if the social goal is to encourage investment in the production of new designs adapted to ever-changing consumer tastes, then the law of passing off, which requires proof of *existing* reputation in the market, falls short. Before such reputation has developed the product is vulnerable to free-riders, imitators who by their actions undermine the innovator's opportunity to develop a reputation in the new product design. In other words protection of reputation by way of passing off is not suitable for monopolising *new* design shapes. It is also easy for an imitator to negate any suggestion of a connection by employing a disclaimer of some sort (whether express or by applying the imitator's own mark) but still derive advantage from copying an attractive new design.

The alternative form of protection is trade mark registration, which can be obtained *without* proving an existing reputation. Since the WTO/TRIPS agreement and the new *Trade Marks Act 1995* (Cth) shapes, including *of products themselves*, have in fact become registrable as trade marks in many jurisdictions, including Australia. In theory such registration could thus afford protection for the shape of *new* designs even before they have acquired actual goodwill. The condition for registration as a trade mark, though, is that consumers can and do distinguish a product from another by reference to the distinctive mark; in this context, by reference to the distinctive new shape of a product. And that is perhaps unlikely, since new consumer product designs tend to be appreciated for their own sake, rather than being seen as 'badges of origin'. The issue of trade mark registration for product shapes is further considered below, in Chapter five.

[Registration and delay] A registration-based system offers advantages in terms of prevention of infringement, and avoidance of overlap and conflicting uses. The Register is also a public database of information concerning new developments in design. General issues relating to a registration model have been considered above in the context of patent grant (see Chapter three); as pointed out there, one disadvantage compared to an automatic subsistence model, such as copyright law, is the cost both of establishing the system and of its administrative and testing functions. Delay between application and grant is also a drawback, particularly so for industries with a quick turnover in designs; for example, fashion. For fashion and similar seasonal goods, an unregistered design system may avoid the delays and costs inherent in the frequent and multiple applications otherwise required. In the European scheme unregistered designs enjoy anti-copying protection against imitation for a period of three years, but this model was not adopted in Australia in the *Designs Act 2003*. Given the fact that registration under the present Australian system is not subject to substantive examination, and can thus be obtained with minimal delay, the need may not be as acute. However, costs are still incurred, and there have been recent calls for the introduction of unregistered design protection here. Whether it is required partly depends on the availability of copyright protection in relation to manufactured articles; as is explained below, in the Australian system a copyright claim relying on underlying artistic works, such as patterns and masks used in the manufacture of clothes, is defeated by section 73ff of the *Copyright Act*. As an alternative solution to the problem of rapid turnover of designs in the fashion industry, it has been proposed that a grace period should be introduced.[10]

[Relationship with the innovation patent] As indicated above, modifications in design can enhance functionality in varying ways. In other words functional advantages may result from changes in appearance of an article. It is then possible to either focus on those functional advantages as the object of legal rights or, alternatively, to focus on the appearance while ignoring resulting functional advantages. If choosing the former approach, the availability of a patent depends on the threshold level of functional advancement that the law sets; thus the inventive-step requirement for standard patents may be a stumbling block for minor functional advances resulting from product design. However, with the introduction of the innovation patent, an alternative is now available only requiring a very low level of inventiveness. The innovation patent only requires 'an innovative step', rather than 'inventive step'. By virtue of section 7 of the *Patents Act*, an invention is taken to lack an innovative step if it only varies from the relevant prior art in ways '*that make no substantial contribution to the working of the invention*'.

In other words, if a design change to an existing product makes a substantial functional contribution, then an innovation patent will be available. Although not limited to it, this form of protection is obviously particularly suited to small mechanical product innovations. A person who designs a product they consider new can thus either apply for design registration – with a maximum term of 10 years – relying on the 'new and distinctive' appearance compared to the prior art; or alternatively apply for an innovation patent – with a maximum term of eight years – if the new aspect makes a substantial functional contribution to the working of an existing product (as to more detail concerning innovation patents, and what may amount to a 'substantial' contribution, see Chapter three). Both innovation patent and design registration are 'first to file', with monopoly rights as the prize, and thus protect against both independent invention and imitation, and in that sense offer similar advantages. Under the old *Designs Act*, prior art information for the purpose of novelty was in practice restricted to only Australian publications and use, whereas for patents grant it has always included publications outside Australia as well. The present standard under the *Designs Act 2003* and the *Patents Act 1990* (as amended by the *Patents Amendment Act 2001* (Cth)) includes publications both within and outside Australia in the prior art, as well as public use within Australia. Public use *outside* Australia is included in the prior art for patent novelty purposes, but not for designs. Before the present Act was introduced, there was no threshold test in designs law other than for novelty, although the old Act made it clear that a standard or obvious variation from the prior art would not be considered novel: see section 17 (1) (a) (b) of the 1906

---

[10] See Rothnie W, 'The vexed problem of Copyright/Designs overlap' (2005) *Intellectual Property Forum* 60, 33, at 35.

Act. Under the 2003 Act, as well as being new, a design must be 'distinctive when compared to the prior art base'. A design is distinctive if it is not substantially similar in overall impression, a standard which focusses on the totality of the design. Further issues relating to novelty under the present Act are considered below.

Designs law in Australia: entitlement

Introduction

[Operation of the old and the present Act] The registration of a design does not, of course, guarantee validity. The revocation of a registration can be sought either by way of a counterclaim in infringement proceedings, or by way of an application by a person to a prescribed court. The provisions of the 1906 Act (referred to as 'the old Act' in the 2003 Act) concerning validity of the registration and concerning infringement of a design continue to apply to designs that were registered or applied for under that Act (see sections 151–156, *Designs Act 2003* (Cth)). The term of validity of such registrations is determined by the old Act – in other words, 16 years maximum, as opposed to 10 years for designs registered under the present Act. That means that the familiar requirements for validity and rules concerning infringement under the old Act will continue to be applied in the courts for a considerable time to come. Any consideration of designs law today thus requires attention to the provisions of both the old and the present Acts, so this work proceeds mostly by contrasting the old and the new provisions. References to section numbers below are to the present Act unless otherwise indicated.

[Procedural innovations under the present Act: registration and certification] The present Act adopts the same procedural approach as applies for innovations patents: that is, it distinguishes between 'registration', which will proceed on the basis of a successful formalities check alone, and 'examination' which can occur at any time after registration. The formalities check is exactly that: it enforces conformity with formalities specified in the Regulations. In terms of *substance* the only relevant aspect of this check is that 'the design application identifies the product or products in relation to which the design is sought to be registered sufficiently to enable each product to be classified in accordance with the Locarno Agreement': see Design Regulations 2004, reg 4.04 (1) (c); in other words there must be something in the application sufficiently clear to be identified as a design of some sort. Successful *examination* at the request of any person (usually the registered owner) or at the Registrar's own initiative, will result in the issuing of a Certificate of Examination. Certification must precede enforcement of the registered design (see section 73 (3) (b)). The term of registration is initially five years from the filing of the application in which the design was first disclosed, with a single renewal possible for a further five years, resulting in a maximum of 10 years. If the application for renewal is in the form prescribed by the Regulations, the Registrar must renew the registration (see sections 46–47); there is no option of opposition to renewal. Broadly speaking, a Certificate of Examination can be refused if the application does not contain subject matter falling within the statutory definition of a design (see section 5); is not novel as required by section 15; or on any other ground prescribed by the regulations (see section 65 (2) (b); also excluded are *inter alia* Olympic signs and Circuit Layouts). Prior to certification a person entitled to be entered as an owner of a registered design can apply for revocation on the grounds specified in section 51ff, and any time after the granting of a Certificate of Examination any person can apply to a prescribed court for an order revoking the registration, on the grounds prescribed in section 93 (3). An applicant also has the option of requesting publication of a design disclosed in an application, rather than registration (see section 35): publication will prevent others from obtaining registration of the design.

Requirements for a valid design

[The statutory definition of design] By virtue of section 5 '"design", in relation to a product, means the overall appearance of the product resulting from one or more visual features of the product'. Use of the terms 'appearance' and 'visual features' makes it abundantly clear that the monopoly does not reside in function (ie the functional advantage inherent in a certain design) but appearance, and resides in visual features rather than in the product as such. For instance, design registration of a security lock employing a new mechanism does not give a monopoly in all security locks employing that mechanism, but simply in a product with the appearance of the particular security lock represented in the application. It is the *overall* appearance that constitutes the design, resulting from either two-dimensional or three-dimensional features (see section 7) or a combination of both, not some specific or isolated aspect of the appearance. Nonetheless an applicant can draw attention to a specific feature in a 'Statement of Newness and Distinctiveness', which then may result in that feature being given more weight in the judgment concerning an alleged infringement (see further below, Infringement of a registered design). Under the old Act, methods or principles of construction were expressly excluded from registration, but the exclusion is clearly inherent in the present Act's definition of a design. In any case this quite naturally flows from the fact that a visual representation (a photo or drawing) defines and circumscribes the design in the application, rather than a verbal description.

[Visual features] By virtue of section 7, '"visual feature", in relation to a product, includes the shape, configuration, pattern and ornamentation of the product'. Thus 2D or 3D features or a combination of both can make up a new design; but tactile rather than visual features of a new design cannot be registered: feel and texture are expressly excluded from registration (see section 7). This may frustrate modern designers whose innovation precisely lies in the materials used rather than the appearance of the product – one can readily imagine examples. In the old Act, only 'features judged by the eye' could be registered, terms now replaced by the simpler 'visual features'. This requires that features should be visible in the sense that they can be perceived – that they are apparent to the eye, even if only with some guidance. Overly subtle features that only become apparent by careful measurement or engineering analysis may therefore be excluded. Under the old Act, only features that could be seen by the *unaided* eye could be registered, but this restriction does not apply under the present Act – if a feature can be seen with the aid of instruments that are common to the relevant trade, then it should be registrable.[11] If it is necessary to break open or destroy an article to observe the visual features concerned, then no registration should be possible; however, if a design becomes visible where an item is used for its intended purpose, the design may be valid: see eg *Ferrero's Design Application* (1978) R.P.C. 473, which related to a two-tone chocolate egg whose internal colour only became apparent upon consumption after purchase. Note that the features of a circuit layout of a computer chip are expressly excluded from registration (see section 43 (1) (c)). Visual features that are regularly repeated (ie appear in a regular pattern) in lengths or bolts of indefinite dimensions are registrable – indeed the oldest form of registered design legislation in the United Kingdom was specifically directed at protecting new textile designs.

[Design protection of functional features] Industrial designs are of course always functional to some extent, in the sense that the visual features are those of a product with some functional purpose. The fact that a visual feature fulfils a functional purpose is not an impediment to its registration – as expressly stipulated in section 7 (2). Consequently, whether the feature adds value because of its visual appeal or because of its functional advantage is irrelevant. Nonetheless it has from time to time been doubted whether a design whose visual features are *entirely* determined by function is a design properly so-called. If no choice is exercised and no concept expressed in determining the shape or configuration of a design, then it could be argued that no process of designing has taken place, and therefore no industrial design in the statutory sense has resulted. However, it is doubtful that there are many designs whose function *absolutely* dictates visible features. In any case, it is striking how many designs infringement actions in Australia actually concern very functional designs – ie designs whose appearance, as distinct from function, would be of no potential significance to a purchaser or consumer.[12]

Nonetheless, whatever the ambition or expectation of the registrant in this regard might be, although a design may be inspired by functional desiderata or criteria, its functionality is not appropriated by design registration. Only the appearance is the subject of monopoly rights, and if function can be replicated without imitating appearance so as to offend against the standards set in designs legislation, no infringement results. An illustration is provided by *Lockwood* (see

---

[11] See ALRC Report No 74, Recommendation 21.
[12] Eg security locks in *Lockwood Security Products Pty Ltd v Australian Lock Company Pty Ltd* [2005] FCA 203; door hinges in *Allen Manufacturing Company Pty Ltd v McCallum Co Pty Ltd* [2001] FCA 1838; mining conveyor belt modules in *Conrol Pty Ltd v Meco McCallum Pty Ltd & Anor* (1996) 34 IPR 517; etc.

above) where it was agreed by the parties that design registration of high-security keys only offered limited protection against unauthorised copying, as 'the parties acknowledged that the scope of design protection for key blanks was limited because a functional equivalent of the key blank could be manufactured without infringing the design monopoly of the key blank' (at FCA [13]). To try to protect the technology inherent in the high-security locking system – and thus to accommodate the security needs of customers – the parties had to develop a whole suite of strategies to prevent the circulation of blanks, as explained in the case at [9]–[14], including emphasising the fact of having IPRs itself: 'both Lockwood and Alco promote the existence of their design registration portfolio and use it as part of their marketing strategies' (at FCA [13]).

[Particular appearance] It was pointed out above that the design *process*, or the process of making, building or constructing a design product, cannot be monopolised by registration of a design – it is rather the appearance or visual features of the resulting product that are protected. This also implies that it is the specific appearance as represented in the application which is protected by registration; not some broad idea, principle, concept or combination of elements, but the way the idea is specifically worked out and appears as a feature visible to the human eye, rather than a non-visual concept in the human mind.[13] This principle goes to what can be registered and also to how a registered design should be construed in an infringement case. It is also inherent in the core content of design applications: not a verbal description of a design, or of a process by which a product or article is constructed to obtain a certain appearance, but a visual representation such as a drawing or photo of the design. Despite the fact that design registration relates to appearance and not function, parties enforcing a registered design frequently appear to strive for some monopolisation of function. Partly this is because it can be difficult to mentally divorce the appearance of a product from its underlying function, concept or idea. Partly it is also due to a misunderstanding of the nature of the system, and arguably the outcomes of such (in-) famous cases as *Firmagroup* (see above) and *Turbo Tek Enterprises Inc v Sperling Enterprises Pty Ltd* (1989) 23 FCR 331 illustrate the disappointments resulting from the misconceptions in the mind of some registered design owners, rather than the failings of the system. The ALRC Report No 74 said that 'Many of those who responded to the Commission's design users survey thought they were receiving design protection for the way a product works' (at [4.44]), but it is questionable whether the changes to designs law wrought by the present Act have substantially addressed this issue. Even though the scope of the monopoly has been extended to include designs 'substantially similar in overall appearance' (see sections 71 and 19), it is still the case that where the design is determined by functionality and not visual appeal, courts must tread a narrow path between the principle that exclusive rights attach to a specific appearance and not an

---

[13] See the High Court in *Firmagroup Australia Pty Ltd v Byrne & Davidson Doors (Vic) Pty Ltd* (1987) 180 CLR 483; as referred to in *Polyaire Pty Ltd v K-Aire Pty Ltd* [2003] SASC 41 by the Supreme Court of South Australia; at FCA [322]–[323].

underlying concept, and enabling a person who invested in registering a valid design to enjoy an effective monopoly.

[Designs must be of articles (old Act) or products (present Act)] Under the present Act the exclusive right is to make products that embody the design (see section 10 (1) (a)), a more straightforward concept than prevailed under the old Act, which referred to the right to apply a design to an article. Nonetheless the longstanding principle that the right resides in the visual features of a product rather than in the product itself persists under the present Act, and in that sense there is still a conceptual dualism. A product under the present Act is a thing (this is the statutory term, not further defined in the Act) that is either manufactured or hand-made; interestingly the ALRC's Report No 74, Recommendation No 10 was that '"Product" should mean anything that is manufactured including something hand made', whereas under the statutory definition a product is either manufactured *or* hand-made. However, under the old Act, articles that were functional, but primarily literary or artistic in nature were excluded by regulation (Regulation 11 of the Designs Regulation 1982; based on the power in section 17 (2) of the old Act). Under the present Act the specific power to exclude items primarily literary or artistic by regulation is comprised within a more general power to exclude *any* product from registration by regulation. The Design Regulations 2004 exclude medals, as was the case under the old regulations, but none of the other items that were excluded in Regulation 11 as being primarily literary or artistic in nature (such as stamps, dressmaking patterns and book jackets). Presumably, neither under the old nor under the present Act, articles or products exclusively artistic in character were excluded from registration (eg a sculpture) since items made by hand could be registered; but there would be little advantage in registering such items, since copyright protection would be lost (see the Copyright–designs overlap provisions discussed further below). There may also be an argument that these are not 'products' properly so-called.

[Textiles] Designs registration is of considerable potential interest to the fashion industry. Naturally garments, as well as patterned textiles, can be registered as industrial designs since they are 'products' by virtue of the statutory definition. But the drawbacks inherent in using the registered design system for fashion have already been highlighted above (see Registration and delay above). An alternative is to rely on copyright in underlying dress patterns and other artistic works generated in the conceptual and preparatory stages. If the dress pattern is not registered as a design, then it will attract copyright, but as was shown in *Muscat v Le* [2003] FCA 1540 (19 December 2003) under the old overlap provisions, as is still the case under the new, reproduction of the two-dimensional patterns in three-dimensional clothes would trigger the defence provided by section 77 (see further below, Copyright–designs overlap). Before the amended overlap provisions of the *Copyright Act* occasioned by the introduction of the present Act were introduced, a plaintiff could still rely on copyright even though the garment concerned had been industrially manufactured, by claiming indirect reproduction of dress patterns or drawings if they could prove that such drawings had been made by a defendant in the course of producing the imitation clothes; this was what happened in *Muscat*. As Rothnie points out, this completely undermined the overlap provisions.[14] Subsequent to the 2003 copyright amendments regarding copyright–designs overlap this issue is addressed by the new section 77A of the *Copyright Act 1968* (Cth), which provides that indirect copying of dress patterns (ie copying via the garment itself) will not infringe where the making of the garment itself benefits from the overlap defence (the same applies to moulds and casts used in a manufacturing process). Thus reliance on copyright will usually not be possible.

An alternative to registering the garment itself as a design is to register the dressmaking pattern. Under the old Act such *patterns* were expressly excluded from designs registration, but they now can be registered. But for the same reasons as rehearsed in relation to design registration of garments themselves (see above Registration and delay) this may only be of very limited interest to the fashion industry: if a new dressmaking pattern were registered as a design this would only allow the designer to restrain others from producing substantially similar *dressmaking patterns*, not from making garments to the dressmaking patterns. Such limited rights may however still be useful if, as under the copyright scenario just described, a copyist, as a stage in the process of making a copy of the clothing made to the dressmaking pattern, themselves produce a pattern which is substantially similar to the registered one.

[Circuit layouts] Circuit layout designs are expressly excluded by virtue of section 43 (1) (c) (i), but they benefit from a separate, copyright-style protection regime: the *Circuit Layouts Act 1989* (*CLA*) (see Chapter five). That form of protection, however, is copyright-like in that it is not registration-based, and establishes an anti-copying rather than a monopoly right. The rights granted by the *CLA* are also subject to a number of significant statutory exceptions that have no equivalent in the present *Designs Act* in Australia; they are addressed in Chapter five below. By contrast, the EU Designs scheme provides exemptions for acts done privately and for non-commercial purposes; and for experimental purposes and for teaching purposes provided this is compatible with fair trading, does not unduly prejudice the normal exploitation of the design and makes mention of the source.[15] The ALRC Report No 74 does not consider in any detail why design registration should not extend to circuit layouts, particularly given the fact that the requirement under the old Act that a design be visible to the naked eye has been omitted in the present Act. The effect of the ALRC recommendation to omit the 'able to be judged by the eye' requirement, which was an element of the statutory definition of 'design' under the old Act, *inter alia* because '[I]t should be possible for a person, including the informed user, [109] to be assisted by the tools and instruments such as microscopes that are relevant or common

---

[14] See Rothnie, above, at 34.
[15] See Council Regulation (EC) No 6/2002 of 12 December 2001 on Community designs (consolidated version), article 20 (1); see also article 13 of the Directive 98/71/EC of the European Parliament and of the Council of 13 October 1998 on the legal protection of designs.

to the trade' [at 4.35] may be that structurally nothing in the Act, other than the express exclusion, would otherwise stand in the way of the registering of circuit layouts, since they are presumably visible with the aid of appropriate instrumentation. It is also accepted that internal surfaces of an object can be registered as designs. Why a specific anti-piracy regime of the kind established under the *CLA* is preferable to a design registration model for circuit layouts is not analysed in the ALRC Report No 74. However, *sui generis* protection for circuit layouts, with its standard limitations and exceptions, has been the norm around the globe since the Washington Treaty on Intellectual Property in Respect of Integrated Circuits of 1989 was signed.

[Screen displays and 'branding assets'] By virtue of the more general statutory threshold tests, rather than by express exclusion, screen displays have not achieved registration as designs in Australia. Naturally copyright law may go some way to protecting original computer displays, although only to a limited extent – as either artistic works or as computer programs (see in that regard, Chapter five). Screen displays (or computer interfaces) were consistently held not to be registrable under the old Act, which provided that a design had to be applied to an article; with screen displays the design *is* the article, and thus there was no application of a design *to* an article. Alternatively, it was argued that the physical screen or monitor is the product, and then no design is applied to it since the appearance of or display on the screen is transitory and not consistent – such reasoning can equally apply under the present Act. As pointed out in *Re Applications by Comshare Incorporated* (1991) 23 IPR 145 at 147, a screen display also does not have a 'particular and individual appearance', but appears as something both ephemeral and changeable. That case also treated screen displays as primarily literary or artistic in nature and thus excluded from registration as a design under the old Act. The Deputy Registrar in *Altoweb, Inc* [2002] ADO 2 (16 April 2002) also refused to register a design consisting of features of pattern/ornamentation displayed on a screen through the operation of software. He referred to a number of decisions: *inter alia Comshare* (above); but also *KK Suwa Seikosha's Design Application* (1982) RPC 166 (UK; Seiko), in which a computer-generated watch screen display was found to be a registrable design, and some other decisions in foreign jurisdictions which had allowed similar registrations. Nonetheless the applicant failed because the design was not *applied to* the 'finished article', ie the computer screen, but was '[. . .] displayed on the computer screen by software that is totally independent of the computer screen as manufactured and as sold' (at [ADO 37].).

By contrast, in the UK in the Registered Design Appeal Tribunal case *Apple Computer Inc v Design Registry*, 24.10.2001, noted at [2002] E.I.P.R. N-40, a screen-displayed icon was found to be registrable, even under the old law which was also based on the 'design applicable to an article' approach. Jacob J found that user interfaces for computer displays were registrable because they were displayed every time the machine was used, the icons being considered inbuilt in the machine. The ephemeral nature of the display was not an obstacle because *every time* the computer is used the icon displays. *A fortiori*, under the present UK law which expressly renders typefaces and graphics registrable as designs, symbols for display on a screen are registrable. In the EU, 'branding assets', eg 'logos, corporate identities, advertising materials and displays' are accepted for registration as Community Designs.[16] Neither typefaces nor graphics, nor branding assets can at present be registered in Australia *as such,* not being visual features of a product. Clearly registration of 'branding assets' is an extension beyond the traditional realm of designs.[17]

[Design registration of components and of interoperable parts] Under both the old Act and the present Act, spare parts or component parts of a complex article can be separately registered. Therefore a car manufacturer, for instance, having developed a new model, could register the overall appearance of the car, as well as the overall appearance of its every separate component. Both visually significant parts, such as body panels, and other parts, such as engine and systems components, for which visual appearance is of no consequence, would be registrable. Such components must of course be 'new and distinctive', which would often not be the case, since they would tend to be identical to, or insignificant variants of existing parts. There is no restriction on the registration of must-fit and must-match (or 'interoperable') parts, which had attracted significant concern about anti-competitive effects.[18] Such parts can by definition not be 'designed around' so that a car manufacturer, for instance, would not only enjoy a monopoly in the upstream market for its car brand, but also in the downstream market for supply of all registered spare and replacement parts (with the exception of enhancements that it did not itself produce and register as designs, such as wings and other attachments, mag wheels, etc). This obviously has the potential to drive up costs of components, and therefore insurance premiums, and to erect considerable barriers against competition by generic parts manufacturers. Although automotive manufacturing has been the totemic issue in this regard, it is also significant for a number of other industries, where product manufacturers may set out to generate considerable income from regular consumable component supplies (eg ink cartridges for photocopiers and printers), as well as from the supply of spare parts used for repairs. The ALRC proposed restrictions on the registration of such parts with a referral mechanism involving the Australian Consumer & Competition Commission. Fortunately the government rejected this burdensome approach, instead continuing to treat component parts like any other designs, but subject to a repair defence in infringement proceedings: see further below. However, the repair defence will have no effect in relation to the supply of consumables, for instance as contained in cartridges and other containers which may constitute 'must-fit' components. In contrast to designs for spare parts which are registrable,

---

[16] See Jose J Izquierdo Peris, 'Registered Community Design: First two-year Balance from an Insider's Perspective' (2006) 28 *EIPR* 3, 146 at 147.
[17] For a more general treatment of interface design issues, see Debra Brown and Euan Cameron 'Designing the interface' (2005), *International Review of Law, Computers & Technology*, 19, 1, 65–81.
[18] See ALRC Report No 74, Chapter 16 'Spare Parts'.

portions or parts of products that are not separate are not registrable other than as part of the overall design.

The novelty test

[Elevating the innovation threshold] Whereas under the old Act a design only had to pass a test of novelty (although the terms 'new or original' were used in the old Act, section 17, 'original' was not thought to add anything), the present Act newly introduced a two-step test, requiring both novelty *and* distinctiveness: see section 15. Under the old Act, a design was not novel if the prior art base contained either an identical design, or a design that only varied in relation to an immaterial detail or the kind of variation common in the trade (section 17 (1) (a) of the old Act). The general perception was that identification of some detailed differences would sustain a finding of novelty, even if these differences hardly affected the overall look of the design. As a consequence, designs were perceived as too readily registered, the concomitant being that they were also very readily circumvented, by making relatively minor changes. The newly introduced distinctiveness requirement is intended to simultaneously address the problems of low innovation threshold and narrow scope of protection. By virtue of section 19 of the present Act, the approach and factors applicable to determining whether a design is sufficiently novel compared to a prior art design are expressly harmonised with those applicable to judging whether an impugned design is too similar to a registered design. Thus at a single stroke of the lawmaker's pen two 'empirical observations' about the old system were to be addressed: the presence of many unmeritorious designs on the Register; and the failure of certain high-profile infringement cases where many felt the defendants had managed to get away with pinching the substance of very innovative registered designs. Those observations, whether solidly based or not, had certainly resulted in a lack of confidence in the system of designs registration in Australia. In this regard, the 2003 Act represents a transition to a more mature design system, less imitative and incremental, and more innovative and attuned to a world in which design innovation has acquired much greater significance than it had when the old Act was born. Nonetheless, this transition must still be seen within the framework of the limitations and constraining factors inherent in design innovation, which were discussed above.

[New and distinctive designs under the present Act] A design is not new if it is identical to a design in the prior art base; and it is not distinctive if it is 'substantially similar in overall impression' to such a design. Under the old Act, detail informs the decision about similarity: is the new design an advance in anything more than irrelevant details? Under the present Act, *overall impression* rather than detailed individual difference is the focal point of the test *ab initio*. By virtue of section 19, factors to be taken into account in the assessment of substantial similarity in overall impression receive express statutory confirmation; no equivalent guidance existed under the old Act. The section applies both in the context of subsistence of a design right, and in the context of infringement: the single standard of 'substantially identical in overall impression' applies to both. The most significant guidance – and departure from the old Act – resulting from section 19 is that similarities are to be given more weight than differences (see section 19 (1) of the present Act). The process of assessing novelty under the old Act resulted in small differences receiving considerable attention and weight. By implication, anything more than an immaterial or common trade variation would get a design over the line, and enumerating individual differences often resulted in a long list which automatically attracted too much weight in the overall assessment.

Under the present Act, in the presence of *substantial* similarity in overall impression, identified small differences should not get a design over the novelty threshold. The *overall impression* one design makes on the mind must be different compared with the *overall impression* the other makes. However, this does not mean that an application should fail because the same underlying idea, concept, method or principle has been applied in a pre-existing design. Even under the present Act, the monopoly must still reside in the specific appearance of the actual representation of the design in the application. In that light it is less clear just how different the approach resulting from the present Act will be; to some extent it will depend on how compacted the design field is. The following quote from Jacobs J's judgment in *Sebel* still applies to designs progression overall, certainly for the kind of common product he was speaking of, viz, a chair:

> I think that it is most important to bear in mind in relation to such an article as a chair, that one cannot and should not expect to find some startling novelty or originality. The element of novelty or originality will of necessity be likely to be within a small compass. I do not mean thereby that any difference of shape, outline, proportion or placement of components will thereby constitute novelty of design, but provided I can see a substantial difference from the fundamental form and from the development in the trade up to the time of the application for registration, then I do not think that it is sufficient to point to a number of elements of similarity to past design in order to show that the design is not new or original.[19]

[What does 'distinctiveness' add?] The present two-tier test requires distinctiveness as well as novelty. Sections 15 (1) & (2), 16 (2) and 19 do no more than establish rules for assessing differences between the design at issue and similar but non-identical designs comprised in the prior art. It is unclear what the use of the cover-all term 'distinctiveness' adds to the substance of the test as identified in section 16 (2), ie whether a design is substantially similar in overall impression in the eyes of a person who is an 'informed user' (see further below). As ALRC Report No 74 points out, certain submissions to the ALRC opposed the use of the term because of its similarity to the trade marks concept. The ultimate touchstone of distinctiveness in trade marks law is the ordinary consumer, and the term implies something striking by which they could tell products apart. But it is not appropriate to import any of that learning into designs law. The EU Designs

---

[19] See *D Sebel & Co Ltd v National Art Metal Co Pty Ltd* (1965) 10 FLR 224 at 226.

Regulation adopts the standard of 'individual character' (see article 6) rather than distinctiveness. Nonetheless the earlier EU *Green Paper*[20] had proposed a second-tier requirement of distinctiveness which deliberately introduced a consumer protection element into designs registration. It is worth quoting from the *Green Paper* at some length to illustrate how different the thinking there was to the approach that was ultimately adopted by way of sections 16 (2) and 19 here in Australia (see *Green Paper* (above) at 5.5.6.2):

> In this second stage of the test what matters is 'the reaction of the relevant public', i.e. of those persons who are supposed to be the purchasers of the products in which the design is or is going to be incorporated. They must not be misled by the similarity of the design with other existing designs and assume that the products in hand are the same even if they show some minor differences or variations. This element of the test brings into the picture the opinion of the ordinary consumer of the products in question. This implies raising the threshold somewhat higher than in the first stage where experts assess whether a design is or is not already known to them. The ordinary consumer may not be aware of minor differences which would be immediately detected by the skilled expert.

So a design that experts regarded as novel would still be excluded, if ordinary consumers could not distinguish it from other existing designs. As is discussed below, the person through whose eyes distinctiveness is to be assessed in Australia is not 'those persons who are supposed to be the purchasers of the products [. . .]', but a more complex character, the 'informed user' in possession of the specific information and observing the rather technical process set out in section 19.

[Other factors of section 19] Apart from the general rule that overall similarity is now to be given more weight than detailed individual differences, section 19 refers to specified factors the decision-maker must have regard to. Three of these factors are intended to introduce flexibility into the test of distinctiveness, ie the ability to adapt the test to the circumstances of and background to the design. The two factors connected to the state of the prior art are 'the development of the prior art base for the design' (section 19 (2) (a)); and the 'freedom of the creator of the design to innovate' (section 19 (2) (d)). The former recognises that in some fields a large body of antecedents exists so there is less room for innovation. The latter tempers the overall test by recognising that for certain products there is 'limited scope for design variation' (see ALRC report No 74 at [5.24]): then small differences are to be given more weight. The ALRC also refers to factors not inherent in the product '[. . .] including the market for the product and marketing constraints' (at [5.24]). In the EC *Green Paper* (see above) on which this ALRC contention is based, reference is had to factors such as standardisation (ie regulatory requirements), and the 'necessity of taking into account deep-rooted marketing requirements by the clients, features imposed by fashion [. . .]'

---

[20] See Commission of the European Communities, *Green Paper on the Legal Protection of Industrial Designs* III/F/5131191-EN (1991).

(at 5.5.8.3). The government's response to the ALRC recommendations used the following terms when accepting that the freedom of the designer should be taken into account: '[...] and take into account the limits imposed by product and marketing constraints on the designer'.[21] The third factor is intended to deal with the thorny problem of a design that differs in part only: then the Act requires that where only a part of a design is substantially similar to another design, regard must be had to 'the amount, quality and importance of that part in the context of the design as a whole' (see 19 (2) (d)).

[Through whose eyes is distinctiveness assessed?] An important question is to whom the design must appear distinctive: as suggested above, a test based on the impression of an average consumer or user may have a very different outcome from a detailed analysis by design experts! Some features of a design may appear striking, ingenious or innovative to a professional designer, but barely noticeable to a person with no intimate knowledge of design evolution. Indeed, one aspect of good design is that complex technical difficulties are overcome in a manner which is *not* obvious to a consumer. Under the present Act, the relevant factors must be assessed through the eyes of the person 'who is familiar with the product to which the design relates', or similar products: the standard of the 'informed user' (see section 19 (3)). These terms are broad and inclusive, covering a varied spectrum of persons, including consumers or users, but also experts. The ALRC (at ALRC [5.17]) proposed the concept as 'flexible enough to incorporate where relevant the views of consumers, experts, specialists and skilled tradespersons. At the same time it does not, and should not, require that the expert or consumer be the test in all cases'; when and how the view of a design expert *should* be sought is not clear.

[The prior art base] Novelty and distinctiveness must be assessed relative to a defined set of pre-existing designs; some must be taken into account and others must be ignored. Under the old Act only local novelty counted; foreign designs not used or published in Australia could not undermine a local application. That approach tended to support imitation of foreign designs as opposed to only local innovation, so under the present Act the prior art base has been augmented to include foreign documentary publications. However, foreign public *use* of a design does not form part of the prior art base, and can therefore be ignored – this makes practical sense. The ALRC proposal that only use *in trade or commerce* in Australia would constitute anticipation was not adopted in the present Act: any use, for instance showing a design to a single member of the public in Australia without the cloak of confidence, would constitute anticipation. If a design is disclosed in a foreign design application, then the question is simply whether it is a 'design published in a document [...]' outside Australia: see section 15 (2). If the design is contained in an Australian application with an earlier priority date, then even if that design is only made public for the first time on or after the

---

[21] See Government Response to the ALRC Designs Review, Released on 16 February 1999 by IP Australia and Mr Warren Entsch MP, Parliamentary Secretary to the Minister for Industry, Science and Resources; Recommendation 37.

priority date of the applied-for design, it will be taken to be part of the prior art base.

Expanding the prior art base has taken the test of novelty to a new level in Australia, comparatively high by international standards, although universal or absolute novelty is not unknown. The novelty standard in the EU Designs Directive is significantly different: only disclosure of the design such that it could reasonably have become known in the normal course of business to the circles specialised in the sector concerned, operating within the Community, constitutes anticipation. But as is pointed out by on the Ladas & Parry website:

> On the question of the novelty test Europe has deviated strongly from BIRPI's model law which would have imposed a universal novelty requirement by providing for exceptions for 1) situations where the events in question 'could not reasonably have become known in the normal course of business to the circles in the sector concerned operating within the' EU and 2) for registered rights disclosures by the designer him or herself or someone obtaining the design from him or her within the twelve month period prior to the filing of the application for the registered right.[22]

[Grace period for designs] Grace periods for designs are one possible way of overcoming the difficulties a registration system causes for high-turnover industries such as fashion, as pointed out above. A grace period (as exists now in relation to patents, still a relative innovation in Australian terms; see above Chapter three) allows disclosures by the applicant to be ignored, if they occur within a certain period prior to filing. In other words, an applicant should ensure that an application is filed within the statutory period following their own first disclosure. Thus if a grace period existed, a designer could test a design in the market for a certain period, before deciding whether or not to apply for registration and incur the consequent costs. However, by analogy with patent grace periods, the registered owner would not have a right of action against imitations that occurred during the grace period prior to filing, which would limit their usefulness in this regard. In its Report No 74 the ALRC recommended against adopting a grace period for designs, indicating that instead a designer could lodge multiple applications, and then only pursue those in relation to designs that had been successful by market standards.

However, in Europe the European Design Regulation provides a one-year grace period for designs.[23] Similarly, the United States has a one-year grace period because designs are included within their patent system. However, the difficulties that already apply to grace periods for patents, notably the lack of international harmonisation which puts applications that take advantage of local rules at risk overseas, remain a disincentive for the introduction of and reliance on grace periods for designs (see further above in Chapter three).

---

[22] See Ladas & Parry, 'Intellectual Property Law, The European Design Regulation in Context', Chapter 5, *The position in Europe* (at www.ladas.com/Patents/PatentPractice/EUDesignRegulation/EUDesi05.html).
[23] See Council Regulation (EC) No 6/2002 of 12 December 2001 on Community designs, article 7.

Nature of the design right

[The old Act and the present Act in general] There are some significant differences between the old and the present Acts in terms of the nature and extent of design rights. The old Act expressly granted a 'monopoly' in the design; the present Act no longer uses that term, but the owner still has the exclusive right to make, import, sell, hire, use for the purposes of trade or business, keep for such purposes or authorise another to do any of those things in relation to a product embodying a registered design (see section 10). The right is still monopolistic in the sense that it excludes all others from so using the design, whether they have copied or not. Under the old Act there was a scaled approach to infringement: either a design article was identical or an obvious imitation, which was determined solely by side-by-side comparison; or it was a fraudulent imitation, which required proof of access and copying of the registered design. Designs with greater differences were included within the monopoly's scope where imitation was fraudulent, ie where there was deliberately disguised copying. Under the present Act establishing access to the registered design becomes irrelevant, but the scope of the design right has been extended to encompass the kind of designs which previously would only be caught if fraudulent imitation could be proven – and maybe more: anything that is a design 'substantially similar in overall impression' by reference to the factors mentioned above in the context of novelty, and in the light of any 'Statement of newness and distinctiveness', as further explored below. The nature of the evidence provided in designs infringement cases may thus change under the present Act, since proof of access and copying was previously an important aspect of cases relating to non-identical designs. Such evidence may still be significant in relation to remedies: the court may refuse to award an account of profits, or refuse or reduce damages, if at the time of the making of the relevant product, the defendant was not aware the design was registered, and had taken all reasonable prior steps to ascertain whether it was. It will be recalled that an infringement action can only be brought after certification of the design: see section 73 (3).

[Who is entitled to register a design?] Any person may apply for a design registration under the present Act (section 21), but only certain persons are entitled to be registered as owner – the person(s) so entitled must be mentioned in the application (see section 13). The designer, ie the creator of the design, is primarily entitled to the registered design, but if the design is created in the course of employment or 'under a contract with another person' (see section 13 (1) (b)), the employer or other person is entitled to the registration, unless otherwise specified in the contract. Thus in relation to designs, the person who commissions the creation of a design under a contract for services is entitled to be registered as its owner, reversing the rule applicable to commissioned artistic works in copyright, where the commissioned author owns copyright unless the contract is to the contrary. More than one person can be entered on the Register as owner of a design; and by virtue of section 118 the Register is *prima facie* evidence of any particulars entered in it. Note that by an interesting innovation, the present Act now provides by virtue of section 35 that an applicant can opt for the design disclosed in an application to be published rather than registered. This provides some form of protection against others obtaining design registration for a design that has been developed but not applied to products or manufactured and published in that manner.

[**The term of the monopoly**] The term of the monopoly under the old Act was maximum 16 years, but under the present Act it has been shortened to a maximum of 10 years (two periods of five years). Australia thus meets the 10-year minimum term requirement under TRIPS article 26 (3). The government rejected the Recommendation of the ALRC Report 74 (No 105) to retain the old term of protection, indicating that it was not in the public interest to have a term longer than the minimum required by international treaty obligations. Neither the Berne Convention – which leaves it up to contracting parties whether to apply copyright to designs or not – nor the Paris Convention prescribe the term of protection of a registered design, Article 5 'Industrial Designs' only providing that 'Industrial designs shall be protected in all the countries of the Union'. Under the UK *Registered Designs Act 1949* (as included in consolidated form as Schedule 4 of the *Copyright, Designs & Patents Act 1988*; and as substantially amended on the 9th December 2001 to conform to the EU Community Design Directive (Directive 98/71/EC)) the term of protection is maximum 25 years. For an unregistered design the period is three years from first making available to the public, as defined in the Design Regulation (see above, art 11 (2)). Thus the 10-year term under the present Act, although in conformity with TRIPS, is much shorter than the EU maximum. The ALRC in its report points out that only about 5% of designs were at that time extended to their full term, which supports a shorter term. The system of an initial short term of registration under the old Act, with no opposition until renewal, was not retained in the present Act. Designs registration now requires renewal after five years, but there is no longer any connection between this renewal and opposition. A design is now registered with no more than a formalities check, and must be examined as to substantive requirements if it is to be enforced. But examination can be requested at any time after registration by any person or undertaken on the Registrar's own initiative, and may result in either certification or revocation. A request for examination from any person may contain material relating to the newness and distinctiveness of the design. By this method the certification – ie deferred examination, effectively – and opposition procedures have been amalgamated. Alternatively, once a design is certified, any person can apply to the court for revocation.

[**Validity of a registered design**] As indicated above, neither registration nor certification guarantee the validity of a design. The validity of a design registration can be attacked in various ways: in the context of infringement proceedings, it is by way of counterclaim for revocation by virtue of section 74 of the present Act. But any person can in fact apply to a prescribed court for an order revoking a design, once a certificate of examination has been issued; the grounds for such an application are listed in section 93 (3). Further, under the present Act, any person can apply to the Registrar to have a design that has been registered at any time examined; the Registrar can also undertake examination *ex officio*: see section 63. Under the old Act only a 'person aggrieved' has standing to attack a design registration other than by counterclaim.[24] Note also the unjustified threats provisions, sections 77–81 of the present Act.

Infringement of a registered design

[The old Act and the present Act: strengthening the design owner's position]
As indicated above, the intention of the present Act was to strengthen the position of the registered design owner. The broader scope of protection reflects the higher novelty threshold: the statutory test for infringement in relation to designs 'similar in overall impression' takes into account the same factors and adopts the same process as the test for novelty. Apart from the factors discussed in that context above, the design owner's hand is also strengthened by clearer provisions as to the use of a 'Statement of Newness and Distinctiveness', identifying individual features of a registered design. Free-riders should not as readily escape liability by adopting the overall appearance of a registered design but making modifications in detail. However, the underlying structure of the designs regime has not fundamentally changed: the fact that registration extends to particular appearance only, and not to an underlying concept, idea or method of making a product continues to inform infringement questions. Despite the higher novelty threshold, design registration is still available for incremental changes of a less fundamental nature, as well as for breakthrough designs. The monopoly will continue to be based on a particular representation, ie a drawing or a photograph of a design as found in the application.

[Forms of infringement] Infringement of a registered design occurs when a person makes, without authorisation, a product which embodies the design: see section 71 (1) (a) of the present Act; under the old Act, where a person so applies the design to an article: section 30 (1) (a). In respect of remedies the present Act makes a distinction between primary and secondary infringement (see section 75): the former relates to making infringing products, the latter to commercial dealing in them (see further below). But unlike in patents law (contributory infringement, see section 117 of the *Patents Act*) and arguably in copyright (authorisation as a form of infringement: see section 36 (1), (2) of the *Copyright Act*), contributory infringement is not provided for in designs law in Australia. The issue is well illustrated by *Foggin v Lacey* [2003] FCAFC 147. The defendant sold the article (an 'orgasmatron' head-scratcher) not in the registered beehive form in which it was to be used but with straightened prongs. Had it been patented, the supply by the defendant, with instructions on

---

[24] See *Lockwood Security Products Pty Ltd v Australian Lock Company Pty Ltd* [2005] FCA 203.

how to shape the prongs into a functional configuration, would most likely have amounted to contributory infringement under section 117 (2) (c) of the *Patents Act*. But applying the *Designs Act 1906*, Emmett J pointed out at FCAFC [75] that:

> [. . .], even if carrying out the Foggin Instruction according to a fair reading of the Foggin Instruction would involve an application of the Design, it is difficult to see how, at the point of sale, there is any infringement, at that time, the Design has not been applied to any article. Nor has any obvious imitation of the Design been applied to any article.

As his Honour pointed out (at FCAFC [78]), by contrast the *Registered Designs Act 1949* (UK) expressly included contributory infringement:

> The rights given to the registered proprietor of a design under s 7 of the UK Act, as originally enacted, included the exclusive right: 'to make anything for enabling any [article in respect of which the design is registered, being an article to which the design has been applied] to be made . . .

As no such provision appears in the Australian Acts, it could be presumed that contributory infringement has been deliberately left outside the scope of the registered design owner's rights. It should be noted that international exhaustion of rights applies to registered designs: if the registered design is embodied in a product with the licence of the registered owner, then its importation cannot be restrained. In other words, parallel importation of legitimate designs is allowed: see section 171 (2) of the present Act. In this regard there is no change from the old Act.

[Non-identical designs under the old Act] Under the old Act (which continues to apply to pre-2003 designs) the registered owner has a monopoly in the design (see section 25), but the test for infringement revolves around the concept of obvious or fraudulent 'imitation' (see section 30). In *Malleys Ltd v J W Tomlin Pty Ltd* (1961) 180 CLR 120 the High Court explained the operation of section 30 (at CLR [13]):

> Turning to s. 30 it is apparent that there is infringement in any one of three cases – that is, where the design which has been applied is: – (i) the registered design (ii) an obvious imitation of the registered design (i.e., not the same but a copy apparent to the eye notwithstanding slight differences) and (iii) a fraudulent imitation (i.e., a copy with differences which are both apparent and not so slight as to be insubstantial but which have been made merely to disguise the copying). Visual comparison will establish (i) or (ii) but a finding of fraudulent imitation must require something more because in such a case visual comparison is not of itself sufficient to establish imitation; otherwise it would be an obvious imitation.

So although the term 'imitation' implies copying, independent evidence of actual copying of a design is *only* relevant to establish 'fraudulent imitation'. In a finding of obvious imitation, which is arrived at on the basis of a visual comparison *alone*, actual copying of a registered design is merely implicit. Copying need not be expressly implied from similarity in such a case, since the design owner's right is in the nature of a monopoly (contrast this with copyright). Alternatively, as suggested in *Polyaire Pty Ltd v K-Aire Pty Ltd* [2005] HCA 32 at [20], obvious imitation implies a process of subconscious copying, although in theory a design registration could be infringed by a person who arrived at the identical or very similar design wholly independently; but in practice, given the specific and particular representation of a registered design, this is unlikely to occur. A good summary of the appropriate approach to infringement questions under the old Act is found in Gummow J's judgment in *Wanem Pty Ltd v John Tekiela* (1990) 19 IPR 435 at 440:

> (i) first impressions are important in determining whether there is an infringement of a design, (ii) an obvious imitation is one which is not the same as the registered design but is a copy apparent to the eye notwithstanding slight differences, (iii) the question must be looked at as one of substance and by examining the essential features of the design, (iv) a closer correspondence between the registered design and the alleged infringing design is necessary to satisfy the test of obvious imitation than that of fraudulent imitation, (v) precise mathematical comparisons or matters of measurements or ratios, which form no part of the mental picture which the eye conveys to the brain of shape or configuration suggested by the design, are not to be applied as the test of infringement; appearance to the eye is the critical issue, and (vi) questions of infringement must not be determined by a narrow or overly technical approach in comparison between the design and the alleged infringement, lest the registration be sapped of its worth to the registered owner.

[Fraudulent imitation] Where the impugned design is not an obvious, ie an immediately apparent imitation or, in terms of the *Malleys* case, where there are 'differences which are both apparent and not so slight as to be insubstantial', a finding of 'fraudulent imitation' is still possible. Such a finding cannot rely on visual comparison alone: extrinsic evidence relating to the derivation of the impugned design will be required. In other words, as well as pointing to similarities between the two designs, the plaintiff must provide evidence of the process of 'imitating' that has resulted in them. However, even in the presence of such evidence, it is still required that 'One must be able finally to say that the product is an imitation visually recognisable as such'.[25] In other words, derivation will not amount to infringement if the design has been sufficiently modified in the process. Thus both a legitimate design innovation and an illegitimate imitation may derive from an existing design, and the overarching distinguishing factor between the two remains the degree of visual similarity, even in the case of 'fraudulent' imitation.

This notion of fraud was introduced to designs law as early as 1842 in the UK but its proper scope was only recently settled in the High Court's decision in *Polyaire Pty Ltd v K-Aire Pty Ltd* [2005] HCA 32 (16 June 2005), which contains a potted history of it at [10ff]. It was always perfectly clear that derivation in itself is not enough, but less certain whether the term 'fraudulent' implied that 'dishonest concealment' by the copyist should be established. The Court (McHugh, Gummow, Hayne, Callinan and Heydon JJ) held in a single judgment that no dishonest

---

[25] Ibid.

intention to disguise copying is in fact required. The implication of the statutory terminology was simply that in circumstances where actual derivation can be shown, a fraudulent imitation may be present even though the imitation was not obvious. No more is required than imitation with knowledge, 'and without any sufficient invention on the part of the imitator'.[26] It is not necessary therefore to establish a fraudulent intent to disguise; and it may be that even where there is a legitimate reason to make changes, a design may still be a 'fraudulent imitation' because it has been knowingly derived from a registered design and the changes made are not sufficient to take it outside the scope of the registered design. As quoted in *Polyaire* by the High Court at [34], the Franki Committee (the Designs Law Review Committee), in its Report on the Law Relating to Designs, February 1973 at 29 had said:

> We are satisfied that the broad protection afforded by section 30 is appropriate and should remove any idea that if a design is copied infringement can be avoided by attempting to disguise copying by making apparent and not insubstantial differences. We do not recommend that there should be any major amendment of it.

The conclusive ruling in *Polyaire* has strengthened the design owner's position, which is striking in the light of the attempt to achieve the same thing by introducing a different test of infringement in the present Act.

[Perceived failings of the old Act] The impetus for reform of the infringement provisions of the old Act largely stemmed from a 'perception that the infringement provisions [of the 1906 Act] are weighted against plaintiffs'.[27] The outcome of some high-profile cases contributed to this perception; in particular, concerns '[. . .] escalated as a result of the decision in *Firmagroup*'.[28] But the registered design in *Firmagroup* – a recessed doorhandle for a 'rolladoor' – was one whose innovation lay principally in the underlying concept, combining certain elements to great functional advantage. The trial judge King J said that it was a 'new concept of design in products of its kind', identifying the 'new main features' as 'a more elongated rectangular shape than was previously known and a recessed handle'. The registered design owner's case fell short even though 'salient features' of construction had been copied. The High Court stressed that (at CLR [6]):

> The only design features that are susceptible of protection are those features which convey the idea of 'one particular individual and specific appearance', to repeat the phrase from Russell-Clarke. No design should be so construed as to give to its proprietor a monopoly in a method or principle of construction.

An underlying concept, idea, method of construction or combination of elements as such was not protected by registration, only the visual appearance of a particular embodiment. The High Court was concerned to limit designs registration to its proper purpose (at HCA [5]):

---

[26] From Edmunds and Bentwich, *The law of Copyright in Designs*, 2nd edn, 1908, as quoted in *Polyaire* at [32].
[27] ALRC Report No 74 at [6.4]).
[28] *Firmagroup Australia Pty Ltd v Byrne & Davidson Doors (Vic) Pty Ltd* (1987) 180 CLR 483 at 489; ALRC, Report No 74, at [6.3]).

When a design satisfies the statutory definition of 'design' by reason of its applicability 'to the purpose of . . . shape, or configuration, of an article', the monopoly conferred by registration does not extend to the features of the design which do not determine the article's unique shape or configuration, and this is so although the design may be applied to make a new and useful article. The Act is concerned with shape and configuration, not function: per Dixon J in *Macrae Knitting Mills Ltd. v Lowes Ltd.* (1936) 55 CLR 725, at p 730.

The express exclusion in the old Act of 'method or principle of construction' (see section 4 'design') added little that was not already inherent in the concept of design registration, as the Court implied (at HCA 5):

> The notion that a feature which does no more than identify a general characteristic of shape is a method or principle of construction and is therefore outside the protection of the Act appears in what this Court said in *Malleys Ltd. v. J. W. Tomlin Pty. Ltd.* (1961) 35 ALJR 352, at p 353 [. . .]

Malleys predated the amendments to the old Act which inserted the express exclusion of a method or principle of construction. The Court quoted with approval the following passage from the trial judge's decision (at HCA [9]):

> In this case salient features of construction are taken, but the whole unit has been so redesigned to incorporate them that a different design has been produced. Thus the change in balance of the features and the lengthening of the article are not mere disguise but are themselves salient features of the defendants' design which are novel and unique in that design.

There was little or no reference to the fact that, as King J recognised, the registered design was a considerable advance on the previous art, admittedly in terms of functionality, but also in appearance. The considerable departure from the prior art was not reflected in a broader scope of protection, the Court focussing very much on listing very specific differences in appearance. Arguably these were slight differences of proportion and detail, and it is doubtful that a successful outcome would have amounted to allowing the functional idea to be monopolised.

In another high-profile case, *Turbo Tek Enterprises Inc v Sperling Enterprises Pty Ltd* (1989) 88 ALR 524, the registered design was also a major development in the design of the kind or article concerned. The judge here *did* expressly state that this was relevant to the scope of the monopoly. 'This, in my opinion, is a major development in the concept of shape and configuration and differences between the Registered Design and the [allegedly infringing] Taiwanese device must be judged accordingly' (at FCA [23]). Nonetheless the incorporation of all the features of the registered design was not enough: the resulting design had, in overall appearance, to be substantially the same as the registered design. In this case a pistol grip was added to a registered design consisting of a spray nozzle incorporating a cylindrical reservoir, and therefore the resulting article was not sufficiently similar. The design protection was not so extensive as to convey 'a monopoly in respect of all designs of spray washers which used cylindrical reservoirs or drums mounted in conjunction with the wands' (*Turbo Tek* at FCA 29). Again, the monopoly lay in a specific appearance, not an underlying idea or concept.

[Methods of construction] *Foggin v Lacey* (see above) affords an example of the issues that can arise in relation to the exclusion of methods or principles of construction. The appellant submitted that the design registration was invalid because the flexible nature of the prongs of the 'orgasmatron' meant that they could be shaped into any number of round or wineglass shapes that would allow the 'orgasmatron' to have its intended effect. The owner of the design seemed to submit that the Design would be infringed if the result is an article that has a shape that can be characterised as a 'cage' or 'inverted wine glass'. Emmett J dealt with the matter as follows (at [53]):

> If that were the Design, the monopoly would not be limited to the particular appearance shown in the certificate of registration of the Design. Lacey, by such contentions is, in effect, seeking to protect features that make the Orgasmatron useful. However, the features that Lacey so seeks to protect are insufficiently precise to convey an idea of unique shape or configuration. The monopoly granted by the Act is not such as to protect features comprising eight malleable prongs attached to a cylindrical handle that can be manipulated in an infinite number of ways, so long as each is manipulated outwards and subsequently inwards, or away and then back towards the line of the cylindrical handle. [54] The grant of registration of the Design gives a monopoly only in the particular shape configuration pattern or ornamentation depicted in the representation attached to the Certificate of registration. On that basis, the Design is validly registered.

Thus the right did not extend to 'non-electrical head massagers' but to one specific appearance as in the representations in the application. As the majority said, there was nothing in the design that made flexibility of the prongs an element.[29]

[Infringement under the present Act] Under the present Act the approach to infringement is simpler: the concept of fraudulent imitation is abandoned. Just two alternatives remain: either the impugned product embodies an identical design, or it embodies a design substantially similar in overall impression. To neither alternative is evidence of actual copying, or disguise, etc relevant – both are a matter of careful side-by-side comparison; but similarity in overall impression is intended to incorporate at least designs that would be considered fraudulent imitations under the old Act. The present Act deliberately expands the scope of protection. It departs from the alleged tendency under the old Act to over-emphasise specific detailed differences in relation to non-identical designs: first, by expressly referring to 'substantial similarity *in overall impression*'; and secondly, by specifically directing a court to attach more weight to similarities than to differences (see section 19). The government response to the ALRC Recommendation relating to the test of similarity in overall impression was as follows:

---

[29] At [27], where the appellant/defendant's submissions are usefully summarised.

> [Recommendation] No 33. Distinctiveness should be assessed by considering the overall impression of the design. Accepted – the courts should not consider minor or insignificant changes to a design relevant if the overall impression remains one of substantial or significant similarity. [. . .].[30]

The Act now also provides greater direction to courts, mandating factors to which they must have regard: the extent of the advance over the prior art (section 19 (2) (a)) and also the freedom to innovate (section 19 (2) (d)); see above, Novelty). Express inclusion of these factors should aid clarity and consistency, but in substance there is no real departure from some of the principles commonly applied under the old Act. For instance, in *Tu v Pakway Australia Pty Ltd* [2004] FCA 1151, a case decided under the old Act, the court quoted from another judgment (at [104]):

> A matter to bear in mind is that the scope of protection afforded by the monopoly conferred by a registered design is to be determined by reference to the prior art at the priority date. When a design has a close resemblance to the prior art, the protection will be limited. In *Dart Industries*, Lockhart J explained at 409: 'Small differences between the registered design and the prior art will generally lead to a finding of no infringement if there are equally small differences between the registered design and the alleged infringing article. On the other hand, the greater the advance in the registered design over the prior art, generally the more likely that a court will find common features between the design and the alleged infringing article to support a finding of infringement.' (Citations omitted).

The potential impact of having more regard to overall appearance than to detailed differences is reinforced by the standard set: that of the informed user, ie any person who is familiar with the design as a user of the design product, and not just an expert designer who might have excessive regard to matters of detail (see also the section above on Novelty). In terms of the *Firmagroup* case (see above), the Law Council of Australia in its submission to the ALRC alleged that that case would have been differently decided if a list of factors had been specified (see ALRC Report No 74 at [6.28]). Indeed, the differences between the registered design and the prior art were greater than those between the registered design and the impugned design, something the ALRC thought should result in a finding of infringement (at [6.30]); there was some freedom for any designer to innovate within the broader constraints of function, use and marketing requirements (eg the recessed part could have been elongated along the bottom with the key-lock placed above); and the overall impression, without an eye to fine detail but for instance from the point of view of an installer of garage doors, was substantially similar (if not substantially identical).

[Statements of Newness and Distinctiveness] Under the old Act, an applicant could file a Statement of Novelty, and/or a Statement of Monopoly; under the present Act, it is a 'Statement of Newness or Distinctiveness'. There was a

---

[30] See Government Response to the ALRC Designs Review, Released on 16 February 1999 by IP Australia and Mr Warren Entsch MP, Parliamentary Secretary to the Minister for Industry, Science and Resources.

perceived risk under the old Act of limiting rather than enhancing the scope of the monopoly by the form of a Statement of Monopoly. As Merkel J put it in *Allen John Wilson v Hollywood Toys (Australia) Pty Ltd* No. VG 326 of 1993 FED No. 126/96 Designs (at AUSTLII [35]): '[A]lthough the Act provides that an application for registration may be accompanied by a statement of monopoly which upon registration appears on the Register ((13) S.20(4) and S.23(3)) the Act contains no express provision as to its function . . .'. Hence Statements of Monopoly generally simply claimed a monopoly in the shape and ornamentation of the article as illustrated – ie *all* aspects of the article rather than a limited number. However, they were sometimes used to disclaim features that were not new. Statements of Novelty identified novel features of a design, particularly where there was close resemblance to the prior art. The Registrar could require one be filed, but commonly none was, again because of reluctance to narrow the monopoly down to the specific features identified. So Statements were little used in any real sense and their status in infringement proceedings remains unclear.

In the present Act this is addressed by specific reference to the use of a 'Statement of Newness and Distinctiveness' in the context of infringement: first, particular regard must be had to those features identified (see section 19 (2) (b) (i)); and secondly, 'if those features relate to only part of the design – have particular regard to that part of the design, but in the context of the design as a whole' (see section 19 (2) (b) (ii)). The ALRC recommended that applicants should be made to identify new and distinctive features of the design, (see ALRC [6.17]) but under the present Act filing such a Statement is optional (though recommended). However, commonly Statements of Newness and Distinctiveness do not identify specific features, but are in terms such as these: 'Newness and distinctiveness is claimed in the features of shape and/or configuration of a [product] as illustrated in the accompanying representations', or 'The shape and configuration of the product is new and distinctive', or 'Each feature of the design considered separately or in combination with any other feature or features', sometimes followed by some feature or another that is to be disregarded (eg the brand name appearing on the product in the representation; or the wearer of a registered garment). None of these types of statements identify any particular feature, which may be because the novelty lies in the overall appearance, or because applicants hold similar concerns as under the old Act. Even though the provisions of section 19 now expressly attach clear advantages to filing Statements, it remains to be seen whether they will prove to have much impact.

[Individual features] That *particular* regard is to be had to features identified in a Statement of Newness and Distinctiveness; that if the features identified relate only to part of the design, *particular* regard must be had to that part; and that if only part of a design is substantially similar to the registered design, that part's size, quality and importance must be considered are all elements that combine to strengthen the hand of the registered owner where a specific feature or part only has been copied, either in a situation where other parts of a design are not reproduced, or in a situation where the rest of the design is commonplace. This position must then be reconciled with two tendencies flowing from section 19 which counteract special attention to specific parts or aspects only of a design: first, that similarity in *overall impression* is the overarching test; and secondly, that section 19 (3) provides that in the absence of a Statement of Newness and Distinctiveness, regard must be had to the appearance of the design 'as a whole'. It is also provided that if the Statement concerns features that relate only to part of the design, although particular regard should be had to those features, this should be 'in the context of the design as a whole' (see section 19 (2) (b) (ii)). It is not clear what real assistance all this provides to a decision-maker ultimately needing to resolve whether there is sufficient similarity *in overall impression*. However, it seems clear enough that, first, in the presence of a Statement identifying particular features that relate to part of the design only, the test of overall similarity is tempered by the decision-maker being encouraged to give somewhat more weight to similarity in the parts identified. Secondly, in the absence of a meaningful Statement, the decision-maker must have regard to the design as a whole, but if only parts of the designs are similar, then must turn their mind to the significance of that part. In other words, where the decision-maker has doubts about overall similarity, the plaintiff may still get across the line, by showing that the parts that are similar are both innovative and a significant part of the design as a whole, in terms of quantity and quality. Hence the impact of the requirement of similarity in overall impression is somewhat tempered where similarity rather lies in a significant part or parts only. The statutory terminology adds up to multifarious and complex guidance; it is unclear how much it will really assist the decision-maker's mental process of comparison. It remains to be seen how section 19 will be interpreted by the courts, but the legislator's intention of strengthening the registered owner's hand might have been just as effectively achieved by simply resting with the rule that more weight should be given to similarities than to differences, possibly combined with a provision that if differences between an impugned design and a registered design were less than those between the registered design and the prior art, infringement should be found.

[General approach] Because a finding of 'fraudulent imitation' under the old Act depended on establishing copying, information about access to the registered design, and about the process of, and influential factors in the creation of the impugned design, was usually in evidence. Under the present Act, this type of evidence, although arguably usefully informing and contextualising a decision about infringement, is no longer relevant. The evidentiary process will shift to a more patent-like, rather than copyright-like approach: how to characterise the informed user, what would the informed user know, what would their overall impression be; and also, the making of the registered design: how does it relate to the prior art, how was the designer constrained by use and function, etc. The question whether there was copying, or knowledge and intention, however, remains relevant in terms of remedies, as it was under the old Act. The court may refuse or, an innovation in the present Act, reduce an award of damages, or refuse to make an order for an account of profits, if the infringer was not aware the design was registered and had taken all reasonable steps to ascertain whether a monopoly in the design existed (section 32B old Act; section 75 present Act). This places a relatively high onus on the defendant, compared to patents law, where it is sufficient for the defendant to establish that there was no reason to believe a patent existed (see section 123 *Patents Act 1990*). But the provision of a public register that all parties can readily access (also now online), and that is relatively simple to consult, lies at the core of designs law, so inspecting the register could normally be regarded as a 'reasonable step' for any person in business.

[Spare parts] As indicated above, registration of spare parts, or 'component parts' of a 'complex product' caused controversy in the lead-up to the introduction of the present Act. The ALRC proposed a 'procedure for referral of potentially anti-competitive designs to the TPC' (see ALRC Report No 74, Recommendation 165), in particular for component parts of durable complex products. But the government opted neither to exclude component parts, nor to impose any special restrictions on their registration; however, the universally higher threshold test of novelty and distinctiveness should prevent registrations of some must-match and must-fit components that might have proceeded under the old Act. Nonetheless, the government has tempered the potentially malign monopolisation of downstream markets for spare parts by introducing a 'repair defence' (section 72 of the present Act. No such defence existed under the old Act). The repair defence applies if a product embodying a registered design is 'used' (as statutorily defined) without the authorisation of the registered design owner, in repairing a complex product so as to restore its overall appearance in whole or in part. The core requirements are that there must be a 'repair', and that the overall appearance must be 'restored' by it. As pointed out in the Explanatory Memorandum, at [107]:

> However, this subclause does not provide a defence against infringement where the use of a component part embodying a design results in the enhancement of the appearance of the complex product. This approach preserves the incentive to innovate by allowing all designs of component parts of complex products to be registered if they meet the innovation threshold, without introducing any risk of subsequent anti-competitive behaviour. This enables original component parts to be protected, while the same or substantially similar component parts may be used for repairs without the risk of infringement.

[The details of the repair defence] The ordinary meaning of the term 'use' is extended by virtue of section 72 (5) to include making, selling, importing, etc as well as actually using a component part to make a repair to a complex product. By virtue of the same sub-section, repair of a complex product includes *replacing* a part, but only where the part being replaced is either damaged or decayed, or the replacement happens in the course of maintenance, or is incidental to restoring or replacing a damaged or decayed component part. So if a part is replaced without it being worn or broken, in the absence of a genuine 'repair' the defence does not operate. The defence is only available if the repair *restores the overall appearance*, either in whole or in part, of the complex product. Thus if the component part enhances, or changes the appearance of the complex product, the defence does not apply in relation to a registered design embodied in the part so used, even if a damaged or decayed part is replaced in the process. For instance, if the wheel hubs on a new car are later replaced with different hubs (eg more sporty or striking ones) then no spare parts defence will defeat the owner of a registered design in the new replacement hub or cap, as long as the overall appearance of the car is judged to be materially different after the replacement.

In other words, enhancements, add-ons, and replacement parts that modify the overall appearance of the complex product are not covered. A repair is to be taken to have restored the overall appearance *as a whole*, if there is no material difference between the appearance of the complex product immediately before and after the repair (see section 17 (3)). It is to be taken to have restored the overall appearance *in part*, if any material difference is 'solely attributable to the fact that only part of the complex product has been repaired' (ibid.). For instance, if a single door panel of an old and generally battered car was repaired by installing a brand-new replacement panel, then the difference in overall appearance of the car as a whole after the repair would be solely due to the fact that one panel looked new compared to the rest of the car. To judge whether the overall appearance has been restored or materially affected, the standard of the 'informed user' is to be applied, ie the standard of a person who is familiar with the complex product, or with products of that sort. The 'informed user' is a concept familiar from the novelty test (see above under Novelty).

As indicated before, the repair defence is available where the replacement part does not restore the appearance of a complex product as a whole, but only does so in part. Presumably this means that the appearance of the area of a complex product immediately surrounding the replacement part will have to be restored. For instance, if the spare part is required to replace a damaged control switch on the dashboard of a car, the defence would be available if the overall appearance of the dashboard is not materially altered by the replacement part. However, reference to the overall appearance becomes more difficult when functional parts – which can be registered as designs in Australia – are considered, for instance, a brake pad or rotor: what then is the part of the overall product to which one must have regard?

[Who will benefit from the repair defence?] The provisions will potentially benefit suppliers of replacement parts, but not suppliers of enhancements: for instance, the owner of the registered design in a spoiler fitted to a new car will encounter the defence if another party makes and installs a replacement spoiler after an accident. However, the owner of a registered design in an enhancement spoiler, such as a car owner might 'retro-fit' to a previously acquired car, will not be affected by the repair defence. The extent to which the legitimate purposes can be imputed to a manufacturer of components is a difficult issue. If authorised to make and supply a component part by a repairer there is no difficulty; but what is the situation in the absence of such authorisation? If they make a component that can only be used to replace another part and restore the overall appearance (eg a must-match car panel), is the making of the spare part covered by the defence even though there is no specific authorisation from the ultimate repairer? Whatever the case may be, the Explanatory Memorandum states that the onus is on the registered design owner to prove that a spare part is not being made, supplied or used for repair purposes; further (at [108–109]):

> To place the onus on the suppliers or manufacturers of spare parts would act as a disincentive for new participants to enter the spare parts market. It would force suppliers and manufacturers of spare parts to track their entire inventory to see whether they all are being used for genuine repair purposes. Nevertheless, if suppliers or manufacturers are knowingly participating in using parts for non-repair purposes, or should have reasonably known that they are doing so, then they should not be able to hide behind the right of repair defence.

[Comparative issues concerning spare parts and monopolies] By contrast with the new spare parts provisions in the *Designs Act*, in copyright the question of a spare parts exception is not settled by statute law, but must if at all be based on general principles of contract and property law. So in cases where copyright *can* be relied upon (ie where the overlap provisions do not operate to provide a defence to copyright infringement: see further below Copyright–designs overlap), copyright provides rights broader in scope (as discussed above; see also Gummow J in *Interlego* (see above)) but also not limited by a statutory repair defence. The fair use doctrine does not extend to accommodate a spare parts exception as it does not conform to any of the statutory purposes (see section 40ff of the *Copyright Act 1968*), and nothing equivalent to the exceptions applying to reverse engineering in computer program copyright (see further below, Chapter five) applies to other subject matter under the *Copyright Act*.

It is thus to the doubtful authority of *British Leyland Motor Corporation Ltd v Armstrong Patents Co Ltd* [1986] AC 577, *Solar Thomson Engineering Co Ltd v Barton* [1977] RPC 537 and *Canon v Green Cartridge* [1997] 3 WLR 13 that one has to turn. The question in those cases was whether a right to repair one's property should or could extend to the right to make a new spare part, and extend further to others who might supply the market for spare parts. As is pointed out by Lord Hoffman in *Canon v Green Cartridge* (at 18–19): 'But in practical terms, the "right to repair" could be of value only if other people could manufacture copy exhausts which the motorist could acquire "in an unrestricted market"'. The Privy Council in *Green Cartridge* was obviously not enthusiastic about the approach taken in *British Leyland,* by either Lord Bridge or Lord Templeman, based on either an implied licence analogy or a non-derogation from grant of property rights theory. Yet they did continue to apply the principles propounded in *British Leyland*, however hard to fathom they found them, but which they thought based on either the analogy with the right to repair, or the stifling of competition arguments. Neither of those was at all convincing in relation to the right to supply replacement cartridges for photocopiers, and their Lordships were uneasy about whether a court of law was the appropriate venue for this sort of competition analysis, and the amendment by judicial fiat of the copyright laws that it implied. But *British Leyland,* despite the criticism, was not overturned.

3 The copyright–designs overlap

[General policy] Even though (particular) regard must sometimes be had to part only of a registered design (see the discussion above, in section 2, Individual features), the determinative test of infringement concerning a non-identical design is still substantial similarity in overall impression. In the context of copyright, the infringement test, ie reproduction of a 'substantial part', has a potentially wider scope than the test 'substantially similar in overall impression' in designs law. Taking only a single feature may amount to reproduction, if it is a 'substantial part' of the source work, even if the overall appearance of the impugned product is not similar. And furthermore, arguably the scope of protection in terms of substantial similarity *overall* is also broader under copyright than under designs law, even under the present Act. Copyright presents other advantages to an innovator policing free-riding: automatic subsistence means no registration is required and thus no expenses are incurred. Also, copyright is not at risk of failure because of non-compliance with technical rules, or because of the stringent novelty requirement: all that is required is that the work has not been copied. The term of copyright protection is also much longer (life of the author plus 70 years vs maximum 10 years from filing). However, copyright is subject to evidentiary difficulties in terms of ownership and object of rights that designs do not suffer because of the effect of the Register. It should be noted that, unlike in some other jurisdictions such as the US and the UK, voluntary registration of copyright is not possible in Australia. Such a system allows the issue of demarcation and ownership of copyright to be at least partially addressed. A further potential disadvantage of copyright is the fact that access needs to be established to prove copyright infringement, ie that the right is not monopolistic in nature. However, this is of limited importance because the resemblance required between registered and impugned design is usually so close that copying can be inferred anyway. Under the old Act the two regimes were even closer in this regard, because the category of fraudulent imitation required proof of copying. On balance, if given a free choice a firm might well choose to rely on copyright. In other cases, it might do so simply because it was ignorant or negligent in relation to obtaining designs registration – and use copyright as a default option. However, statutory policy in Australia does not allow a free choice: it prevents either reliance on copyright or dual protection in relation to imitation of manufactured products – ie in relation to innovation in product design *in industry*.

From a public policy perspective designs registration offers the advantage of certain demarcation and clarity about rights, and easy verification of other firms' entitlements – something unregistered rights do not allow. Its narrower scope and clearer demarcation is also appropriate to the industrial context with its incremental and constrained innovation and change. For firms, this means that generally speaking they are compelled by the law (sections 74ff of the *Copyright Act*) to rely on designs registration to protect themselves against imitation of their manufactured goods. If a design is not registered, copyright will only be available in relation to limited categories of copyright materials excepted from the operation of the overlap provisions, such as works of artistic craftsmanship (see below).

[How the policy is put into effect] The policy of restricting access to copyright remedies in industry is put into effect in the form of a defence against infringement of copyright by way of manufacturing products embodying artistic works (see section 74ff of the *Copyright Act*). In other words, where the defence applies, an owner of copyright in either underlying 2D artistic works – drawings primarily – or relevant 3D works – sculptures and engravings (see above) – cannot obtain a remedy against another person who makes or sells a product which either directly or indirectly reproduces his 3D work, or the underlying 2D work. Some significant exceptions do apply, and the provisions have undergone some tweaking over time. The innovator whose product is being imitated either will have registered a design, in which case whatever remedies available under that regime can be pursued; or else will be left without a remedy, unless the copyright material falls within one of the excepted categories. Unsurprisingly where the defence is raised, litigants will try hard to find ways around it. This is particularly so where as here the defence itself is subject to significant exceptions – in other words, there are a number of situations in which a litigant *can* continue to rely on the underlying copyright in a work incorporated in an industrial product. Gummow J gives a good historical account of the overlap provisions and how developments in copyright and designs law gave rise to them in *Interlego AG v Croner Trading Pty Ltd* (1992) 11 ALR 577 at 582ff. The overlap provisions in the *Copyright Act* were most recently amended upon the introduction of the new *Designs Act 2003*, but the substance of their operation was not changed. Commentary below addresses the provisions as amended.

[More detail concerning the overlap provisions] As indicated in the previous paragraph, the general defence is subject to significant limitations and exceptions. First, the defence only applies if the features of *shape and configuration* (ie the three-dimensional features) of a product embody an artistic work; in other words, it does not apply where an artistic work is simply reproduced on the surface of a product. For instance, the defence will operate if a product constitutes a three-dimensional reproduction of technical drawings; or if it reproduces a model which is a sculpture under the Act. But if the product simply has a 2D artistic work flatly reproduced on its surface, for instance a drawing on the outside of a coffee mug, copyright remains available for a plaintiff seeking redress against an alleged imitator of the mug, *unless* a design for the mug including the 2D work has been registered. The new provisions, introduced to coincide with the new *Designs Act 2003*, clarify when an artistic work is deemed to be embodied in a product, as opposed to merely being reproduced on the surface of a product. 'Embody' is given an expansive meaning, in that it includes woven into, impressed on or worked into the product (section 74 (2)). So if an artistic work is simply applied to a flat surface, there is no product embodying the work, and copyright rights are not limited by the defence. As the Explanatory Memorandum points out:

> a 'corresponding design' can include artistic works exploited in products such as tapestries, knitted items and carpets. The amendments therefore clarify the circumstances where copyright protection will be lost and design registration would be necessary for a corresponding design to receive statutory protection.[31]

[When a corresponding design is registered] When a design is registered for a product that embodies an artistic work the *Copyright Act* cannot be relied upon in relation to an unauthorised reproduction of the product (section 75). This rule prevents dual or alternative protection, and it applies in relation to all artistic works, including buildings and works of artistic craftsmanship (which are otherwise exempted from the operation of the overlap provisions in cases of 'industrial application'; see below). However, it does not apply if the registered design does not embody the artistic work, but merely has an artistic work applied to its surface (see above): in such cases dual protection is available. Fixed buildings or structures are not considered products and for that reason are not registrable as designs. Hence they remain protected by copyright, either as such or on the basis of copyright in underlying house-plans or models, despite the definition of 'corresponding design' in section 74 (1); in other words, a plan or model reproduced as an actual building does not constitute a corresponding design because its visual features are not embodied in a 'product' – the last limb of the definition of 'corresponding design' is simply not applicable. Buildings can only be registered as designs if they are removable or kit-based, and such buildings, once registered, will lose copyright protection in the sense described above.

In truth reliance on copyright is restricted, not just when a design is registered, but in accordance with section 77, when a complete specification that discloses a product made to the corresponding design is first published in Australia; or a representation of a product made to the corresponding design and included in a design application is first published in Australia (section 77 (2) (b), (c)). Section 75 refers to registration of a design, not certification, so the design will not necessarily have been examined for novelty, and may in fact be uncertifiable. If a design is not registered or refused certification for lack of novelty, or for some other reason was not capable of registration under the present Act, then copyright will still be lost if the relevant artistic work was 'industrially applied' (see section 77).

[Industrial application] Designers might find it attractive, given the restrictions on copyright remedies upon registration of a design, to forgo designs

---
[31] See Designs (Consequential Amendments) Bill 2002, Explanatory Memorandum.

registration altogether. But as indicated above, the policy of the law is not only to prevent dual or alternative protection, but also to prevent reliance on copyright if a corresponding product has not been registered but has been industrially manufactured. In other words, it is not open to act against free-riding on the basis of artistic copyright in underlying plans or drawings, or in a three-dimensional artistic work such as a sculpture or engraving, where a product is designed for industrial production or manufacture. This aspect of the policy is put into effect by section 77 of the *Copyright Act*. As the Explanatory Memorandum puts it: 'The provision provides a defence to copyright infringement where another person reproduces the artistic work in three-dimensional form when applying a corresponding design to a product'.[32] As indicated above, if artistic works constitute features of pattern or ornamentation applied to the surface of a product, the operation of copyright is without limitation. Section 77 provides that when a design is not registered, or is not registrable, but a product incorporating the design is or has been produced (or 'applied' industrially, what is referred to in the Explanatory Memorandum as 'mass produced'), and is sold, let for hire or offered or exposed for sale or hire, whether in Australia or elsewhere, the protection of copyright is lost in the same manner as would be the case if the design were registered, and that from the moment of the first sale, etc. By virtue of Regulation 17 of the Copyright Regulations 1969 a design is taken to have been industrially applied when more than 50 products embodying the design are produced (although the regulations still use the old terminology of applying designs to articles), or the product is produced in regular lengths or pieces, unless, in the latter case, they are hand-made products. However, the regulation is not exhaustive in this respect, and the court in *Kevlacat* held that manufacture of a product (a large one: a yacht) could be in fewer copies and still amount to the industrial application of an artistic work.[33] As indicated above, a result equivalent to industrial application follows from the inclusion of artistic works as representations in a patent or design application, from the date of the publication of the specification or application. In other words, the same defence against copyright infringement will be available from that time, in relation to the reproduction of the representations included in either specification or application. Such inclusion is deemed to be equivalent to an industrial application (see section 77 (1A)).

[Unregistrable designs] Whether a corresponding design (ie a product embodying an artistic work) is capable of being registered as a design or not does not matter: if it is 'industrially applied', the defence will operate. Any doubt about the question before the 2003 amendments has been laid to rest by section 74 (1). Most commonly a design may be incapable of registration because it lacks novelty (eg it has been publicly exploited prior to the lodging of an application for registration). In such cases the effect of this part of the provisions is fair and in fact essential to the integrity of the system as a whole – otherwise simply publishing

---

[32] Ibid.
[33] See *Kevlacat Pty Ltd v Trailcraft Marine Pty Ltd* (1987) 11 IPR 77.

the design would avoid the operation of the overlap provisions. However, products that cannot be registered as designs because of their exclusion by operation of the Designs Regulations continue to enjoy copyright protection: see section 77 (3). Such items were previously excluded by regulation by virtue of section 17 (2) of the *Designs Act 1906*, as items that were 'primarily literary or artistic in character'. But many items listed in the regulations consisted of two-dimensional artistic works applied to the surface of an article and, from the introduction of the *Copyright Amendment Act 1989* (Cth) (see section 10 of that Act), had escaped the effect of the overlap provisions in any case.

In the present Act, the reference to works of primarily literary and artistic character has been subsumed within by a general regulatory power to prescribe certain designs (see section 43 (1) (a)). Excluded by the Designs Regulations 2004, reg 4.06 are medals, scandalous designs, and a number of official or currency-related representations. If an application concerning a design has been refused by virtue of this regulation, then this fact is conclusive that the design is not capable of registration under the regulation, at least if no appeal has been allowed or was pending before the commencement of proceedings in copyright infringement (see section 77 (3)). If this is not the case then it shall presumably be a matter for the defendant to prove, since the question arises in the context of a defence to copyright infringement.

[Designs not capable of registration for other reasons] The consequences that flow from a design not being capable of registration for a reason other than anticipation or regulatory exclusion vary. If it is because it does not concern a 'product', for instance a fixed building, the defence will not operate (see also above). But where a product does not fall within the definition of a registrable design, for instance in the rare case where the shape of the product is exclusively determined by its function,[34] the overlap provisions will operate under the present Act. In such a case a plaintiff is – seemingly unfairly – entirely deprived of a remedy, no registration being available and a copyright action being defeated by the defence. Nonetheless the opposite solution, ie a design unregistrable because of pure functionality benefiting from full copyright protection, is also somewhat unsatisfactory, because it is exactly those kinds of very functional items which are inappropriate for copyright protection. After all, as Gummow J points out in *Interlego* (at 598), the appropriate starting point is: '[. . .] that authors who intended to use works for multiplication by an industrial process should not receive in full the extensive rights now to be given by the copyright law, particularly in respect of three dimensional reproduction of drawings, for a lengthy period'. Gummow J pointed out that historical amendments to copyright law that had expanded the rights of the copyright owner to include reproduction in all material forms and in all dimensions were ultimately the source of the difficulty that copyright, by way of drawings as artistic works (and later also by way of expansive interpretation

---

[34] Eg as discussed in *Hosakawa Micron Pty Ltd v Michael Fortune* (1991) AIPC 90-754/97 ALR 615 26 FCR 393/19 IPR 531.

of certain three-dimensional artistic works), entered the field of industrial manufacturing or mass production.

[Exclusions from the 'industrial application' provision] By virtue of section 77 (1) (a), buildings, models of buildings and works of artistic craftsmanship are excluded from the operation of the overlap provisions, in respect of industrial application. In other words, even if such works are industrially applied, copyright will continue to operate to its full extent. Both buildings and works of artistic craftsmanship are hybrids of a sort: industrial, but not truly 'manufactured', even though multiple exemplars of one design may in the end be produced. Architecture has long been a core area of copyright law, and fixed buildings have always been excluded from designs registration – they are not considered 'products' that are mass produced by manufacturing. Works of artistic craftsmanship straddle the fence between copyright and designs because they combine artistic intent and craftsmanship with utility. In other words, rather than pure art, a work of artistic craftsmanship is a useful thing such as a chair or pot, but not normally manufactured in factories by mass reproduction of identical copies. Copyright therefore continues to apply to them. In fact the category of 'works of artistic craftsmanship' in the *Copyright Act* might have been condemned to obscurity were it not for the overlap provisions: most will also qualify as a different category of artistic work, or be based on 2D works. But as is wont to happen, because categorisation as such permits a copyright remedy to be obtained, litigants have sought to extend the boundaries of the category beyond what the initiators of the arts and crafts movement might have had in contemplation. Because the effect of the overlap provisions can be severe, leaving parties with no remedy at all where they have failed to register a design, litigation concerning the provisions, and then, in particular, about categorisation of a work as something that escapes their operation, is relatively common.

[Buildings and models of buildings] The excision of buildings from the operation of the overlap provisions is limited by section 77 (5) which provides that a 'building or model of a building does not include a portable building such as a shed, a pre-constructed swimming pool, a demountable building or similar portable building'. In other words, traditional architecture relating to fixed buildings is excluded from the overlap provisions, whether reliant on copyright in underlying plans or in buildings or models of buildings as such. This is unsurprising: architecture is not an aspect of industrial design! In terms of the statutory approach, architecture is not concerned with 'products' under the present Act, or 'articles' in the sense of the *Designs Act 1906* (Cth). In *Re Concrete Ltd's Application* (1939) 57 RPC 121, Morton J held that the article to which the design is to be applied 'must be something which is to be delivered to the purchaser as a finished article'. Thus a fixed building structure (a concrete air-raid shelter) was not an article.

He did not, however, hold that a building or structure could *never* be an article. In *Re Christopher Russel John Hansly* (1988) AIPC 90-465, the Assistant Registrar of Designs held that the design of a building which was intended to be a fixed, not a portable structure, was not an article. But portable or movable structures *are* subject to the operation of the overlap provisions. The limitation of section 77 (5) or equivalent did not appear in the *Copyright Act* prior to the introduction of the present *Designs Act*; indeed it may seem superfluous, because it would require a movable structure to be a 'building' under the *Copyright Act* for section 77 (5) to be at all necessary. But precisely that had in fact previously – rather permissively – been held: in *Kruhse Enterprises* (see above) a fibreglass pool shell was a 'building', and a plug used in the manufacture of such a shell, a 'model of a building'. Such products then benefited from continued copyright protection even if mass produced, notwithstanding the fact that they could also be registered as designs, since they were movable: in *Tefex Pty Ltd v Bowler* (1981) 40 ALR 326, Rath J held that the plaintiff's fibreglass swimming pools which were sold either as fibreglass units or in kit form, but were not installed by the plaintiff, were 'articles'. Now, because of the operation of section 77 (5), only fixed buildings continue to enjoy copyright protection even when industrially applied (for instance, project homes). However, if such works are embodied in a design that is registered, the defence will operate by virtue of section 75, as with any other artistic work.

[*Kruhse Enterprises* after the introduction of the new provisions] The result of the express inclusion within the operation of the overlap provisions of portable buildings and the like is that cases such as *Kruhse Enterprises* (see above) are not likely to reoccur so frequently, as portable structures such as prefabricated fibreglass pools are now subject to the copyright defence of section 77. In that case it had been held that a building need not be a fixed structure, but that it could be a structure which was *intended* to be fixed and which could be removed, and that the expansive definition of buildings in section 10 of the *Copyright Act*, which expressly includes 'structures of any kind', could accommodate a fibreglass pool. It was also held in that case that the plug and mould fell within the terms 'model of a building', and so were also excluded from the operation of the overlap provisions. But as indicated above, copyright owners of such movable structures are, under the new Act, no longer able to benefit from the permissive construction of the terms 'building or a model of a building' in cases such as *Kruhse*. The exclusion of portable buildings in section 77 (5) is peculiar in its drafting in that it appears somewhat circular, but it is difficult to envisage it not catching every structure that could be held to be a building under the permissive approach in copyright but is prefabricated, manufactured elsewhere in preparation for installation on site, or is demountable. The term 'demountable' is not further defined, but presumably it means that the building can be removed by reducing it to remountable parts, and without destroying it in some manner. However, many sheds would not fall under this definition, and the requirement of demountability does not seem apt for such structures.

[Works of artistic craftsmanship] Works of artistic craftsmanship are the other artistic works excluded from the operation of the overlap provisions. The proper limits of this category of works have been somewhat controversial of late.[35] Drummond J's 1998 decision in *Coogi* revised arguably accepted learning, extending the category's boundaries, as is discussed further below.[36] Nonetheless the amendments to the overlap provisions in 2003 have left the exclusion untouched. The original incorporation of 'works of artistic craftsmanship' as copyright works resulted from the influence of the arts and crafts movement at the time of the passage of the 1911 UK *Copyright Act*. The rationale was that copyright should not be restricted to the fine arts – artistic expression for its own sake – but should also accommodate functional objects if their appearance was the result of an artistic process of creation or intent. Hence a level of artistic quality *is* required by the Act (see section 10) for such functional objects to attract copyright.

From that perspective it makes sense that such works remain within the realm of copyright, rather than being forced into the registered designs regime, which in Australia is neither universally concerned with artistic quality nor with craftsman-like as opposed to industrial production. The exception only applies to the objects themselves, and not to any plans or drawings for those objects; they like other artistic works do not have to display artistic quality, and remain subject to the operation of the overlap provisions. However, due to the nature of, and usual production processes for, arts and crafts, such underlying works are perhaps less likely to exist, since works of artistic craftsmanship are normally 'designed in the making'.

[The *Coogi* case] Prior to *Coogi* 'works of artistic craftsmanship' were commonly described as utilitarian objects with artistic merit, hand-made by a person who combined artistic intent with craft skill in the process of creation. But a careful examination of the case reports revealed less restrictive conditions to the court in *Coogi*, which courts in subsequent cases have also chosen to apply.[37] *Coogi* held that the craft skill and the artistic merit could emanate from separate persons; that the object need not be made by hand with traditional hand tools, but could be made with the aid of machines with any degree of sophistication and automation; and that although the artistic intent behind the creation was critically important, the artistic quality of the resulting object was also significant, the latter having to be assessed by the judge, whether or not with the help of experts in the relevant field. As a result a bolt or 'first run' of Coogi fabric produced on an industrial knitting machine amounted to a work of artistic craftsmanship. Probably the most controversial aspect of the decision, however, was that something that was only a constituent part (a bolt of fabric) of a finished product (a garment), was considered to be a work of artistic craftsmanship. However, every bolt of fabric, due to the particular method of textile manufacture of the plaintiff, was unique; in other words, further bolts of fabric were not simply identical copies of the bolt considered to be a work of artistic craftsmanship. That work

---

[35] See for instance Dan Hunter, 'The Curious Case of the Computer-created Fabric', 37 *Intellectual Property Forum*, 10–15 (1999).
[36] See *Coogi Australia Pty Ltd v Hysport International Pty Ltd* [1998] FCA 1059.
[37] See eg *Muscat v Le* [2003] FCA 1540; *Sheldon v Metrokane* [2004] FCA 19.

was not in that sense a prototype or model of a final product to be manufactured *en masse*. In other words, it is not the case that each prototype or model produced by a craftsman as an initial step in a manufacturing process will qualify as a work of artistic craftsmanship, a situation that would severely undermine the overlap provisions' intent. The fabric produced by the defendant, although similar in style and technique (bold colours in thickly textured layers), was for similar reasons not found to be a reproduction of the work of artistic craftsmanship either. Note that, in the alternative, a claim could be based on copyright vesting in a garment itself, as a 'work of artistic craftsmanship'; in that case the overlap provisions do not apply to afford a copyist a defence. Textiles are considered in more detail above.

[Artistic quality] One crucial distinguishing characteristic of a work of artistic craftsmanship is artistic quality; the other is that the article be 'crafted'. As to artistic quality, one would be tempted to require little more than that the appearance of the article not be entirely determined by function. Such a standard could readily be addressed by evidence. However, the Court in *Coogi* rejected this approach (at FCA p 11):

> But one thing is clear enough: the presence of non-functional features cannot be the test since, as Lord Simon observes in *Henscher* at 93B-C the anthesis [sic] between function and beauty is a false one, especially in the context of the Arts and Crafts Movement.

Rather the Court set a higher standard (see *Coogi* at FCA p 10):

> a work will qualify as one of artistic craftsmanship only if it has an element of real artistic, ie aesthetic quality, whether or not it is a utilitarian work.

On the other hand, relying again heavily on *Henscher* as all cases in this area do, the Court in *Coogi* also pointed out that (at FCA p 10):

> [...] the article need not have such a high level of aesthetic quality as to make it a work of fine art.

This certainly excludes articles whose appearance is entirely determined by function, but requires something else; unfortunately, what else is required is hard to predict – certainly a fine aesthetic sensibility is called for! The Court in *Coogi* also rejected the approach suggested by Laddie, Prescott and Vitoria[38] that it should be objectively ascertained whether the visual appearance of the article is such that at least some members of the public 'wish to acquire and retain [i]t "on special account" thereof'. This would be setting the threshold too high and in any case artistic quality and popularity with the average consumer are two different things. Instead *Coogi* upheld the proposition that the court itself must make the judgment, on the evidence before it, which can include expert evidence.

---

[38] Laddie, Prescott and Vitoria, *The modern law of Copyright and Designs*, 2nd edn, at 208, as quoted in *Coogi* at pp 10–11.

[The craft process] Crafts skills must also have been applied in making the work of artistic craftsmanship. Significant is that the work of artistic craftsmanship is authored *in the making*; in other words, if the article is made on the basis of pre-existing drawings and technical specifications by workers following instructions, then there will be no work of artistic craftsmanship. In any case such an article would arguably not be original and would thus not attract copyright in its own right, since it would be a copy of the underlying drawings. Prototypes and models made on the basis of drawings and technical specifications are thus excluded. However, if the article is created in the process of application and experimentation with a machine, not to a pre-existing design, then a work of artistic craftsmanship can result. As *Coogi* rightly points out, the sophistication of machines used, whether traditional hand tools or programmed electrical devices, matters not; what is required is 'pride in sound workmanship' (*Coogi* at p 11) and exercise of skill in using the materials and the implements or machines employed. Further, the creator must have the intention to make something that is not merely pleasing to the eye or attractive, but represents his or her artistic concept or idea. In other words, a process not merely focussed on finding an appearance that is pleasing to consumers and that is in synch with current design trends and consumer expectations. In *Coogi* a fine line was drawn, but it was arguably drawn correctly; on balance the Court found that Coogi did have copyright in the first embodiment of the author's skill and labour, ie 'in that portion of the first roll of fabric produced by it in which the XYZ design was first completely embodied'. This constituted a work of artistic craftsmanship, but all other lengths produced to the same design were not. However, the Court in *Coogi* drew a further inference from its conclusion that nothing should turn on the nature of the tool or machine used (FAC at 11–12):

> Once it is accepted, as I think it should be, that 'works of artistic craftsmanship' are not confined to hand-made objects, there is no reason why it should be essential for such a work to be the product of a single person, ie of an artist-craftsman. It is enough that it satisfies the two criteria of craftsmanship and aesthetic quality.

Sound as all this may seem, one is left to question whether the result is consonant with the views of Morris, the father of the arts and crafts movement, which according to Rushton were 'that a factory cannot produce art, and that the aim of art is to enrich life for both the buyer and the creator, [. . .]'.[39]

[Sheldon v Metrokane] In *Metrokane* (see above), which concerned a new 'Rabbit' corkscrew design, the Court had to deal with some of the implications flowing from *Coogi*, in particular the finding that machine tools are a legitimate part of art and craft. The Court also found that there was an absence of consensus in cases prior to *Coogi*, so it adopted the *Coogi* approach. It accepted

---

[39] See Rushton M, 'An Economic Approach to Copyright in Works of Artistic Craftsmanship' [2001] *Intellectual Property Quarterly* 3, 255–74; see also Hansmann H and M Santilli, 'Authors' and artists' moral rights: A comparative legal and economic analysis' (1997) 26 *J Legal Stud* 95; and Denicola R, 'Freedom to Copy' (1999) 108 *Yale L. J.* 1661, p 1671 (as quoted in Rushton).

that it was legitimate to look at the first corkscrew produced rather than at the prototypes, which had been lost and could not therefore be produced in evidence, and ask whether that first corkscrew manufactured was a work of artistic craftsmanship. But the alleged author was not much concerned with or involved in the supervision of the initial manufacturing. What contribution he did make did not amount to a contribution of skill and labour to the production of the work itself sufficient to make him, rather than unidentified workers in the Chinese factory, into an author. The Court accepted that the workers in China could be craftsmen and thus authors; however, the designer who was rarely present there was not – he did not contribute sufficient craftsmanship. Significant is that the author of an underlying design, for instance expressed in technical drawings, is not thereby an author of the work of artistic craftsmanship: for that, a practical involvement in the actual making of the article, contributing both skill and the implementation of the author's own artistic concept, is required.

In other words, the process of making the first article in accordance with drawings, etc and technical specifications supplied by a designer will not amount to authoring a work of artistic craftsmanship. In such circumstances, the work will constitute a non-original reproduction of underlying artistic works; or alternatively, the worker(s) have not made an authorial contribution to the making of the article – they did not contribute skill and originality of expression. This point disposed of the case but the Court nonetheless went on to consider whether the resulting product had the necessary aesthetic qualities – which task was undertaken by reference to expert evidence concerning the design of the Rabbit corkscrew. In the event the Court placed more emphasis on the intention behind the creation than on the aesthetic or artistic merits of the result. It found that the intentions of the company behind the creation of the corkscrew were not to create a work of artistic craftsmanship *per se*.

[What the defence applies to] Apart from not applying to certain kinds of artistic works, the extent of the defence is also limited: it does not apply to every act comprised in the copyright. At its heart it applies to the manufacturing of products that reproduce the artistic work: 'it is not an infringement of that copyright to reproduce the work by embodying that, or any other, corresponding design in a product' (sections 75 and 77 (2)). But the defence also applies in terms of section 77A, which was introduced to overcome the kind of problem exposed by the result in *Muscat v Le* (see above). In the process of copying and then manufacturing a product that embodies an artistic work, the copyist will commonly generate artistic works such as technical drawings and patterns, moulds and dies which themselves will constitute indirect copies of the underlying artistic works of a plaintiff. In the absence of section 77A, the plaintiff, although barred from complaining about the reproduction of his works in the product itself, could still sue for infringement of copyright in the shape of the various preliminary works. Section 77A blocks this route by providing that the production of casts and moulds or other intermediate artistic works such as drawings does not constitute an infringement if the product they are used in making itself enjoys the protection of sections 75 and 77. The details and implications of this provision are usefully analysed by Rothnie.[40]

---

[40] See Rothnie W, 'The vexed problem of Copyright/Designs overlap' (2005) *Intellectual Property Forum* 60, 33 (see also above).

5

Sui generis regimes and trade mark registration

Introduction

[The contents of this chapter] Chapters one to four considered various legal regimes that are technology-neutral; ie whose subject matter is not limited to a specified technology or product. The majority of intellectual property law is of this nature, promulgating abstract standards that apply to a wide range of products and processes, innovations and technologies to determine whether they are entitled to some form of legal protection. However, two regimes are technology-specific: layouts of integrated circuits are the subject matter of the *Circuit Layouts Act 1989* (Cth) and plant varieties are covered by the *Plant Breeder's Rights Act 1994* (Cth); these regimes are known as *sui generis*, in that they are tailored to a specific product.

The emergence of computer programs triggered a debate on the adequacy and suitability of existing technology-neutral regimes, and the option of crafting a new special regime; but ultimately the alternative of adapting the rules of copyright to accommodate computer programs prevailed. Nonetheless, since computer programs are *functional*, unlike any other copyright subject matter, statutory rules and judicial approaches have since been adapted, so that computer program copyright has developed into a '*sui generis* system within a system'. This is one reason for covering the topic here, but this also permits comparing computer program copyright with software patents, the other available option. After initial resistance, over time the suitability of patent protection has become accepted, so software patents are now more common. Computer programs are central to the functionality of computers, but so are computer 'chips' or integrated circuits. Their emergence resulted in a different form of legal protection: that of a *sui generis* statutory regime with copyright-like characteristics but also divergent rules. As well as these technology-specific regimes, this chapter examines the possibility of obtaining some protection for new products by way of a remedy for harm to reputation, and for consumer deception, ie the extent to which passing off but more relevantly trade marks registration can allow new product shapes to be monopolised. Recent changes to trade marks law allowing the registration of product shapes as trade marks have created considerable interest in this option, although as we shall see, the real protection that can be so obtained is quite limited.

[Technology-neutral vs *sui generis* regimes] Technology-neutral protection regimes have obvious advantages: no recurrent amendment of the regulatory framework is required to accommodate unavoidable changes in technology and innovation. Rather than by frequent modification of the regulatory mechanism, the necessary adaptability is achieved by flexible decision-making within broad standards or tests. The various technology-neutral regimes have adapted well to changes in science and technology over time. Nonetheless some entirely new departures in technology or radical innovations are not easily accommodated within their existing regulatory framework. The reason for this may simply be that the subject matter is not of a kind that warrants legal protection; but in other cases new technologies or products expose genuine gaps in an existing regime which, in the interests of consistency, should be filled by extending coverage analogously within the existing framework. Technology-specific regimes, on the other hand, suffer from inflexibility and multiplicity (ie many different regimes or statutes will be required). Such multiplicity of protection regimes increases transaction costs because of users' knowledge deficit when confronted with variable new regimes. But *sui generis* regimes have the advantage of precision – ie of accurately tailoring regulatory structures to the subject matter and to policy requirements. In other words, such regimes can be more responsive to the specific nature of a technology and also of an industry; it is also easier to so avoid redundant regulation.

[The two *sui generis* regimes] The introduction of the existing two *sui generis* schemes, for circuit layouts and for plant varieties, resulted from the perception that the coverage of general regimes fell short, and was also inappropriate or ill-adapted to the subject matter. This could be dealt with by amending existing regimes, but that risks inconsistency and subversion of established principles. In the case of circuit layouts, the microscopic nature of the circuitry makes it ineligible for designs registration – and in any case the appearance of the layout is irrelevant: the nature of the circuitry is relevant to functionality. Computer chips that incorporate an inventive product or process could always be patented, but advances in functionality such as operating speed are more a matter of incremental capacity growth and adaptations in manufacturing than of fundamental breakthroughs. This model of innovation, not so much based on inventiveness but rather on systematic research and gradual capacity growth within known parameters, requiring considerable investment and technical skill, is something that chips and plant varieties have in common. New plant varieties, as they are developed by the systematic application of commonly shared techniques of cross-breeding, are both expensive to produce, not inventive to a patent law standard, and easy to replicate. For both, the costs of development are high, the imitation threshold low, and the technology-neutral rule structures not accommodating, hence the introduction of *sui generis* regimes. Furthermore, even though the regimes are technology-specific, they relate to subject matter that is not so narrow as to preclude continuous and significant variation and improvement. In the case of integrated circuits, the WIPO Washington Treaty on Intellectual Property in Respect of Integrated Circuits, 26 May 1989 provided the multilateral impetus for the introduction of circuit layouts legislation in Australia. The international instrument in relation to plant variety rights is the International Convention for the Protection of New Varieties of Plants, commonly referred to as UPOV. However, UPOV does not mandate domestic protection. Article 27.3 (b) of WTO/TRIPS, on the other hand, provides that member countries can exclude plant varieties from patent protection, as long as a *sui generis* form of protection is available. Australia has not adopted the option of excluding plant varieties from patent protection, and hence either a plant breeder's right (PBR) or a patent is in theory available for a new plant. The different threshold requirements and strategic issues will determine what a firm decides to opt for.

[Computer programs: a *sui generis* scheme within copyright?] When computer programs arrived on the scene, judicial decisions and legal commentary around the world called into doubt the suitability of both copyright *and* patents. Nonetheless, rather than a *sui generis* solution, adapting copyright developed as the global norm. The *Apple* decision[1] in Australia held that computer programs in digital form (object code) did not constitute a literary work or other subject matter under the *Copyright Act* – they afford no instruction or literary enjoyment. At the same time, computer programs, being mathematical or reliant on mathematical algorithms, were also thought to be unsuitable for patenting; courts in the United States took this view, and it was accepted around the world. Misguided as this probably was in retrospect, it was only with the decision in *International Business Machines Corporation v Smith, Commissioner of Patents* (1992) AIPC 90-853 that the Australian patent office approach was modified to permit software inventions to be patented here. Arguably it is in the patents sphere that computer programs belong, since they are *functional* subject matter: as the definition in the *Copyright Act* says, they are intended to make a computer perform in a certain way. This lies at the heart of the conceptual and practical problems resulting from inclusion of computer programs in copyright, as the High Court said: 'difficulties . . . arise from accommodating computer technology protection to principles of copyright . . . but the Act now expressly requires such an accommodation'.[2] All other works serve the goal of providing information or enjoyment, not of operating or controlling a machine. In terms of infringement, that means that copyright cannot be called upon to appropriate functionality – only

---

[1] *Apple Computer Inc v Computer Edge Pty Ltd* (1984) 1 FCR 549; 53 ALR 225.
[2] *Data Access Corp v Powerflex Services Pty Ltd* [1999] HCA 49 (30 September 1999) at HCA 25; (1999) 73 ALJR 1435.

the form of literary expression. By analogy, copyright in a recipe does not confer any exclusive right on its author to make the dish; and copyright in a computer program does not confer an exclusive right to cause a computer to function in a certain way. A person who achieves the same functionality but with a computer program with different code does not infringe copyright, even if their ideas are derived from a source program's functionality, look and feel or operation. Hence the modern interest in the alternative option of patent protection, and acceptance that software belongs to an economic field of endeavour as required by *National Research Development Corporation v Commissioner of Patents* (1959) 102 CLR 252 at 275–77. But that option is subject to high threshold requirements of novelty and inventiveness, administrative costs and bureaucratic impediments.

[Is copyright not enough?] But, as raised in Chapter one, a more fundamental underlying issue is whether or when the incentive of a patent monopoly is essential to encourage innovation in software development. It may be that copyright, with its narrower scope and limited as it is to an anti-copying right, is better adapted to provide the level and kind of incentive required. There appears to be little evidence that in the era before software patents there was a dearth of innovation in the software sector; in fact there is evidence of very rapid substitution of new software solutions. In an industry with many dispersed independent actors, an increased risk of innocent infringement because of others' monopoly rights has a potential chilling effect. It will also be difficult to effectively research and determine novelty and inventiveness. Furthermore, in an industry with network effects, there are considerable first mover advantages, which result in high barriers to entry; patents in such an environment may simply be superfluous, and the success of 'open source' is telling in this regard.

[Computer programs and circuit layouts] Whereas computer programs were initially accommodated in copyright, circuit layouts were not – a *sui generis* regime was preferred. However, the nature of this regime is close to copyright: a non-registration system with automatic subsistence, anti-copying rather than monopoly rights, and with a term calculated from making or first exploitation rather than from filing. However, there is a significant difference in relation to exceptions, which are more extensive and specifically tailored to the subject matter. Nonetheless, the inclusion of computer programs in copyright also necessitated the subsequent introduction of tailored exceptions. These address issues rather analogous to those arising in the circuit layouts regime, principally concerned with the problem of reverse engineering. All intellectual property regimes tend to favour the diffusion of ideas, information and data, while restricting their use in specific ways to provide creators some return on their investment and intellectual effort. Thus in copyright, reading a book is not an act comprised in the exclusive rights of the copyright owner, nor is extracting and using ideas or information from it. In patents, the exclusive rights are subject to an obligation to publish details of the invention from which anybody can learn, as long as they do not do or make that which the patentee claims. The main difficulty with computer programs is that such programs in binary form are incomprehensible – the underlying ideas, be it programming styles or solutions, architecture or structure, can only be revealed to a programmer by reverse engineering or decompiling it – a form of reproduction of the work which a programmer, in the absence of special exceptions, is not entitled to engage in without the agreement of the copyright owner! This problem gives rise to the exceptions in sections 47ABff of the *Copyright Act* and sections 20ff of the *Circuit Layouts Act*. In the context of the latter, certain actions that would otherwise impinge on exclusive rights are allowed for the purpose of obtaining information concerning the eligible layout for study and further development.

[The incidental relevance of reputation] The *sui generis* regimes discussed above all have in common that they provide exclusive rights in a product or process *per se*. But this chapter also considers how the legal protection of reputation or goodwill may be relevant to a firm seeking to use the law to appropriate some of the returns flowing from product innovation; in other words, seeking to restrain imitation of new product appearance. This admittedly both relies on a wholly different conceptual approach, and as will be seen, is only possible in rather limited circumstances. It is quite obvious that the tort of passing off (and section 52 of the *Trade Practices Act*) and trade marks registration are not aimed at or structured for the purpose of monopolising the appearance of some new product, or preventing free-riding. If they do it at all they therefore do it incidentally, and to a limited extent. Nonetheless the ability to register the shape of a product as a trade mark has galvanised firms and advisers into considering the advantages that might flow from goodwill protection in relation to product designs, and also to 'push the envelope' to take advantage of what opportunities the law may offer. The changes in registered trade marks law have also drawn attention to the potential of passing off in this regard, but as passing off only protects established reputation, it is of scant relevance to *new* products. To achieve some form of monopolisation of product shape via reputation, the main requirement is that consumers see a certain product shape as serving the purpose of distinguishing the goods coming from one trader from those coming from another, and that it actually does so. This is rarely the case, because consumers tend to see *new* product shapes as either offering some functional advantage or being aesthetically pleasing or both – not as distinctive badges of origin. But the possibility is worth some further investigation, as undertaken below, in relation to registered trade marks.

1 Computers

[Matters considered in this section] This section considers three issues; although all are connected to computers each is different in character. First, computer program copyright: the subsistence and infringement of copyright in computer programs is addressed, including so-called 'look and feel' cases, taking into account the specific statutory defences and exceptions, and the evolution in judicial approach. The relevance of computer program copyright to computer games and video games is also considered, which requires some exploration also of other relevant areas, in particular film copyright. Secondly, the patenting of computer programs is considered, in the context of computer-implemented inventions in general. In particular the issues concerning patentability and relevant distinctions with copyright in computer programs are rehearsed in this section. And thirdly, the circuit layouts regime will be reviewed in general outline, while also exploring the relationship with copyright and with designs registration.

Computer program copyright

[The statutory definition] As indicated above, section 10 (as amended by the *Copyright Amendment (Digital Agenda) Act 2000* (Cth)) now extends the meaning of 'literary work' to include computer programs, further defined as 'a set of statements or instructions to be used directly or indirectly in a computer to bring about a certain result'. At the core of the definition lies functionality: it is their 'use to bring about a certain result in a computer' that distinguishes programs from ordinary literary works. Other provisions make it clear that copyright subsists irrespective of the form of the computer program, in source or in object code, visible or invisible, and also of the programming language in which it is expressed. This overcomes the difficulty confronted in *Apple* (see above). But although a computer program is defined in terms of its function, the exclusive rights in a computer program do not extend to functionality, only to the form of 'literary' expression, ie of expression in a programming language or notation – a matter further explored below. It is not required that a computer program is to be used to operate what is traditionally known as a computer, eg a PC, laptop or mainframe. If code is used in the operation of some other machine with digital capabilities, such as an automated knitting machine, it is also a computer program under the Act.[3] A computer program need not consist exclusively of commands; it may be accompanied by or closely integrated with data – for instance, the look-up table in *Autodesk Inc v Dyason (No 2)* [1993] 176 CLR 300, or the knitting patterns in *Coogi*. The present statutory definition refers to 'statements or instructions', and as Gaudron J put it in *Autodesk* at 329, in words relating to the pre-amendment definition but still applicable: 'it is, in my view, clear that that expression directs attention to an entire instruction or, more accurately, an entire set of instructions, and not merely those parts that consist of bare commands'; and further, data could be integral to a computer program because 'in many cases it will be necessary for instructions to be accompanied by related information if those devices are to perform quite ordinary computer functions'. This does not detract from the fact that statements or instructions are only a computer program if they serve to operate a computer. An important distinction must thus be maintained,

---

[3] See *Coogi Australia Pty Ltd v Hysport International Pty Ltd* [1998] FCA 1059 (2 August 1998).

between on the one hand a 'set of statements' to be used to operate a computer, and on the other hand statements, simply stored or created on a computer, that are *not* to be so used. The latter are literary works, but in the traditional sense: for instance, texts that provide information or literary enjoyment.

[Circumscribing a computer program] Software ranges from short sequences of code to large complex programs, consisting of multiple, relatively integrated and interdependent parts, maybe forming suites or packages. At one end of the spectrum lies the question of when statements or instructions amount to a 'set'. In *Data Access* the High Court held that single reserved words of a computer language did not amount to a 'set' of instructions and were thus not a computer program.[4] At the other end of the spectrum lies the question of whether a constellation of statements or instructions amounts to one single program or a compilation of separate computer programs. It may be important to determine where an individual computer program in the statutory sense begins and ends, as this can have a significant impact in determining whether a 'substantial part' has been reproduced. Because quality rather than quantity determines what is a 'substantial part', even if a large but commonplace or unoriginal part of a program is copied there will ordinarily be no infringement. However, the Court in *Accounting Systems 2000 (Developments) Pty Ltd v CCH Australia Ltd* (1993) 42 FCR 470; 114 ALR 355 accepted that it may be appropriate to *infer* that when a large proportion is taken a qualitatively, not just quantitatively important part must have been reproduced. But a proportion of what? This is a matter of fact and depends on all the circumstances, but that a set of statements or instructions is functionally separate will go some way towards establishing that it is a computer program in its own right.

[Infringement of computer program copyright] An allegation of software copyright infringement will generally be framed either in terms of copying actual code sequences or in terms of copying program structure or 'architecture'. Where only a fraction of the actual code has been literally reproduced the question arises: does that fraction amount to a substantial part? This was essentially the question at issue in *Autodesk* (see above), which concerned the security features of an AUTOCAD package. The High Court held that a part of a computer program was substantial in the copyright sense if it was an 'essential' or a 'critical' part. In circumventing the AUTOCAD hardware lock, the defendant Dyason had only reproduced the look-up table, a minuscule part of the Autodesk program. But because the whole package would not operate without the responses generated by the look-up table, it was essential and thus a substantial part of the program. Pumfrey J in the later UK case *Cantor Fitzgerald International v Tradition (UK) Ltd* [2000] RPC 95 pointed out that this approach is problematical (at [75]): 'It seems to me, with all respect, that this reasoning would result in any part of any computer program being substantial since without any part the program would not work, or at best not work as desired. It seems to me with all respect

---

[4] See *Data Access Corp v Powerflex Services Pty Ltd* [1999] HCA 49 at [28]; 73 ALJR 1435, 166 ALR 228.

that such an approach is simplistic'. Rather, in determining whether some small part was substantial in copyright terms, given that copyright protects the skill and labour expended by an author: '... a copyist infringes if he appropriates a part of the work upon which a substantial part of the author's skill and labour was expended', or, in other words, 'it is necessary to look at the substantiality of the skill and labour expended on that which is taken'. This approach was then adopted in *Data Access*, the High Court reversing *Autodesk* (at ALJR 1450; ALR 248). The best approach to ascertain what were material features of a program was to have regard to the originality of those parts (at ALJR 1450–1; ALR 249):

> ... that being so, a person who does no more than reproduce those parts of a program which are 'data' or 'related information' and which are irrelevant to its structure, choice of commands and combination and sequencing of commands will be unlikely to have reproduced a substantial part of the computer program. We say 'unlikely' and not 'impossible' because it is conceivable that the data, considered alone, could be sufficiently original to be a substantial part of the computer program.

['Look and feel' of a computer program] Where the allegation is that the overall structure or architecture of a program rather than actual code has been reproduced, a different approach is called for, somewhat analogous to dramatic work infringement. These are the so-called 'look and feel' cases (eg the *Cantor Fitzgerald* case mentioned above) because the result of imitation at the structural level may be that the interface and attendant functionality of a computer program (its 'look and feel') are rather alike, without the underlying code sequences being the same. Pumfrey J in *Cantor Fitzgerald* certainly accepted that structure, compilation or architecture of a program was an element of expression, rather than underlying idea or functionality, and therefore attracted copyright. In *Ibcos Computers Ltd v Barclays Mercantile Highland Finance Ltd* (1994) 21 FSR 275; (1994) 29 IPR 25 functions which it was common ground would have to be carried out by any relevant system had been allocated between various programs, and Jacob J accepted copyright subsisted in the 'compilation of (the plaintiff's) programs' (at FSR 289, IPR 38). In *Data Access*, the Court said that: 'The structure of what was allegedly taken, its choice of commands, and its combination and sequencing of commands, when compared, at the same level of abstraction, with the original, would all be relevant to ... determining whether a substantial part was reproduced'.

However, there are some important reservations concerning this approach: first, where the similarity lies at the level of architecture or structure, one must determine whether that is due to copying or to some other reason, for instance, because of the consistent programming style of the author of both programs, as alleged in *Cantor Fitzgerald*. In other words, similarity at that level of abstraction may not be a sufficient basis to infer access and copying: separate evidence may be required. Secondly, if similarity lies at too high a level of abstraction, the danger is that copyright strays into functionality: thus in *Admar Computers*

Pty Ltd v Ezy Systems Pty Ltd (1997) 38 IPR 659; [1997] AIPC ¶39–644, the plaintiff attempted to use 'pseudocode' analysis to prove reproduction of structure and programming logic. But pseudocode being an abstraction of the functionality of a program, similar pseudocodes could easily result from similar functions. Pseudocode analysis was therefore inappropriate and instead, when looking at structural design features, courts should be held to 'analysing the contents and arrangement within the four corners of the literary work' (at IPR 670; AIPC 39,653). Maintaining the line between function and expression lies at the heart of Dawson J's warning in *Autodesk* (see above, at CLR 344; ALJR 238):

> Indeed, the significance placed by Northrop J [the trial judge in the case] upon the function of the two locks would appear to be in disregard of the traditional dichotomy in the law of copyright between an idea and the expression of an idea.

[A unique approach to infringement in computer program cases?] That computer programs are functional (or as Mason CJ said in *Autodesk* at 305, are means to an end rather than ends in themselves) creates unique complexities in the infringement context. The 'but for' test adopted by the majority in *Autodesk* (but for a certain code sequence the program would not operate, therefore that sequence is a substantial part) had evolved from the established copyright method of determining whether something was a substantial part by asking whether it was an 'essential' or 'material' part of the work as a whole. But as indicated above this test was rejected in *Data Access* because it perversely results in virtually any and every part of a computer program being 'substantial' – instead regard had to be had to the originality of the part taken. This prompted the following comment from the Full Federal Court in *Tamawood Limited v Henley Arch Pty Ltd* [2004] FCAFC 78 (31 March 2004) at [54]:

> We do not accept Tamawood's submission that in *Data Access* the High Court intended to lay down a new test of 'substantial part'. *Autodesk* and *Data Access* concerned computer programs. Every digit in a computer program is essential to the successful operation of the program. The High Court was concerned in those cases to reject the notion that this meant that every such part also necessarily constituted a substantial part of a computer program regarded as a literary work for copyright purposes. [. . .]

In other words, where the test for substantiality in relation to other works may fix on how significant, material or important a part is in the context of the overall work, or to the appreciation of that work, in the context of computer programs this approach may have perverse results. Instead the focus should therefore be on the originality of the part reproduced only, in the sense of the degree of authorial skill and labour comprised in its expression. In *Data Access*, Gleeson CJ, McHugh, Gummow and Hayne JJ put it as follows (at [85]): '. . . the originality of what was allegedly taken from a computer program must be assessed with respect to the originality with which it expresses [the] algorithmic or logical relationship or part thereof'. Or to put it in the rather ingenious but roundabout way Mason CJ did in *Autodesk*, whether a part is material or significant in the context of computer programs depends on the level of its originality.

[Reverse engineering] The 'copyright conundrum' in relation to computer programs is that a person cannot ascertain how a computer program works (other than by observing what it does), unless source code is made publicly available; and that is not normally done. Even operating a program causes reproduction (in RAM), and although there may be an implied or express (and now statutory, see below) licence to so reproduce it for its intended purpose, such authorisation may not extend to reproduction in the course of operating it for the purpose of detecting its underlying characteristics. Furthermore, the only way to gain access to underlying ideas, information, data, structure or architecture, freely accessible in any other copyright work, is by decompilation or disassembly, necessarily involving reproduction or adaptation in the statutory sense. After all, by virtue of section 21 (5):

> For the purposes of this Act, a computer program is taken to have been reproduced if: (a) an object code version of the program is derived from the program in source code by any process, including compilation; or (b) a source code version of the program is derived from the program in object code by any process, including decompilation; and any such version is taken to be a reproduction of the program.

Note also that the copyright owner has the exclusive right to make an adaptation of a computer program, and by virtue of section 10:

> 'adaptation' means: . . . (ba) in relation to a literary work being a computer program – a version of the work (whether or not in the language, code or notation in which the work was originally expressed) not being a reproduction of the work.

But the difficulties experienced are not restricted to the perhaps rather theoretical attenuation of the traditional idea/expression dichotomy; they also extend to the significant practical and economic issue of interoperability. How constraining, in the absence of specific statutory exceptions, the law is in this regard is apparent from one aspect of *Data Access* (see above; this case predates the statutory exceptions discussed below). The Dataflex software contained a Huffman compression table, an original literary work as a 'table' stored on a computer. The impugned program, PFXplus, required the default Huffman compression table to be replicated so that Dataflex files could be compressed and decompressed by PFXplus. The author of PFXplus, carefully avoiding decompiling Dataflex, instead used complex steps to obtain the required copy of the table. However, as the High Court pointed out (at HCA [124]; ALJR 1455–6):

> The fact that Dr Bennett used an ingenious method of determining the bit string assigned to each character does not make the output of such a process any less a 'reproduction' than if Dr Bennett had sat down with a print-out of the table and copy-typed it into the PFXplus program.

The Court went on to say (at HCA [125]; ALJR 1456):

> The finding that the respondents infringed the appellant's copyright in the Huffman table embedded in the Dataflex program may well have considerable practical consequences. [. . .], it may also have wider ramifications for anyone who seeks to produce a computer program that is compatible with a program produced by others. These are, however, matters that can be resolved only by the legislature reconsidering and, if it thinks it necessary or desirable, rewriting the whole of the provisions that deal with copyright in computer programs.

To some limited degree only, the concerns expressed by the High Court are addressed by the *Copyright Amendment (Computer Programs) Act 1999* (Cth) and the further amendments in the *Copyright Amendment (Digital Agenda) Act 2000* (Cth).

[Statutory exceptions for certain reproductions of computer programs] In fact the provisions introduced in 1999 and amended in 2000 do not establish a broad reverse engineering or interoperability exception – they are very specific and circumscribed, in a manner analogous to the other fair dealing sections. By virtue of section 47B (1) (a), the reproduction of a program 'made in the course of running a copy of the program for the purposes for which the program was designed' does not infringe. Section 47B (3) extends this somewhat by providing that where copies are made in the course of ordinary operation of a computer program *for studying underlying ideas or function* no infringement occurs either. However, section 47D probably has the greatest intended practical impact, as it permits a legitimate owner or licensee to reproduce or adapt a program for the purpose of obtaining information necessary to enable the *independent* making of another program or article, to connect or be used together with, or interoperate with the original or any other program. The interoperability exception only applies if the information required was not previously readily available (see section 47D (1) (e)) and only to an extent reasonably necessary to obtain the information and produce the interoperable program (see section 47D (1) (c) and (d)). The provision is manifestly limited in scope, which attracted criticism from the IPCRC; by making just the relevant parts of the code reasonably available the copyright owner avoids its operation.

[Computer programs and computer games] As said above, by virtue of section 47B (1) (a) reproduction of a *computer program* in the course of normal use does not constitute an infringement of copyright in that program. However, products rarely coincide with rights: many computer programs are incorporated or integrated with other copyright works or subject matter. Computer games are a commercially significant example of this. Burchett J in *Sega Enterprises Ltd v Galaxy Electronics Pty Ltd* (1996) 69 FCR 269 at 273–274 held *video* games (and by extension computer games) to be cine films under Part IV of the *Copyright Act*. The games incorporated moving images. The fact that, unlike a traditional film, they were interactive meant that the succession of images was to some extent determined by the player. But this was not an obstacle to them being films, because the video game could only develop in a finite number of ways, effectively predetermined by the maker. Burchett J's liberal approach was endorsed by a Full Federal Court (*Galaxy Electronics Pty Ltd v Sega Enterprises Ltd* (1997) 75 FCR 8). Computer games will often contain other components as well, such as copyright-protected films (see *Australian Video Retailers Association Ltd v Warner Home Video Pty Ltd* [2001] FCA 1719. If in the playing they are reproduced or copied *in a copyright sense*, then the user may be performing acts comprised in the copyright; if so the copyright owner's control would be considerably extended.

[Use as infringement] The question revolves around reproduction or copying in RAM. Two issues arise: does this constitute reproduction or copying in a form from which the copy can be reproduced; and secondly, does whatever is replicated in RAM amount to a reproduction or copy of a 'substantial part'? Whereas the reproduction of the computer program may fall under the exclusion of section 47B (1) (a), reproduction of associated subject matter does not fall within this exception. If the answer to both questions is yes, an exclusive right comprised in the copyright is potentially exercised whenever the product is used in the normal manner. The owner's exclusive rights would extend to every use, each implementation or exploitation of the process or method which triggers reproduction of associated works and subject matter in RAM. As to the first question, before the amendments to the *Copyright Act* by virtue of the Free Trade Agreement (USFTA) with the United States, the definition of 'copy' in Part IV of the Act included only material forms of storage from which the subject matter could in turn be reproduced. This presented obvious difficulties for reproduction in RAM which is by its nature ephemeral, temporary and not reproducible, as was recognised by the High Court in *Stevens v Kabushiki Kaisha Sony Computer Entertainment* [2005] HCA 58 (the 'modchip' case). However, the USFTA amendments have removed this requirement: see now section 10(5) and 10(6). This opens the way to every copy in RAM (other than of a computer program) being an act comprised in the copyright. However, a further issue remains: does the copy or reproduction in RAM constitute reproduction of a 'substantial part' of the work or subject matter? This question has not been definitively resolved, but the High Court in *Stevens* (see above, HCA at [65]) did not take issue with the trial judge's finding that a substantial part of the computer game was reproduced in RAM during play.

[Straying into the path of patents] Normally copyright limits rights to copying and does not extend to *implementation*, ie to use or exploitation; it is limited to expression and does not extend to function. Thus as indicated above, a recipe including instructions does not give the copyright owner the exclusive right to implement, apply or exploit the instructions and make the dish, only the right to copy them in material form as he expressed them. Similarly the expression (or if you like, precise description) of a computing process or method – whether in a source or object code, or any computer language – does not give the author the exclusive right to implement that kind of process. However, because of a quirk of technology using or exploiting a computer program necessarily involves reproduction in RAM of the program itself or associated works and subject matter, as explained above. If this amounts to reproduction in the copyright sense, then the copyright owner indirectly extends his control beyond traditional limits and into *exploitation* of the program. This effect is mitigated by the provisions of Part IVA in relation to computer programs, but not in relation to associated copyright material. In this way computer program copyright potentially strays into the sphere of patents, as a patent's purpose is exactly to give the patentee an exclusive right over the *exploitation* of the process that is a computer program. With this potentially broad scope of copyright law, what are the remaining attractions of the main alternative for computer program protection, ie patents law? One is in relation to computer programs not associated with other copyright material; another is avoiding the uncertainty of the extension of copyright to RAM reproductions; and a further is the fact that patent protection results in monopoly rights, rather than in the grant of a mere anti-copying right. Furthermore, while copyright might restrain direct derivation, it will not stop – apart from the reverse engineering conundrum – a competitor extracting the core ideas, functionalities, methods or process without infringing copyright.

Patents for computer programs

[When can a patent for a computer program be obtained?] So is a computer program patentable subject matter? In some jurisdictions, notably in Europe, the patenting of computer programs *as such* has been subject to express statutory limitations. Predictably enough this has resulted in the development and partial acceptance of various legal and drafting circumventions. Recent attempts to remove or reduce the scope of the limitation have been controversial and bitterly contested. In Australia the patentability principles expounded in *NRDC* (see above, Chapter three) must be applied: no special rules or limitations adhere to computer program inventions alone. As the *Patent Manual* points out:

> [T]he particular statement of this test, formulated in *CCOM v Jiejing*, for determining the patentability of computer software related inventions is whether there is: 'a mode or manner of achieving an end result which is an artificially created state of affairs of utility in the field of economic endeavour'.[5]

On the one hand, a pure mathematical formula or algorithm is clearly not patentable as such: it is a theoretical method not claimed to achieve some practical end. At the other end of the spectrum lie clearly patentable method patents such as that claimed in *IBM v Smith* (see above): the algorithm was an integral part of the practical process claimed, directed at improving the presentation of a curve on a computer screen. In the same way operational steps or methods to be performed on computers or machinery with some practical benefit are clearly

---

[5] *Patent Manual of Practice and Procedures*, 2.9.2.7.

patentable subject matter. More problematical is the patentability of an algorithm which calculates an end result in the shape of a figure, sum or amount, where 'real world values' are used and the resulting value has practical significance. The *Manual* (as above, ibid.) gives as a patentable example 'an applied algorithm or mathematical formula, eg a claim to a method of determining the length of a road (L) in metres by applying the formula: [the formula follows]'. The *Manual* distinguishes this from a clearly unpatentable theoretical formula: 'a pure mathematical formula (unapplied), eg a claim to a method of calculating a value c, where: $c = e^x \sin(t)$. Note: c, x, and t are pure variables with no defined significance to the real world'. There is some apparent inconsistency in this: the process of calculating the length of a road, presented as patentable, is not itself a practical, technological or scientific process that is applied in a physical sense at all. Even if what is intended to be described is the calculation method as incorporated in a computer program, this still does not give it that character. The result of the calculation may be able to be used in some practical way, but that practical method of use is not claimed. There is no *practical* process for solving a practical, real world, technological problem.

[Should programming solutions be patentable inventions?] Computer program patents are often referred to in the same breath as business method patents. However, a distinction must be drawn between computer processes and programs used in business; and patents that claim business methods, schemes, plans, etc. The core question is whether software such as accounting software, business administration software, financial software, etc is patentable subject matter; the question of business methods patents is better dealt with separately (as to that issue, see above Chapter three). At the core of the computer programs issue is whether coding, writing or software programming solutions should be patentable. The writing of code, or 'programming', is a practical art – code is not written to be read but to be used in a computer, so in theory there may not be much of a 'suitability' problem in terms of *NRDC*. One is reminded here of the words of the High Court: computer programs seem 'to have more in common with the subject matter of a patent than a copyright'.[6] But there are obviously *other* validity issues with allowing programming solutions to be patented: if common languages and techniques are used, inventiveness may be lacking in most cases. Novelty, ie whether programming codes or sequences have been published or publicly used, will be very difficult to ascertain. Thus patent examiners will often be ignorant of anticipations, allowing ultimately invalid patents onto the books, with potentially chilling effects on competition. An inefficient impost on business may result, certainly in circumstances where there is no evidence of a dearth of innovation or development in computer programming. Copyright, on the other hand, arguably presents a more balanced solution: inadvertent infringement is

---

[6] *Data Access Corp v Powerflex Services Pty Ltd* (1999) AIPC 91-514; [1999] HCA 49 (30 September 1999) at [20].

not possible, copying being required, and thus programmers working independently are not at risk (procedures to avoid copying are commonly deployed by programmers). Under patents law there is no interoperability exception, so that the potentially monopolistic effect of patent grant can spread into secondary markets for application software – not a desirable effect. If a technical standard is patented, then anti-competitive effects become even more marked.

Furthermore, programming solutions are not the kind of technical inventions which require considerable investment in practical experimentation, R&D infrastructure and the like which are put at risk by independent invention. Software itself is also easy to manufacture and reproduce, so patent protection is not required for significant investment in manufacturing capacity. Developers also have a readily available user infrastructure: computers in business and community are widespread and readily available. Development can easily be carried out in secret. There are thus strong arguments against programming steps or sequences being patentable; as well, it is arguable that patents protection is not appropriate for pure calculus software programs, even if the result calculated can afterwards be put to practical use. Widespread adherence to the open-source software movement demonstrates that a significant sector of industry can get along without proprietary solutions in relation to software anyway – cooperation trumping competition as a more efficient way of building a software infrastructure for common use.

Circuit layouts

[Microprocessors before the *CLA*] Microprocessors lie at the heart of the digital revolution, and increases in processing speeds underpin efficiency gains in all branches of business and industry. Innovation in design and layout of the circuitry incorporated in a microprocessor (a 'computer chip', or 'semiconductor chip') requires capital investment and intellectual know-how. However, prior to the introduction of the tailored regime of the *Circuit Layouts Act 1989* (Cth) computer chips were not readily accommodated by existing IP regimes. The layout could not be registered as a design, since its appearance was not visible to the unaided eye, as was then required by the *Designs Act 1906* (Cth) (see above, Chapter four). Patents were and continue to be potentially relevant, but each new advance in layout design, while it may result in increased processing speed, does not necessarily involve an inventive step embodied in the computer chip (rather than perhaps in manufacturing methods). Nonetheless, an inventive product or processes incorporated in a microprocessor could always attract a standard patent. Petty patents were of no greater utility than standard patents when microprocessor protection first became an issue, since they required the same level of inventiveness. Innovation patents, which recently replaced petty patents, require only an innovative step (ie a substantial contribution to the working of the invention; see Chapter three, above), so they may be more applicable. Copyright may well subsist in the development drawings, 2D layouts or manufacturing specifications as artistic works, theoretically offering some avenues of protection, as does copyright in a computer program incorporated in a microprocessor. However, the copyright–designs overlap provisions present a potential hurdle to the enforcement of artistic work copyright, and even if copyright did apply, the concept of reproduction is not well adapted to this subject matter, certainly if it is from a 2D plan to a 3D layout. Computer program copyright was a doubtful proposition before it was expressly included in 1984; and under the *CLA*, reliance on copyright in computer programs embodied in a processor is restricted (see below).

[The essential nature of *CLA* protection] The US Congress introduced a *sui generis* protection scheme by virtue of the *Semiconductor Chip Protection Act 1984*. The subsequently concluded WIPO Washington Treaty on Intellectual Property in Respect of Integrated Circuits, 26 May 1989, mirrored that *sui generis* model. Protection is now required by virtue of article 35–38 of TRIPS/WTO. Australia introduced legislation based on the Washington Treaty: the *Circuit Layouts Act 1989* (Cth) (the *CLA*), providing formality-free, copyright-style, limited term protection for 'eligible layouts'. Essentially the *CLA* introduced an anti-piracy regime for microprocessors. It has copyright characteristics, but is more analogous with Part IV protection for subject matter other than works, than with protection for artistic works in Part III: rights vest in makers, not authors, the term of protection is calculated from making or first exploitation, and the exclusive right is to 'copy' rather than to 'reproduce'. In this sense the solution for circuit layouts differs markedly from the approach to computer programs, ie inclusion in Part III as literary works. With the introduction of a special regime, design registration of a layout covered by the *CLA* was expressly excluded, as continues to be the case under the *Designs Act 2003* (Cth) (see section 43 (1) (c) (i)). The exclusion from designs registration also has the effect of precluding reliance on copyright in underlying 2D artistic works (sometimes described as a 'plan' of a layout). Any other result would be perverse; in any case, the *CLA*, as well as protecting actual microprocessors against copying, expressly provides rights in underlying 2D plans. In *Centronics Systems Pty Ltd v Nintendo Co Ltd* (1992) 39 FCR 147 at 147–8; 111 ALR 13 at 15–16, Northrop J offered the following 'precis' of the system:

> [The *Circuit Layouts Act*] creates rights in the nature of intellectual property rights and which are described as EL [eligible layout] rights. The Act contains many technical expressions, but in essence EL rights are rights conferred on the owner of an original circuit layout which can be described as the drawing of a plan, in a material form, for an integrated circuit, the purpose of which is to perform an electronic function and being a circuit in which the active and passive elements, and any of the interconnections, are integrally formed in or on a piece of material. An integrated circuit is the device made in accordance with a circuit layout. Thus, there is a similarity between the drawings of a plan prepared by an architect for the construction of a building and a circuit layout prepared for the construction of an integrated circuit. The EL rights apply both to the circuit layout and to an integrated circuit made in accordance with the circuit layout. Integrated circuits form part of electronic equipment such as computers and electronic games.

[Layouts eligible for protection under the *CLA*] By virtue of section 5 of the *CLA* an 'eligible layout' is an original circuit layout, whose maker was at the time the layout was made an eligible person, or which was first commercially exploited in Australia or another eligible foreign country. Thus protection extends to subject matter that was neither made nor published in Australia, nor made by an Australian citizen or resident: a layout first put on the market in Japan or the US (eligible foreign countries, where most microprocessors are developed) will therefore be protected in Australia. This is an advantage obtained by foreign EL developers by virtue of the Washington Treaty's provisions. A circuit layout 'means a representation, fixed in any material form, of the three-dimensional location of the active and passive elements and interconnections making up an integrated circuit' (section 5). An EL must be original and in material form. 'Originality' here has a markedly different meaning from that concept in relation to works in Part III of the *Copyright Act*. Section 11 of the *CLA* provides that a circuit layout shall be taken *not* to be original if its making involved no creative contribution by the maker, or it was commonplace at the time it was made. In other words, a layout is taken to be original unless a defendant can demonstrate either that it was commonplace (a concept not further defined) or that no creativity was involved in its making.

[Exclusive rights under the *CLA*] The maker (and thus owner) of the eligible layout, is the person who first 'fixed it in material form', which includes making and storing it on a computer; if a computer is so used, the person who used the computer is considered the maker (see section 10). By virtue of section 16, the employer owns the EL if it is made in the course of employment. By virtue of section 17, the owner of the EL rights has, during the protection period (10 years from either making or first commercial exploitation), the following exclusive rights:

> a) to copy the layout, directly or indirectly, in a material form; b) to make an integrated circuit in accordance with the layout or a copy of the layout – an integrated circuit made in accordance with a layout includes an integrated circuit made in accordance with a substantial part of a layout: see s 13(c); c) to exploit the layout commercially in Australia.

In other words, anti-copying rights adhere both to underlying plans and to a microprocessor's circuitry as such; as to importation, by virtue of section 8 a circuit layout is taken to have been commercially exploited if an integrated circuit (a microprocessor) incorporating it is imported whether as such or incorporated in a product. However, various provisions of the Act mean that parallel importation of legitimate integrated circuits is permitted. Copyright in an incorporated computer program cannot be relied upon as an alternative to prevent importation; in any case the recent relaxation of parallel importation rights for computer programs under the *Copyright Act* has undermined the ability to rely on copyright to restrain parallel importation of computer programs, as of most other copyright material. The knowledge element required for liability by commercial exploitation (ie dealing in infringing copies, as opposed to copying) is dealt with in section 19 (3) and also section 20.[7] By virtue of section 27, damages are unavailable in certain cases of innocent infringement.

[Innocent commercial exploitation] A unique complicating factor in relation to circuit layouts is that a person acquiring or dealing in a complex product may be wholly unaware of the presence of a microprocessor, let alone of any issues related to the legitimacy of incorporated layouts. As the *CLA* provides automatic protection, there is no verifiable register. In that light *Nintendo* (see above) explains the legislative policy behind section 20, which relates to 'innocent commercial exploitation':

> ... to make special provision for circumstances in which it would be unjust to impose liability for infringement on a person who innocently acquires and subsequently deals with an unauthorised integrated circuit. One can readily envisage circumstances in which an ordinary person who innocently acquires, and subsequently commercially deals with, an item of electronic equipment would have no means of knowing or ascertaining that some concealed integrated circuit in the article was an unauthorised copy of an eligible circuit layout in which EL rights subsist.

Most purchasers of computer equipment would not be able to ascertain in accordance with which EL an integrated circuit incorporated in a machine was made. According to Christie,[8] *Nintendo* means that liability for unauthorised commercial exploitation follows only if the person knew or ought reasonably to have known who was the owner of the EL rights, and that that owner had not licensed the defendant to exploit the layout. This tends to take persons who deal in otherwise seemingly legitimate products incorporating microprocessors outside the sphere of potential liability.

[The exceptions regime] The exceptions and limitations regime for circuit layouts differs markedly from that in copyright; mostly its aim is to provide access to information embodied in protected chips which would otherwise be difficult to obtain legally, while preserving effective exclusive rights. Circuit layouts suffer from the same reverse engineering conundrum as computer programs: to learn anything about their composition, operation, structure, etc they need to be copied in a decompilation-type process. Therefore the *CLA* expressly permits copying for the purpose of 'evaluation and analysis' (see section 23). But furthermore, copying is also expressly permitted for 'research or teaching purposes' (section 22), 'private use' (section 21), and 'purposes of defence or security' (section 25). Section 23, which permits the making of a copy or copies of a layout for the purpose of evaluation and analysis, further provides that the making of an original circuit layout on the basis of the evaluation or analysis carried out with the use of the copy or copies of a layout does not constitute an infringement. There are clear parallels here with the provisions introduced by the *Copyright Amendment (Computer Programs) Act 1999* (Cth) relating to the reverse engineering conundrum

---

[7] See also *Nintendo Ltd v Centronics Systems Pty Ltd* (1994) 181 CLR 134; 68 ALJR 537.
[8] See Christie A, *Integrated Circuits and their Contents: International Protection*, LBC Information Services, Sydney, 1995, p 120.

inherent in copyright in computer programs (see *Copyright Act 1968* (Cth) section 47Bff; and above).

2 Plant varieties

Introduction

[The place of plants] The place of plants in the intellectual property firmament has evolved considerably over a relatively short time, from lying outside the realm of IPRs to being firmly ensconced within. Plant intellectual capital originally resided, and to an extent still does, with farmers using traditional methods based on observation and experience to select out plants and cross-breed. As Rangnekar points out, structures of cooperation and exchange between farmers in local areas dominated the improvement process.[9] The variable characteristics of seeds supplied to farmers by public or collective institutions undertaking plant improvement work was not necessarily seen as detrimental, since it was in close cooperation with farmers that seeds were selected out, improved and assimilated over time. But the advent of commercial breeders as additional seed suppliers resulted in greater emphasis on homogeneity and generational retention of genetic characteristics, which in turn supported farmers having to return to seed suppliers each season. As Rangnekar says (at 128):

> Not until the beginning of the twentieth century did breeding transform itself from craft to science by focusing on maintaining the genetic improvements achieved in parents through successive generations in the form of uniform pure lines. Plant breeders differentiated their activity from that of farmers by insisting that farmers return to breeders for fresh seeds after each harvest on the grounds that breeders were the only people capable of maintaining plant varieties at their true (genetic) potential.

This is reflected in the so-called DUS requirements (distinctiveness, uniformity and stability) which lie at the heart of plant variety protection, and are legitimised by UPOV (see further below). However, it is significant that a variety is assessed against the threshold DUS standards on the basis of its physical characteristics and not on the basis of its agronomic advantages. Therefore nothing in the system guarantees that a DUS variety will be any more efficient or productive for a farmer. The first wave of change wrought by the advent of commercial breeders who standardised traditional breeding techniques was later overhauled by innovation based on new technologies, in particular plant genetics. This enabled the development in new plant varieties of characteristics drawn from a potentially very wide gene pool, but genetic modification is neither a cheap and easy nor an inconsequential process; unlike with traditionally bred varieties, environmental and other regulatory issues become significant barriers.

[Farm-saved seeds] Seeds are primarily food, but saving and reusing seeds are also core farming practices: for both reasons there is resistance to unlimited

---

[9] See Rangnekar D, 'Technology paradigms and the Innovation-Appropriation interface: An Examination of the Nature and Scope of Plant Breeders' Rights' (1999) 17 *Prometheus* 2, 125.

property rights in seeds. The age-old practice of using farm-saved seeds for seasonal replanting has generally been preserved by the law, and UPOV allows member countries to exempt it. However, as it is often considered inimical to the interests of plant breeders because it removes the need for seasonal re-purchasing, the legal status of the exemption has come under sustained pressure. Breeders have also deployed technological and contractual means to disallow the practice. Patent protection with its far more absolute monopoly, with no farm-saved seed exception, is also an attractive alternative legal option, but more suited to genetically modified organisms (GMOs) than to traditionally bred plant varieties (PVs) which generally lack inventiveness.

[Plant breeder's rights (PBRs) and patents in Australia] Australia's position in relation to plant intellectual property is challenging. For export revenues Australian agriculture is dependent on local adaptation of foreign introduced varieties, some of which are relatively underdeveloped, while many are quite mature. Compared to these introduced high-volume varieties, relatively little research and development has been done on indigenous plants. Since cash crops for export are an important economic contributor, it makes sense to encourage domestic investment in the development of more productive varieties. The importance of attracting foreign transfers of improved plant varieties also supports a solid domestic protection regime. In recent times, in particular with the 2002 amendments to the *Plant Breeder's Rights Act,* the rights of PBR grantees have indeed been strengthened, but the system is still subject to traditional derogations. The most important of these are the farm-saved seed exemption and the breeding exemption. The former allows farmers to retain and use seeds produced by protected varieties for replanting in subsequent seasons; the latter allows a protected variety to be used in the development of further new varieties, mainly by cross-breeding. Compared to patenting of plants this adds up to a significantly less complete monopoly; but as well as reflecting traditional farming and breeding methods, the more limited PBR rights also match a lower threshold test for subsistence. Rather than having to prove an inventive step in the development of a new plant, as well as its utility, the grantee can obtain a PBR in a PV produced by thoroughly well-known methods, as long as it varies in one or more characteristics from previous varieties (see further below). Although the new variety must also be DUS, that alone does not guarantee that the variety is agronomically advantageous; in fact a new variety's utility need not be proven at all.

Plant patents are significantly harder to obtain, and whereas PBRs number in the thousands, plant patents are few and far between in Australia. Nonetheless the High Court in *Grain Pool of WA v The Commonwealth* [2000] HCA 14 had little difficulty in finding that PBR protection is analogous to patent protection and thus falls within the scope of the IP power in section 51 (xviii) of the Commonwealth Constitution. PBR protection clearly favours investment in the adaptive development of incremental additions to the stock of plant varieties, rather than fundamental research. Patenting, on the other hand, potentially stimulates research into gene-based and analogous methodologies of universal application, potentially resulting in considerable improvements to local varieties but also generating foreign currency flows from licensing local innovations abroad. By contrast, locally bred varieties are only rarely adapted to foreign markets sufficiently to generate PBR revenue flows from overseas – there is a better return from selling crops for food than from selling varieties for planting.

[The utility of PBR protection] The Advisory Council on Intellectual Property (ACIP) recently announced a 'Review of enforcement of Plant Breeder's Rights (PBR)', which demonstrates that ongoing concern exists about the effectiveness and viability of the PBR system. Alexandra, Lee & Vanclay[10] do not give the system the ringing endorsement the government reserves for it in the Explanatory Memorandum of the 2002 Amendment Bill. Having pointed out that empirical data are required to assess economic impact, ie whether the system has provided an additional stimulus resulting in the development of desirable new plant types, they say (at 55):

> [their own research] does provide reasons to be skeptical that [PBRs] are demonstrably superior to what would have been achieved under the previous system. With the possible exception of access to some overseas germplasm (and even this is not uncontroversial) most of the good consequences of the new system would have occurred under the old system, [. . .].

But ultimately, as the authors point out, international obligations (the UPOV Convention) leave Australia no real choice. The usefulness of the PBR system depends on the size and value of the market for specific crops and also on the extent of farm saving. As is pointed out by Alexandra et al (see above) the latter is itself dependent on the quantities of seed required and on generational retention of desirable agronomic characteristics such as disease resistance. The authors argue that the room for plant improvement and the need to change management techniques are also determining factors. Some kinds of plants are not suitable for PBRs, eg annuals, because they become so quickly obsolete. Although the number of plants that meet all these criteria may be relatively low, clearly PBR protection, reflecting traditional practices and adapted as it is to existing breeding techniques, has its place in local plant innovation.

Also very significant for plant-breeding firms, and favouring PBRs, certainly in Australia with its large-scale introduced cash crops, is access to a wide foreign gene pool. A strong PBR structure can encourage foreign inward transfers, but it also allows the introduced varieties to be used in the local breeding of new PVs, properly adapted to Australia's unique local conditions. However, although PBRs are generally useful to encourage improved cross-bred and traditionally bred varieties, there is a limit to the ability to continue to improve varieties by these methods. The patent regime can additionally serve to encourage plant improvements achieved by the introduction of genes from a far wider, non-variety-specific gene pool. From this perspective, Australia's approach of having both plant patenting and a relatively strong PBR system, which is not the universal norm, makes some sense. A further significant factor favouring plant patents is that a patent

---

[10] In Alexandra A, J Lee and F Vanclay, 'Innovation, exclusion and commodification of plant types: A social and philosophical investigation of Plant Variety Rights in Australia', (2004) *Rural Society*, 14, 1.

can be obtained over a method or process, eg used in genetic modification of a plant. The process patent then also extends exclusive rights to all the products resulting from the process, eg the resulting GMOs. Lawson presents a usefully wide-ranging analysis of the arguments concerning access to genetic diversity and the economics of plant IPRs.[11]

The *Plant Breeder's Rights Act 1994*

[Demarcation of subject matter] The PBR system is examination- and grant-based, and is administered by the Registrar of PBRs who maintains a Register of Plant Varieties. The subsistence requirements reflect the terms of the principal international instrument relating to plant varieties, the International Convention for the Protection of New Varieties of Plants, adopted in Paris in 1961 and revised in 1972, 1978 and 1991, and commonly referred to as the UPOV Convention. The subject matter of a PBR is any plant variety that is distinctive, uniform and stable (the DUS factors; see section 43 (1) (b)–(d)). Physical characteristics define a plant variety, and it must be distinguishable from all commonly known varieties by at least one of those characteristics. They must be heritable: the basic parameters of PBR-protected plant varieties are uniform characteristics stable across generations and across all plants within the variety; no heterogeneity is tolerated. A plant variety must not, or only recently, have been exploited, (see section 43 (1) (5) and (6); see below). As well as being DUS, a plant variety must also have a breeder; ie it must have been bred in the statutory sense. Breeding includes both selective propagation so as to enable the development of a new plant variety, and discovery (see section 5). Discovery cannot be present if the variety is commonly known. It is the breeder who is entitled to the PBR over the plant variety (see section 43 (a)); and for the plant variety to be 'discovered' the breeder has to come upon it independently rather than obtaining it from some other person. Selective propagation requires a comparison between the plant variety concerned and the parents or population from which it is developed, showing a clear difference in at least one characteristic. As an example, finding a mutant branch on a plant and propagating a variety from it would be an eligible form of breeding. PBR covers plants derived by any breeding technique, be it gene insertion (biotech breeders) or traditional methods. In December 2002 an Expert Panel convened by the Registrar of PBRs published a report *Clarification of Plant Breeding Issues under the Plant Breeder's Rights Act 1994* (the 2002 *Report*), which clarified issues related to the concepts of 'breeding' and 'essentially derived varieties' under the Act. The Report provides examples as well as explaining the various tests in an accessible manner.

[The novelty requirement] Novelty in the context of a PBR requires that the variety has not been sold (or 'exploited') in Australia before the application date (except recently: see sections 6–7C). In the case of *Sun World International Inc*

---

[11] See Lawson C, 'Patents and plant breeder's rights over plant genetic resources for food and agriculture' (2004) 32 *Federal Law Review* 107.

(Formerly Sun World Inc) v Registrar, Plant Breeder's Rights [1998] 1260 FCA quite minimal sales were held to be an 'exploitation', and it is clear that a grower cannot offer the variety for sale for the purpose of cultivation. However, the 2002 amendments have clarified the meaning of sales as excluding certain sales made in the process of development. The new variety must have a different characteristic in comparison with all varieties 'whose existence is a matter of common knowledge', and thus be distinct. As pointed out in the 2002 *Report* at [12]: 'In situations where the source population/parent is also the most similar variety of common knowledge, breeding and distinctiveness can be tested and satisfied simultaneously'. The onus is on the applicant to establish that a plant variety is different from some source population in which it was found, and they will have to provide, as part of the material description, particulars of distinguishing characteristics and also evidence of test growing having been carried out (see section 34). As the 2002 *Report* also points out:

> While at least one clear difference is required to qualify for protection, economic/aesthetic/performance/values are not, per se, relevant for PBR protection. PBR is primarily a registration scheme based on perceived 'physical difference(s)' (eg a morphological, phonological or physiological difference) that distinguishes the candidate variety from all others. The difference may result in characteristics that have no agronomic value relevant to the registration process.

[Scope of exclusive rights] Two core issues affect the scope of the exclusive rights to plant varieties protected by a PBR. First, the extent to which dealing with or using seeds lies within the monopoly of the grantee – this is dealt with in the next paragraph; and secondly, where the outer limits of the protected variety lie. Declaration of an Essentially Derived Variety (EDV) is the critical legal measure in relation to the second issue. It allows a line to be drawn between illegal copycat activity resulting in an EDV, and legitimate further breeding from a protected plant variety resulting in a different variety. The right to use a protected plant variety in further breeding is a core distinguishing aspect of plant variety rights protection. Section 4 provides that an EDV must be predominantly derived; have the same essential characteristics; and have no important (ie more than cosmetic) differentiating features. A PBR grantee can apply to the Registrar to have a certain variety declared an EDV. The 2002 *Report* explains:

> 'important' would probably be taken to denote significant changes that affect performance, value or place in the market. For example, purple anthers in wheat, which do not affect performance or value of the crop, might fall into the category of a cosmetic feature. [...] The current provisions of the *PBRA* regarding essential derivation go further than the relevant UPOV 1991 provisions by: 1. Defining 'essential characteristics' as 'heritable traits . . . that contribute to the principal features, performance or value of the variety' (see *PBRA* section 3(1)); 2. Requiring that important differences (more than cosmetic) must be demonstrated if the second variety is not to be regarded as an EDV; and 3. Stipulating that the PBR Office should make decisions in relation to a declaration that a variety is essentially derived.

Essentially the EDV test is in substance a novelty standard, although it actually arises in the context of infringement – ie in determining the scope of the PBR. Claims that a variety is an EDV can be defended by showing important differences between the two. The category of EDV may be quite narrow; as the 2002 Report points out:

> Real progress in plant innovation – which must be the goal of intellectual property rights – relies on access to the latest improvements and new variation. As a general rule, the easier the access, the more incremental breeding is promoted. Incremental breeding refers to the breeding of an unlimited series of new varieties with each subsequent variety being bred from, and relying heavily on, the characteristics of the previous varieties. The differences between the previous and subsequent variety can be large, small or very small, with the latter being the most common. [. . .] Any proposition to strengthen the first breeder's power by extending EDV to all incrementally bred varieties (and not just copies) would go to the fundamentals of the PBR system, with profound implications for the community of breeders, for consumers and for Australia's national interests. [. . .] In the context of PBR, incremental breeding is associated with 'freedom to operate' (more formally known as the 'breeder's exemption', or the 'research exemption'), which prescribes free access to PBR varieties (see *PBRA* section 16) for the purpose of research or breeding a new variety and, in virtually all (non EDV) cases, the commercialisation of that new variety.

[What is comprised within the exclusive rights of the grantee?] The term of the PBR is calculated from the day the grant in the plant variety is made, and varies from 25 years for vines and trees to 20 years for any other varieties. The grantee has the exclusive right to produce, reproduce or condition propagating material; and deal commercially in the material (see section 11). Prior to the 2002 amendments, section 18 exempted any dealing in the material for the purpose of food, etc, but with the decision in *Cultivaust Pty Ltd v Grain Pool Pty Ltd* [2005] FCAFC 223 (the *Franklin Barley* case) it became apparent that this had such a limiting effect as to potentially render the grantee's rights nugatory. Instead, section 23 now provides for the exhaustion of the grantee's rights, once he has sold the propagating material (seed), except for the right to further reproduce or to export the material.

[Farm-saved seeds] However, the grantee's right to further reproduce the material is attenuated by the farmer's exemption, which allows farmers to gather seed from plantings and re-use it for sowing: see section 17. But regard should be had to section 14, which extends the PBR to harvested material in circumstances where the grantee has not had a reasonable opportunity to exercise his rights. Furthermore, the farmer is not allowed to on-sell the farm-saved seed to other farmers, but breaches of the legislation in this regard are said to occur frequently because selling saved seed and exchanging it is a common farm practice (so-called brown-bagging). End-point royalty systems (which are dependent on contract rather than on the existence of a PBR, but are commonly associated with it) reduce the effect of farm practices on returns to the PBR grantee: it becomes easier to detect that a farmer selling a protected plant variety did not buy seed for it. The

1991 revision of UPOV made the use of farm-saved seed an optional exclusion, whereas previously it was a core aspect of plant variety protection. Under the European Community Plant Variety Rights system the farmer pays a royalty on saved seeds. The farm-saved seed exception has also had some arguably perverse effects, as it encourages innovators to develop techniques and technologies that stymie or prevent the re-use of plant varieties, such as terminator genes.

[Use of a protected plant variety in breeding] The patent system does not have a farm-saved seed exception, nor does the exception allowing use of the protected variety for breeding purposes have a patent equivalent (see section 16 *PBRA*). This way a PBR does not stand in the way of the continued improvement of plant varieties, effectively preserving a public domain of available lines. However, two concerns flow from the exception. The first is addressed above in relation to EDVs: essentially the same variety can masquerade as a variety in the derivation of which a protected variety has legally been used, but which is supposedly new. The other concern relates principally to genetic modifications: that using a successful protected variety and inserting some modifying gene will result in a variety which is legally new but takes unfair advantage of the development work that underlies the protected variety. However, this view is predicated on the insertion of new genetic traits being somehow both a simpler and a less worthwhile process than more traditional breeding techniques: this is not a universally accepted view. The exclusion of acts done 'for private, experimental or breeding purposes' (see section 16) is further supported by the requirement of reasonable public access to plant varieties covered by a PBR (see section 19).

[PBR and patent rules] There are clear differences between patent and PBR in terms of exemptions, as mentioned above – farm saving cannot be accommodated under patents law, nor can use for further cross-breeding: the licence of the patentee would be required (and may indeed be forthcoming). But there are also differences in scope, as explained by the 2002 *Report*, in the part 'Incremental Breeding, Benefit Sharing, Gene Patenting':

> [. . .] There is a view that favours extending the rights of the first breeder to cover the development and commercialisation of all incrementally bred varieties (as opposed to essentially derived varieties as defined under the Act), whether or not those varieties exhibit important differences. The Panel notes that this view, while bringing PBR more into line with patents, is fundamentally inconsistent with UPOV principles. The Panel understands that this push for benefit sharing across varieties derives from the perceived threat that 'biotech' breeding springs easily off 'traditional breeding' without recognising the true contribution of 'traditional', or first, breeders. It is also held that bio-technicians gain an unfair advantage when they insert patented genes into 'traditional' varieties. This is because the new gene inserted PBR registered variety may not be accessible for further research/development/commercialisation (because of patent considerations) while all other registered varieties without patent complications are available for further research/development/commercialisation. This situation is said to highlight the 'imbalance' of rights between PBR and patents. The real effects of this imbalance need to be verified before changes to the 'core' of the PBR system could be considered. The view of the Panel is that changes to EDV cannot resolve the

fundamental differences between patent and PBR principles. Patents give the capacity for almost total lockup of the invention while PBR gives free access. The wisdom of recreating those elements of the patent system that PBR was specifically designed to address, is questionable. While broad empowerment of the individual breeder, in terms of exclusive right over incrementally bred varieties, has the potential to bring patents and PBR more into line, it would not resolve the underlying fundamental differences, and such a move would be a major shift negating the checks and balances envisaged by Parliament in introducing the PBR system by moving the balance of power more in favour of the individual, and away from public-good interests, [. . .].

[PBR, CLA and the need for *sui generis* regulation] The relative merits of *sui generis* and technology-neutral IPR models were touched upon at the outset of this chapter (see above in the Technology-neutral vs *sui generis* regimes section). The 2002 *Report* addresses that broad issue in the context of PBRs (at 26):

> Plant Breeder's Rights' regimes have been developed specifically to meet the particular needs of intellectual property in plants. Accordingly there are some differences between the two systems. Consequently, it is not possible to apply all of the concepts associated with industrial patents to plants. Moreover, since the *PBRA* policy intent is to promote the development of new varieties of plants, any proposals that may hinder that intent would need to be examined carefully.

But opponents of *sui generis* solutions might argue that it *is* possible to adapt an existing system, as was done for computer programs in copyright. The *PBRA* and *CLA* schemes arguably owe their existence to singular political and economic imperatives at the time of their introduction, but they seem to be supported by common systemic insights, the first of these being that the technology concerned is somehow inherently different from others. Further, it can be argued that R&D and innovation proceed on a fundamentally different footing, in particular by gradual advancement on the basis of generally known methods systematically applied to a finite underlying resource, primarily requiring major investigative resource allocation, but also some intellectual contribution. And lastly, that the existing regimes are ill-adapted to the subject matter, to existing and valuable traditions or to underlying presumptions (in particular concerning access to information). Therefore both different threshold tests and unique exemptions and limitations are required.

However, there are some difficulties with all these arguments. Firstly, no technology is truly unique, or alternatively, *every* technology is unique, although stronger traditions have admittedly grown up around innovation in some areas than in others. Also, some 'unique' subject matter *has* been accommodated within existing regimes: computer programs were inserted into copyright, with some modification of rules. Secondly, R&D and innovation is by its nature adapted to the particular industry and technology with which it is concerned; arguably there is not a single innovation system, but multiple industry-based models that coexist. It is exactly to deal with this variety that a system of general application makes sense. Thirdly, even in the face of often bitter resistance, additional exemptions *can* be accommodated within existing regimes, even those that are more monopolistic in character. For instance, Bastarache J in the Canadian case of *Harvard College v Canada (Commissioner of Patents)* [2002] SCC 76 (at [171]) suggested the introduction of a farmers' rights exemption in patents law; the Supreme Court of Canada has also crafted an exclusion from patenting for higher life forms. Finally, a broader problem bedevils the adoption of *sui generis* regimes: where to draw technological boundaries? For instance, why is there a unique regime for plant varieties, but not for biotechnology, which many have argued is a special category of invention? Might the dividing line between modification of existing regimes and introduction of *sui generis* models simply result from disparate lobbying power?

3 Reliance on trade marks registration to monopolise new product shapes?

[Innovation and reputation] There is a complex relationship between innovation and the legal protection of reputation. Whereas innovation is about the introduction of new products, hitherto unknown to consumers, reputation (or 'goodwill') is derived from goods' previous market exposure. Reputation is often referred to as 'secondary meaning', an association established in consumers' minds by repeat experience. Central to consumer perception in relation to goodwill is distinctiveness; whereas in relation to innovation it is a product's inherent qualities that count. Distinctiveness and thus goodwill do not usually inhere in a product itself, but rather in some sign used in association with a product, a 'trade mark' that consumers perceive as serving the purpose of distinguishing certain products from others. To promote its reputation, a firm normally chooses a sign that is easily recognised and clearly distinguished from others, in which to develop and reinforce goodwill by various strategies. By innovating, a firm's primary goal is to develop a product that is inherently more useful and/or more visually pleasing than competing or preceding ones, and that consumers will pay more for; hence legal protection of innovation focusses on the inherent functional or aesthetic aspects of the goods *themselves*. However, the protection of reputation focusses on the legal status of distinctive, usually functionally or aesthetically insignificant signs (trade marks) associated with those goods; it does not normally focus on aspects of the goods themselves. Nonetheless, clearly innovative goods that are inherently more desirable *can* enhance corporate reputation. If the law comes to accept that this reputation can reside in the appearance of the goods themselves, the two regimes overlap, and trade mark protection can potentially serve the purpose of monopolising the shape of goods.

[General issues relating to trade marks] Because the protection of goodwill under the general law is based on proof of reputation, ie consumer recognition, it has no significant role in terms of product *innovation* – *new* products have by definition not been in the market long enough to build a reputation. Therefore remedies for passing off, one of the requirements for which is proof of *actual* reputation, are not apt to prevent a competitor from copying a product that has only recently or not quite yet been introduced into the market. If the imitator can introduce his copy quickly, then he can disrupt the innovator's chances of establishing a unique reputation in the shape of the product. In any case, passing off is dependent on proof of consumer deception, so if a competitor uses his own trade mark on imitation goods, he will usually escape liability. However, the *Trade Marks Act 1995* (Cth) allows a trade mark, if it is inherently distinctive in some way, to be registered even before it has acquired a reputation in the market. Thus by registration a *newly adopted* sign can be protected against imitation by competitors. If the shape of a product *itself*, in part or in whole, can be considered a distinctive sign, then a new product shape could theoretically be protected against imitation by way of trade mark registration, and that at the time of its first introduction into the market. Crucial therefore is the law accepting that shapes, including the whole shape of products, can be registered as trade marks. However, a longstanding rule required that a trade mark should be something separate from the goods, like a device, tag or brand: '[T]he goods [are] assumed to have an existence independently of the mark'.[12] But as is discussed below, with the introduction of the *Trade Marks Act 1995* (Cth) (*TMA*) it is now reasonably clear that the shape of a product itself, as opposed to only separate signs, can be registered: by virtue of section 6 of the *TMA*, a 'sign' registrable as a trade mark includes a 'shape', which has been held to include product shape.

[Trade marks and designs] This more permissive approach to shape mark registration has motivated firms to explore the potential of trade marks to usurp or bolster the role of designs registration for new product shapes. Designs registration is of course the usual and preferable legal method for monopolising new product appearance. However, a design application may encounter difficulties, in terms of novelty (maybe the design has already been used) or for other reasons. In any case, designs registration only ever offers short term (maximum 10 years) protection against imitation; so trade mark registration may be an attractive substitute, since as long as the mark remains in use it can generally speaking remain on the Register. Alternatively, an innovative firm may consider both registering a design *and* applying for trade mark registration, in particular for a consumer product with a striking, distinctive, individual appearance likely to influence purchasing behaviour. If so, the design must be filed for first, to avoid anticipation by its inclusion in the trade mark application.

[Signs capable of distinguishing goods] However, even if the shape of a product itself can be registered as a 'sign' (see section 17 *TMA* definition of a trade mark), other legal obstacles need to be overcome to proceed to trade mark registration of a new product shape. Although an unused trade mark can be registered, this depends on whether a trade mark examiner (and ultimately a court) judges it to be *capable of distinguishing* the goods (see section 41 *TMA*). This effectively requires an estimation of average consumers' perception – could they ever come

---

[12] See *SKF Laboratories (Aust) Ltd v Registrar of Trade Marks* (1967) 116 CLR 628.

to see the mark (the product's shape in this case) as a badge of origin, as something that is there to identify the distinct origins of the goods? Distinctiveness is a requirement inherent in the statutory definition of a mark (see section 17), but must be examined in the step-wise manner set out in section 41. The overarching test is that a trade mark which is not capable of distinguishing the goods for which it is sought to be registered from those of other persons should be rejected (section 41 (2)). Where a new sign has not yet been used and has no actual reputation, ie has not *acquired* distinctiveness or secondary meaning, the matter is to be resolved on the basis of *inherent* distinctiveness – do its inherent characteristics render the sign capable of distinguishing goods? Courts have generally approached this question by asking whether other traders could legitimately expect to be free to use the sign in the course of ordinary business: if the sign is a product's shape, could others legitimately expect to be able to adopt that shape? In *Kenman Kandy Australia Pty Ltd v The Registrar of Trade Marks* [2001] FCA 1047, trade mark registration of a new shape of a biscuit (or 'piece of confectionary') was initially refused. However, this was overturned on appeal in *Kenman Kandy Australia Pty Ltd v Registrar of Trade Marks* [2002] FCAFC 273. Ultimately the shape was found to be capable of distinguishing the goods: although reminiscent of a real bug it was so stylised that it did not deny other traders the use of real animal shapes, common in confectionery. Stone J, in the majority, made it very clear that although the 1995 Act did *not* intend to change the fundamental policy of trade marks law, the whole shape of a product did not therefore *ipso facto* remain unregistrable. Her Honour said (at [142]): 'I [...] see no reason why a shape that is the whole shape of a good should for that reason alone be incapable of registration as a trade mark. The test must be whether it has the capacity to distinguish'. Earlier (at [137]) her Honour had said:

> The concerns expressed in both *Philips v Remington (Aust)*, FC and *Philips v Remington (Eng)* about the prospect of trade marks creating monopolies related only to the registration of trade marks that would restrict access to functional features or innovations, and for this reason were well founded. It is this concern that finds expression in the requirement that a trade mark be something added to the inherent form of goods. The 'inherent form' of goods, in my view, can only refer to those aspects of form that have functional significance. Were the 1995 Act to enable the registration of a trade mark that would give the owner a monopoly over functional features it would indeed have made a radical change to trade mark law.

In other words, where the pre-1995 rule was that trade marks must be separate from goods the rule has been subtly modified to provide that trade marks must be something added to the 'inherent form' of goods.

['Aesthetic functionality' no bar to registration] Elsewhere her Honour held that, by analogy with traditional marks, the fact that a shape evokes a positive emotional response should not be regarded as the kind of 'aesthetic functionality' that some argue should also prevent registration. That the product's features were attractive to children did not render them unregistrable, as long as those features did not belong to the stock in trade of all businesses interested in such products. Her Honour said (at [156]):

> In addition they show, especially in the comments made in *Mark Foy's* and *Wella*, that, at least in relation to word trade marks, it is not an obstacle to inherent adaptation that the trade mark is also designed to elicit a positive emotional response. The fact that the 'sign' that comprised the trade mark in those cases had a dual function was not seen to be inconsistent with the sign acting as a trade mark in respect of certain goods. I see no reason why the attractiveness of a shape should be considered differently. Moreover, I also see no reason why an invented shape should be regarded as different from an invented word in terms of assessing its inherent capacity to distinguish a trader's goods.

French J accepted like Stone J that the whole shape of goods was not *a priori* excluded from registration. He agreed that the fact that a shape was aesthetically attractive should not always stand in the way of registration either.

[Functional product shapes] French J in *Kenman* held that a shape that goods have because of their nature or 'for a particular technical result' (at [45]) 'could not operate as a trade mark'. Section 39 of the short-lived *Trade Marks Act 1994* (Cth), which in fact never came into operation, provided as follows:

> An application for the registration of a trade mark in respect of goods must be rejected if the trade mark consists wholly or principally of: (a) the shape, or some other characteristic, possessed, because of their nature, by the goods; or (b) a shape, or some other characteristic, that the goods must have if a particular technical result is to be obtained.

But Stone J in *Kenman* (at [137]) pointed out that nothing should be read into the omission of this exclusion from the 1995 Act:

> This is because a trade mark that would be rejected if s 39 applied is a trade mark that would not be capable of distinguishing and therefore would also be rejected under s 41(2). Therefore no significance can be attached to the omission of this section from the 1995 Act.

Thus under the 1995 Act, a functional shape is unlikely to be capable of registration, precisely because functionality should not be monopolised by trade mark registration. In *Koninklijke Philips Electronics NV v Remington Products Australia Pty Limited* [2000] FCA 876 severe doubt was expressed that the trade mark, which related to a functional feature of the hand-held shaver, should ever have been registered, even on the basis of *acquired* distinctiveness. Naturally, whether or not certain characteristics of shape are functional will not always be easy to determine.

[Infringement by adopting or imitating product shape] But does registration of a product shape as a trade mark have much use? In other words, could product imitation amount to an infringing use of a registered shape mark? For various reasons this is unlikely to be the case. The principal difficulty is that the adoption of a shape by a competitor would not necessarily be treated as trade mark use (or 'use of a mark as a mark'), as is required by section 120. Consumers would not see the shape, if it has some functionality or attractiveness, as being there to serve as a badge of origin, in other words as serving the purpose of distinguishing the goods from others. They would not view product imitation as 'use of a mark as a mark', and therefore imitation would not infringe trade mark rights. A further question is whether any of the defences may apply, for instance where registration of the shape mark is obtained subject to a limitation. It is only if the imitator makes too much of the shape *per se* that there could potentially be trade mark use – eg by repeatedly representing the shape prominently in advertising, without also drawing attention to the functional or aesthetic advantages of the shape; this is a matter considered in detail in the *Philips* case (see above) which is an interesting example of the interaction between and limitations of trade marks law, passing off and designs registration in practice. This requirement of use *as a mark* is also an obstacle to product shapes achieving registration on the basis of acquired rather than inherent distinctiveness: only use of a mark *as a trade mark* can be the basis for proof of acquired distinctiveness.

[Register a design first, then a trade mark?] Underlying the question of trade mark use is the issue of the proper separation between the various regimes, and their underlying policy goals. There is little doubt that the obstacles to effectively using trade mark registration to prevent imitation are considerable; nonetheless, the potential effect of shape marks is a permanent monopoly in the appearance of a product, usurping the policy goals underlying and carefully calibrating the designs registration scheme. To use the words of Lord Templeman in *Re Coca-Cola Co* (1986) 6 IPR 275 at 276–277: '[The possibility of registering the shape of a coke bottle as a trade mark] raises the spectre of a total and perpetual monopoly in containers and articles [. . .]'. Should concurrent registration therefore be excluded by statute, or even *subsequent* registration as a trade mark, for a shape that has been registered as a design? There is a relevant precedent for the latter approach, relating to word marks which have been used as the name of patented products. By virtue of section 25 of the *Trade Marks Act*, if a word mark has been the name of an article or substance formerly exploited under a patent, the patent has expired for at least two years, and the word is the only commonly known name of the product, the trade mark owner loses his exclusive right to use the name. This is particularly significant for pharmaceutical names, for compounds that have been subject to a patent. The trade mark goodwill built up exclusively over the patent term cannot be relied upon effectively to extend the patent monopoly because the product has become exclusively associated with that name.

Bibliography

Chapter one: Introduction

Alford W, *To steal a book is an elegant offence: intellectual property law in Chinese civilisation*, Stanford University Press, 1995.
Allison J and M Lemley, 'Empirical evidence on the validity of litigated patents' (1998) *AIPLA Quarterly Journal* 26, 185.
Aoki K, 'Authors, inventors and trademark owners: Private intellectual property and the public domain' (1993–4) 18:1 *Columbia-VLA Journal of Law and the Arts 1*; and Part II in 18:3–4.
Arrow K, 'Economic Welfare and the Allocation of Resources for Innovation', in R Nelson (ed), *The Rate and Direction of Inventive Activity*, Princeton University Press, 1962.
Arup C, *Innovation, policy and law*, Cambridge University Press, 1993.
Australian Bureau of Statistics (ABS), 1370.0, *Measures of Australia's Progress*, 2004.
Australian Law Reform Commission (ALRC), Report No 74, *Designs*, 1995.
Bain J, *Barriers to New Competition*, Harvard UP, 1956, Chapter IV.
Bankman J and RJ Gilson, 'Why start-ups?' (1999) *Stanford LR*, 51, 189.
Bar-Gill O and G Parchomovsky, 'Intellectual Property Law and the Boundaries of the Firm' (2005) U of Penn, Inst for Law & Econ Research Paper 05-10; NYU, Law and Economics Research Paper No. 04-06 (April 2005).
Berliner J, *The Innovation Decision in Soviet Industry*, MIT Press, 1976.
Boisot MH, *Knowledge assets: Securing competitive advantage in the Information Economy*, Oxford University Press, 1998.
Bureau of Industry Economics, *The Economics of Intellectual Property*, BIE Other Publication, June 1995.
Burk D, 'Intellectual property and the firm' (2004) *The University of Chicago Law Review*, 71, 3.
Caine E and A Christie, 'A quantitive analysis of Australian intellectual property law and policy-making since federation' (2005) 16 *AIPJ* 4, 185.
Castells M, *The rise of the Network Society*, Blackwell, 1996.
Chamberlin E, *Theory of Monopolistic Competition*, Harvard University Press, 1959.
Conceicao P et al (eds), *Science, technology and innovation policy: opportunities and challenges for the knowledge economy*, Quorum Books, 2000.
Coombe RJ, 'Objects of property and subjects of politics: intellectual property laws and democratic dialogue' (1991) *Texas LR* 69, 1853.
Corones S, 'Reconciling Intellectual Property Rights and Competition Law: the Magill TV guide case' (1992) 20 *Australian Bus LR* 265.
Coulter M, *Property in ideas*, Thomas Jefferson University Press, 1991.
David P, 'The evolution of intellectual property institutions' MERIT Research Memorandum 93-009 (1993).
Denicola R, 'Freedom to Copy' (1999) 108 *Yale LJ* 1661.
Drahos P, 'The regulation of public goods' (2004) *Journal of International Economic Law*, 7, 2, 321.
—*A Philosophy of Intellectual Property*, Dartmouth, 1996.
—'Intellectual Property Law and Basic Science: Extinguishing Prometheus?' in C Arup (ed), *Science Law and Society* (1992) 10 Law in Context Special Issue 56.
Duysters G, *The Dynamics of Technical Innovation*, Edward Elgar, 1996.

Edvinsson L and M Malone, *Intellectual Capital*, HarperBusiness, 1999.
Fitzgerald B and A Fitzgerald, *Intellectual property in principle*, LBC, 2004.
Flueckiger G, *Control, information and technological change*, Kluwer, 1995.
Gans J, DH Hsu and S Stern, 'When does start-up innovation spur the gale of creative destruction?' (2002) *Rand Journal of Economics*, 33, 4, 571.
Geller PA, 'Dissolving intellectual property' [2006] *EIPR* 139.
Granstrand O (ed), *Economics, Law and Intellectual Property*, Kluwer Academic Publishers, 2003.
Green J and S Scotchmer, 'On the division of profits in sequential innovation' (1995) 26 *Rand J Econ* 20.
Hall P, *Innovation, Economics and Evolution: Theoretical Perspectives on Changing Technology in Economic Systems*, Harvester Wheatsheaf, 1994.
Hall P and G Lea, 'Standards and Intellectual Property Rights: An Economic and Legal Perspective' (2004) *Information Economics and Policy* 16(1) 67.
Holmstrom B and P Milgrom, 'The firm as an incentive system' (1994) *The American Economic Review*, 84, 4, 972.
Hope J, *Open Source Biotechnology project*, RSSS, ANU, available at: http://rsss.anu.edu.au/~janeth/home.html
Horibe F, *Managing knowledge workers: new skills and attitudes to unlock the intellectual capital in your organization*, Wiley, 1999.
Imparato N (ed), *Capital for our time: the economic, legal and management challenges of intellectual capital*, Hoover Institution Press, 1999.
Industrial Property Advisory Committee (IPAC), *Patents, Innovation and Competition in Australia* (August 1984).
Intellectual Property & Competition Review Committee (IPCRC), *Review of Intellectual Property Legislation under the competition Principles Agreement* (Final Report, 30 September 2000).
Kelly RJ, 'Private Data and Public Knowledge: Intellectual Property Rights in Science' (1989) 13 *Legal Studies Forum* 365.
Kingston W, 'Reducing the cost of resolving intellectual property disputes' (1995) *European Journal of Law and Economics* 2, 85.
— 'Intellectual property needs help from accounting' [2002] EIPR, 11, 508.
Klein A, *The strategic management of intellectual capital*, Butterworth Heinemann, 1999.
Laddie, Hon Mr Justice, 'Copyright: Over-strength, Over-regulated, Over-rated?' [1996] 5 *EIPR* 253.
Lamberton D, *Science, technology and the Australian economy*, Tudor Press, 1970.
Lange D, 'Recognizing the Public Domain' (1981) 44 *Law & Contemporary Problems* 4, 147.
Lasch C, *The true and only heaven: progress and its critics*, WW Norton, 1991.
Leijonhufvud A, 'Information costs and the division of labour' (1989) *International Social Science Journal* 120, 165–76.
Lemley M and D McGowan, 'Legal implications of Network Economic Effects' (1998) *California Law Review* 86, 481.
Lemley M, 'Ex ante versus ex post justifications for intellectual property' (2004) *The University of Chicago Law Review*, 71, 129.
Levin R et al, 'Appropriating the returns from industrial research and development' (1987) 3 *Brookings Papers on Econ. Activity* 783.
Link A and F Scherer (eds), *Essays in Honor of Edwin Mansfield*, Springer, 2006.
Litman J, 'The Public Domain' (1990) 39 *Emory LJ* 965.
Long P, 'Invention, authorship, intellectual property, and the origin of patents: notes toward a conceptual history' (1991) *Technology & Culture*, 846–84.
Mansfield E, 'Academic Research and Industrial Innovation' (1991) 20 *Research Policy* 1.
—*The Economics of Technological Change*, Norton & Co, 1968.
McGinnis P, *Intellectual Property Commercialisation: A Business Manager's Companion*, Butterworths, 2003.
McKeough J, A Stewart and P Griffith, *Intellectual Property in Australia*, Butterworths, 2004.

Melzer A, J Weinberger and M. Zinman (eds), *History and the idea of progress*, Cornell University Press, 1995.
Merges R, 'Intellectual Property Rights and the New Institutional Economics' (2000) 53 *V and L Rev* 1957.
Merges RP, 'Property rights theory and the commons: the case of scientific research' (1996) 13 *Soc Phil & Policy* 145–67.
Metcalfe S, *Evolutionary Foundations of Technology Policy*, Edward Elgar, 2000.
Mokyr J, *The lever of riches*, Oxford University Press, 1990.
Neef D, 'Rethinking Economics in the Knowledge-based Economy', in *The Economic Impact of Knowledge*, Butterworth Heinemann, 1998.
—*A little knowledge is a dangerous thing: understanding our global knowledge economy*, Butterworth Heinemann, 1998.
—*The knowledge economy*, Butterworth Heinemann, 1998.
Nelson R, *Understanding Technical Change as an Evolutionary Process*, North Holland, 1987.
Nelson R and S Winter, *An Evolutionary Theory of Economic Change*, Harvard University Press, 1982.
Nonaka I and H Takeuchi, *The Knowledge-creating Company: How Japanese Companies Create the Dynamics of Innovation*, Oxford University Press, 1995.
Pavitt K, Technology, *Management and Systems of Innovation*, Edward Elgar, 1999.
Petrusson U, *Intellectual Property and Entrepreneurship*, CIP Gothenburg, 2004.
Porter R, *The enlightenment*, 2nd edn, Paragon, 2001.
Prager FD, 'A History of Intellectual Property Law from 1545 to 1787' (1944) 26 *JPTO* 712.
Rassokhin VP, 'Centralisation and Freedom of Creativity in Science and Technology' (1988) 27 *Soviet Law and Government* 55.
Reichman J, 'Of Green Tulips and Legal Kudzu: Repackaging Rights in Subpatentable Innovation' (2000) 53 *Vanderbilt Law Review* 174.
Rescher N, *Unpopular essays on technological progress*, University of Pittsburgh Press, 1980.
Reynolds R and N Stoianoff, *Intellectual Property: Text and Essential Cases*, The Federation Press, 2005.
Ricketson S, 'The Future of Australian Intellectual Property Law Reform and Administration' (1990) 1 *AIPJ* 3.
—*The law of intellectual property*, LBC, 1984.
Roos J, G Roos, L Edvinsson and N Dragonetti, *Intellectual capital: Navigating in the New Business Landscape*, NYUP, 1998.
Rose M, *Authors and owners*, Harvard UP, 1993.
Rushing F and C Ganz Brown (eds), *Intellectual Property Rights in Science, Technology, and Economic Performance: International Comparisons*, Westview Press, 1990.
Sackville R, 'Monopoly vs Freedom of Ideas: the expansion of intellectual property' (2005) 16 *AIPJ* 65.
Sahal D, *Patterns of Technological Innovation*, Addison Wesley, 1981.
Schumpeter JA, *Capitalism, Socialism and Democracy*, Harper, 1975 [orig. pub. 1942]) (at pp. 82–85: 'gale of creative destruction').
Shavell S and T van Ypersele, 'Reward versus intellectual property rights' (2001) *The Journal of Law and Economics*, 44, 525.
Sherman B and L Bently, *The making of modern intellectual property law*, Cambridge University Press, 1999.
Shulman B, *Owning the future*, Houghton Mifflin, 1999.
Staff of Senate Subcommittee on Patents, Trademarks and Copyrights, 85th Congress, 'An economic review of the patent system: study No 15 (Comm Print 1958; Fritz Machlup concluded that it would be irresponsible to create a patent system if the US did not have one, but also irresponsible to abolish the one they had).
Standing Committee on Science and Innovation, Inquiry into Business Commitment to Research and Development in Australia, *Riding the Innovation Wave: The Case for Increasing Business Investment in R&D* (23 June 2003).
Steindl J, 'Technical progress and evolution', in: D Sahal (ed), *Research, development and technological innovation*, Lexington, 1980.

Sullivan PH, *Profiting from Intellectual Capital: Extracting value from innovation*, John Wiley & Sons, 1998.
Suthersanen U and G Dutfield, 'The Innovation Dilemma: Intellectual Property and the Historical Legacy of Cumulative Creativity' [2004] 8 *Intellectual Property Quarterly* 379–421.
Todd E, *The causes of progress*, Basil Blackwell, 1987.
van Caenegem W, Butterworths Tutorial Series, *Intellectual Property*, 2nd edn, 2005.
—'Intellectual property law and the idea of progress' (2003) *IPQ* 3, 237.
—'Intellectual property and intellectual capital' (2002) *Intellectual Property Forum* 4810.
—'The public domain: scientia nullius?' (2002) 24 *EIPR* 324.
—'Inventions in Russia: From public good to private property' (1993) 4 *AIPJ* 232.
Whitley R, 'Competition and pluralism in the public sciences: the impact of institutional frameworks on the organization of academic science' (2003) *Research Policy*, 32, 6, 1015.
Whitt LA, 'Indigenous peoples, intellectual property and the new imperial Science' (1998) *Oklahoma City University Law Review* 211.

Chapter two: Trade secrets

Ancori B, A Bureth and P Cohendet, 'The economics of knowledge: the debate about codification and tacit knowledge' (2000) *Industrial and Corporate Change*, 9, 2, 255.
Blackler F, 'Knowledge, knowledge work and organizations: an overview and interpretation' (1995) *Organization Studies*, 16, 6, 1021.
Butler D, 'A Tort of invasion of privacy in Australia?' (2005) *Melbourne Law Review* 11.
Casselman R and D Samson, 'Moving beyond tacit and explicit: four dimensions of knowledge', IPRIA Working Paper, June 2004.
Cohendet P and W Steinmueller, 'The codification of knowledge: a conceptual and empirical exploration' (2002) *Industrial and Corporate Change*, 11, 2, 195.
Cooper DP, 'Innovation and reciprocal externalities: information transmission via job mobility' (2001) *Journal of Economic Behaviour and Organization*, 45, 4, 403.
Cowan R, P David and D Foray, 'The explicit economics of knowledge codification and tacitness' (2000) *Industrial and Corporate Change*, 9, 2, 211.
Darby M, Q Liu and L Zucker, 'Stakes and stars: the effect of intellectual human capital on the level and variability of high-tech firms' market value', NBER Working Paper Series No 7201 (1999).
Dean R, *The Law of Trade Secrets and Personal Secrets*, 2nd edn, Law Book Company, Sydney, 2002.
Di Gregorio D and S Shane, 'Why do some universities generate more start-ups than others?' (2003R) *Research Policy*, 32, 2, 209.
Freedman CD, 'The Extension of the Criminal Law to Protecting Confidential Commercial Information: Comments on the Issues and the Cyber-Context', 14th BILETA Conference: "CYBERSPACE 1999: Crime, Criminal Justice and the Internet", at p 5 (available at www.bileta.ac.uk).
Friedman D, W Landes and R Posner, 'Some Economics of Trade Secret Law' (1991) *Journal of Economic Perspectives*, 5, 1 61–72.
Friedmann D, 'Restitution for wrongs: the basis of liability' in WR Cornish et al (eds), *Restitution: Past present and future*, Hart, 1998.
Gray B, 'Ocular Sciences: a new vision for the doctrine of breach of confidence?' (1999) *Melbourne University Law Review*, 23, 1, 241.
Gurry F, *Breach of Confidence*, Oxford University Press, 1990.
Johnson B, E Lorenz and B-A Lundvall, 'Why all this fuss about codified and tacit knowledge' (2002) *Industrial and Corporate Change*, 11, 2, 245.
Law Commission of England and Wales: 'Legislating the criminal code: misuse of trade secrets', Consultation Paper 150, 1997.
Merges R, 'The law and economics of employee inventions' (1999) *Harvard Journal of Law & Technology* 13, 1.

Monotti A, 'Who owns my research and teaching materials: my university or me?' (1997) *Sydney Law Review*, 19, 4, 425.
Narayanan S, 'The economics of intrapreneurial innovation' (2005) *Journal of Economic Behavior & Organization*, 58, 4, 487.
Nelson R, 'On the uneven evolution of human know-how' (2003) *Research Policy*, 32, 6, 909.
Nightingale P, 'If Nelson and Winter are only half right about tacit knowledge, which half? A Searlean critique of "codification"' (2003) *Industrial and Corporate Change*, 12, 2, 149.
Polanyi M, *Personal Knowledge: Towards a Post-critical Philosophy*, Routledge and Kegan Paul, 1958.
—'The logic of tacit inference' (1966) *Philosophy*, 41, 1.
Riley J, 'Who owns human capital? A critical appraisal of legal techniques for capturing the value of work' (2005) *Australian Journal of Labour Law* 18, 1, 1.
Roberts J, 'The drive to codify: implications for the knowledge based economy' (2001) *Prometheus*, 19, 2, 99.
van Caenegem W, 'Inter-firm migration of tacit knowledge: law and policy' (2005) *Prometheus* 23, 3, 285.

Chapter three: Patents

Advisory Council on Intellectual Property (ACIP), *Should plant & animal subject matter be excluded from protection by the innovation patent?* (November 2004).
—Final Report, *Patents and Experimental Use* (October 2005).
—*Review of crown use provisions for patents and designs* (November 2005).
Australian Law Reform Commission (ALRC), Report No 99, *Genes and Ingenuity: Gene Patenting and Human Health* (2004).
Barton J, 'Patents and antitrust: a rethinking in light of patent breadth and sequential innovation' (1997) *Antitrust Law Journal* 65, 449.
—'Reforming the Patent System', *Science*, Vol 287, 17 March 2000, 1993.
Blows J and D Clark, 'Is an innovative step so easy that "any fool could do it"?', (2006) *Australian Intellectual Property Law Bulletin*, 18, 8, 129.
Brennan D, 'Springboards and Ironing Boards: Confidential information as a restraint of trade' (2005) *Journal of Contract Law* 71.
Bucknell et al, *Australian Patent Law*, Butterworths, 2004.
Bureau of Industry Economics, *The Economics of Patents*, BIE Occasional Paper, Feb. 1994
Burk D and M Lemley, 'Policy levers in patents law' (2003) 79 *Va L Rev* 101.
—'Is patent law technology specific?' (2002) *Berkeley Tech. Law Journal*, 17, 1155.
Christie A, 'Some Observations on the Requirement of Inherent Patentability in the Context of Business Methods Patents' (2000) *Intellectual Property Forum* 43.
Dreyfuss R, 'Are business method patents bad for business?' (2000) *Santa Clara Computer & High Technology Law Journal* 16(2).
Drummond D, 'Are the courts down under properly handling patent disputes?' (2000) *Intellectual Property Forum* 42, 10.
Duffy J, 'Rethinking the prospect theory of patents' (2004) *The University of Chicago Law Review*, 71, 439.
Ellis T, 'Distortion of patent economics by litigation costs', in Hill et al (eds), CASRIP, *Streamlining International Intellectual Property*, 1999.
Garde T, 'Legal certainty, *stare decisis* and the doctrine of equivalents' [2005] *EIPR* 365.
Gee O, 'The description-claims relationship – "A fair balance?". A comparison of the Australian, USA and EPO jurisdictions' (2006) *IP Forum* 64, 44.
Grady MF and JI Alexander, 'Patent law and rent dissipation' (1992) 78 *Virginia Law Review* 305.
Grushcow J, 'Measuring secrecy: a cost of the patent system revealed' (2004) *The Journal of Legal Studies*, 33, 59.
Haines T, 'Patenting legal strategies – Does the utility justify the ends?' (2005) *Intellectual Property Forum* 62, 24.

Hauhart R, 'The origin and development of the British and American patent and copyright laws' (1983) 5 *Whittier L R* 539.

Heath C, 'Remuneration of employees' inventions in Europe and Japan', *AIPPI: Bimonthly Journal of the International Association for the Protection of the Industrial Property of Japan*, Vol. 27 No. 6, November 2002, pp 398–407.

Heller M and R Eisenberg, 'Can Patents Deter Innovation? The Anti-commons in Biomedical Research' (1998) 280 *Science* 698.

House of Representatives Standing Committee on Industry, Science and Technology, 'Genetic manipulations: the threat or the glory?' (1992).

IPAustralia, Issues Paper, *Review of the Innovation Patent* (September 2005).

—*Review of Patent Grace Period* (August 2005).

Janis M, 'Patent Abolitionism' (2002) 17 *Berkeley Technology Law Journal* 899.

Jensen PH and E Webster, 'Achieving the optimal power of patent rights', IPRIA Working Paper No 15/04, December 2004.

Kingston W, 'Why harmonization is a Trojan horse' [2004] 26 *EIPR* 10, 447–60.

—'Innovation needs patent reform' (2001) *Research Policy* 30, 3, 403.

Kitch EW, 'The nature and function of the patent system' (1978) *J of L & Eco* 20, 165.

Lamberton D, Dissenting Statement, 'Patents, Innovation and Competition in Australia', Industrial Property Advisory Group, Attorney General's Department, 1984.

Lemley M, 'Reconceiving patents in the age of venture capital' (2000) *The Journal of Small and Emerging Business Law* 137.

—'The economics of improvement in intellectual property law' (1997) *Texas Law Review* 75, 989.

Levin R et al, 'Appropriating the returns from industrial research and development' (1987) 3 *Brookings Papers on Economic Activity* 783.

Lithgow T, 'Patent infringement immunity for medical practitioners and related health care entities' (1997) *Jurimetrics Journal* 251.

Lo VI, 'Employee inventions and works for hire in Japan: A comparative study against the US, Chinese and German systems' (2002) 16 *Temp Int'l & Comp LJ* 279.

Long P, 'Invention, authorship, "Intellectual property" and the origin of patents: Notes toward a conceptual history' (1991) *Technology and Culture* 32, 846.

Loughlan P, 'Of patents and professors: IP, Research Workers and Universities' [1996] 6 *EIPR* 345.

Macdonald S, 'When Means Become Ends: Considering the Impact of Patent Strategy on Innovation' (2004) *Information Economics and Policy*, 16, 1, 135.

Machlup F, 'Patents' in D Sills (ed), *The international encyclopaedia of the social sciences II*, Macmillan, 1968, pp 468–71.

Macleod C, *Inventing the industrial revolution: the English patent system 1660–1800*, Cambridge University Press, 1988.

Mandeville, Lamberton, Bishop, *The economic effects of the Australian Patent System*, 1982.

Mandich G, 'Venetian Patents (1450–1550)' (1948) *JPTOS* 30, 166.

Mansfield E, M Schwartz and S Wagner, 'Imitation costs and patents: an empirical study' (1981) *The Economics Journal* 91, 907–18.

Martin DL, 'Reducing anticipated rewards from innovation through patent: or less is more' (1992) 78 *Virginia Law Review* 351.

McBratney A, 'Does the fair basing "problem child" escape Lockwood?' (2005) 16 *AIPJ* 4, 210.

—'The Problem Child in Australian Patent Law: "Fair" Basing' (2001) 12 *AIPJ* 4, 211.

Merges R, 'As many as six impossible patents before breakfast: property rights for business concepts and patent system reform' (1999) *Berkeley Technology Law Journal* 14, 577.

—'The law and economics of employee inventions' (1999) *Harvard Journal of Law and Technology* 13, 1.

—'Rent control in the patent district: observations on the Grady-Alexander thesis', 78 (1992) *Virginia Law Review* 359.

Merges R and R Nelson, 'Market structure and technical advance: the role of patent scope decisions', in T Jorde and D Teece (eds), *Antitrust, innovation and competitiveness*, Oxford University Press, 1992.

—'On the complex economics of patents scope' (1990) *Columbia Law Review* 90, 839.
Mills O, *Biotechnological inventions: Moral Restraints and Patent Law*, Ashgate, 2005.
Monotti A and S Ricketson, *Universities and Intellectual Property, Ownership and Exploitation*, Oxford University Press, 2003.
Mossinghoff G, 'Remedies under patents on medical and surgical procedures' (1996) 78 *JPTOS* 789.
Parchomsky G and R Polk Wagner, 'Patent portfolios' (2005) *University of Pennsylvania Law Review* 154, 1, 1.
Pendleton M, 'Construe Widely and Face Invalidity – Construe Narrowly and Miss Infringements: The Dilemma of Interpreting Patent Specifications', *Murdoch University Electronic Journal of Law*, Volume 11, Number 3 (September 2004).
Scotchmer S, 'Standing on the shoulders of giants: cumulative research and the patent law' (1991) *Journal of Economic Perspectives* 5, 29.
van Caenegem W, 'The technicality requirement, patents scope and patentable subject matter in Australia' (2002) *Australian Intellectual Property Journal* 13, 309.
Van Overwalle G, *The legal protection of biotechnological inventions in Europe*, Leuven Law Series, Vol 10, Leuven University Press, 1997.
Walterscheid E, 'The early evolution of the United States Patent Law: Antecedents' (Part I) (1994) *JPTOS* 697; (Part II) (1994) *JPTOS* 849.
Weatherall K and P Jensen, 'An empirical investigation into patent enforcements in Australian courts' (2005) *Federal Law Review* 33, 2, 239.

Chapter four: Copyright and designs

Australian Law Reform Commission (ALRC), Report No 74, *Designs* (1995).
Bently L, 'Visuality and Textuality in Nineteenth Century Intellectual Property Law: The Utility Designs Act 1843' (1997) *Intellectual Property Forum*, Issue 29.
Brown D and E Cameron, 'Designing the interface', (2005) *International Review of Law, Computers & Technology*, 19, 1, 65–81.
Bureau of Industry Economics, The Economics of Intellectual Property Rights for Design, BIE Occasional Paper, June 1995.
Commission of the European Communities, *Green Paper on the Legal Protection of Industrial Designs*, III/F/5131191-EN (1991).
Franzosi M and G de Sanctis, 'Moral Rights and New Technology: Are Copyright and Patents Converging?' [1995] 2 *EIPR* 63.
Fraser G and K Hall, 'Copyright protection for works of artistic craftsmanship' (1999) *Law Institute Journal* 73, 9, 47–9.
Golder T, 'Australian Designs Law – A Commentary on the Lahore Committee Report and the Need for Legislative Reform' (1993) *Intellectual Property Forum Journal* 19.
Gotzen F (ed), 'The green paper on the legal protection of industrial design', *CIR* Leuven (1992).
Hansmann H and M Santilli, 'Authors and artists' moral rights: A comparative legal and economic analysis (1997) 26 *J Legal Stud* 95.
Haungs MJ, 'Copyright of Factual Compilations: Public Policy and the First Amendment' (1990) 23 *Colum J L & Soc Problems* 347.
Izquierdo Peris JJ, 'Registered Community Design: First two-year Balance from an Insider's Perspective' (2006) 28 *EIPR* 3, 146.
Ladas and Parry, 'Intellectual Property Law, the European Design Regulation in Context', Chapter 5, *The position in Europe*, available at www.ladas.com/Patents/PatentPractice/EUDesignRegulation/EUDesi05.html
Laddie, Prescott and Vitoria, *The Modern Law of Copyright and Designs*, 2nd edn 1995.
McGowan G, Paper concerning the new Designs Act, available at: www.vicbar.com.au/pdf/CLESeminar_30062004GMc.pdf
Posner RA and WM Landes, 'An Economic Analysis of Copyright Law' (1989) 18 *Journal of Legal Studies* 325.

Ricketson S, *The Berne Convention for the Protection of Literary and Artistic Works, 1886–1986,* Kluwer, 1987.
Rothnie W, 'The vexed problem of Copyright/Designs overlap' (2005) *Intellectual Property Forum* 60, 33.
Rushton M, 'An Economic Approach to Copyright in Works of Artistic Craftsmanship' [2001] *Intellectual Property Quarterly* 3, 255.

Chapter five: *Sui generis* and trade mark registration

Abbot J, 'Reverse engineering of software: Copyright and interoperability' (2003) *Journal of law and information science* 14, 7.
Advisory Council on Intellectual Property (ACIP), Review of enforcement of Plant Breeder's Rights (Current; 2006).
—*Patents & Experimental Use*, Options Paper (Dec 2004); Final Report (Oct 2005).
—*Should plant & animal subject matter be excluded from protection by the innovation patent?* (Nov 2004).
Alexandra A, J Lee and F Vanclay, 'Innovation, exclusion and commodification of plant types: a social and philosophical investigation of Plant Variety Rights in Australia' (2004), *Rural Society* 14, 1, 46.
Australian Centre for Intellectual Property in Agriculture (ACIPA), 'Understanding PBR's', available at www.acipa.edu.au/frame_pbr.html
Australian Law Reform Commission (ALRC), Report No 99, *Genes and Ingenuity: Gene Patenting & Human Health* (2004).
Bently L and R Burrell, 'The requirement of trade mark use' (2002) *AIPJ*, 18, 1.
Burchfield KJ, 'The Constitutional Intellectual Property Power: Progress of the Useful Arts and the Legal Protection of Semiconductor Technology' (1988) 28 *Santa Clara LR* 473.
Christie A, 'Final Report of the Copyright Law Review Committee on Protection of Computer Software – An Overview of Recommendations and Issues In relation to Copyright in computer programs' (1996) *Intellectual Property Forum* 27.
—*Integrated Circuits and their Contents: International Protection*, LBC Information Services, 1995.
Copyright Law Review Committee, *Final Report on Computer Software Protection* (1995).
Davis J, 'To Protect or Serve? European trade mark law and the decline of the public interest' [2003] *EIPR* 180.
Davis M, 'Death of a Salesman's Doctrine: A critical look at trademark use' (1985) 19 *Georgia LR* 233.
Economides N, 'The Economics of Trademarks' (1988) 78 *Trademark Reporter* 523.
Eisenberg R, 'Proprietary Rights and the Norms of Science in Biotechnology and Research' (1988) 97 *Yale LJ* 2 177.
Expert Panel on Breeding, 'Clarification of plant breeding issues under the *Plant Breeder's Rights Act 1994*', Report, December 2002.
Folie A, 'Trade-offs in trade mark protection: an economic analysis' (2004) *AIPJ* 15, 2, 87.
Forsyth M, 'Biotechnology, Patents and Public Policy: A Proposal for Reform in Australia' (2000) 11 *AIPJ* 202.
Helth TS, 'Beer with lime? A trade mark assembled by the bartender *AIPJ* (2005) *Australian Intellectual Property Law Bulletin*, 18, 6, 93.
Honey R and P Sinden, 'The Interface between Trademark, Designs and Passing Off under Australian Law: The Philips Case' (2000) *Murdoch e-law Journal* Vol 7 No 4.
House of Representatives Standing Committee on Industry, Science and Technology, 'Genetic Manipulation: the Threat or the Glory', Canberra (1992).
Hughes S, 'Protection of Shape Marks in Australia: Extending the permanent monopoly' (2002) 49 *IP Forum* 28.
Janis M, 'Sustainable Agriculture, Patent Rights, and Plant Innovation' (2001) 9 *Indiana Journal of Global Legal Studies* 91.

Jones N, 'Biotechnology patents: a change of heart' [1994] 1 *EIPR* 37.
Kang PH and K Snyder, 'A practitioner's approach to strategic enforcement and analysis of business method patents in the post-State Street era' (2000) *IDEA – The Journal of Law and Technology* 40, 267.
Landes WM and R Posner, 'Trademark law: an economic perspective' (1987) 30 *J of Law & Eco* 265.
Lawson C, 'Patents and plant breeder's rights over plant genetic resources for food and agriculture' (2004) *Federal Law Review* 32, 107.
—'Patenting Genes and Gene Sequences and Competition: Patenting at the Expense of Competition' (2002) 30 *Federal Law Review* 97.
Lemley M and JE Cohen, 'Patent scope and innovation in the software industry' (2001) 89 *California Law Review* 1.
Lemley M and D McGowan, 'Legal Implications of Network Economic Effects' (1998) 86 *California Law Review* 479.
Marschak J, 'The economics of language', in D Lamberton (ed), *The Economics of Communication and Information*, Edward Elgar, 1996.
McCutcheon J, 'Monopolised product shapes and factual distinctiveness under s 41(6) of the *Trade Marks Act 1995* (Cth)' (2004) 15 *AIPJ* 1, 18.
Moens A, 'Streamlining the Software Development Process Through Reuse and Patents' [2000] *EIPR* 22(9) 418.
—'The Use of Copyright and Patents for Software Protection' (1998) 4 *Computer & Telecommunications Law Review* 35.
Nicol D, 'On the legality of gene patents' [2005] *MULR* 25.
Nicol D and J Nielsen, 'The Australian Medical Biotechnology Industry and Access to Intellectual Property: Issues for Patent Law Development' (2001) 23 *Sydney Law Review* 347.
Nott R, 'The proposed directive on biotechnological inventions' [1994] 5 *EIPR* 191.
Nuffield Council on Bioethics, 'The Ethics of Patenting DNA – A Discussion Paper' (2002).
Outterson K, 'The vanishing public domain: antibiotic resistance, pharmaceutical innovation and intellectual property law' (2005) *University of Pittsburgh Law Review*, 1, 67.
Png I and D Reitman, 'Why are some products branded and others not?' (1995) 38 *Journal of Law & Economics* 207.
Rangnekar D, 'Technology paradigms and the Innovation-Appropriation Interface: An examination of the nature and scope of Plant Breeders' Rights' (1999) 17 *Prometheus* 2, 125.
Registrar of Plant Breeder's Rights, *Clarification of Plant Breeding Issues under the Plant Breeder's Rights Act 1994* (2002).
Rimmer M, 'Franklin Barley: patent law and Plant Breeders' Rights' (2003) *Murdoch e-Law Journal* 10 4.
Roberts C, 'The prospects of success of the National Institute of Health's Human Genome Application' [1994] 1 *EIPR* 30.
Roberts T, 'Broad claims for biotechnological inventions' [1994] 9 *EIPR* 371.
Schulze C, 'Registering colour trade marks in the EU' [2003] 25 *EIPR* 2, 55.
Smith C, 'Trade mark protection for product shape – Where does the public interest lie?' (2005) *Intellectual Property Forum* 63, 32.
Suthersanen U, 'The European Court of Justice in Philips v Remington: Trade Marks and Market Freedom' [2003] 7 *Intellectual Property Quarterly* 257–83
Turkevich L, 'An end to the "Mathematical algorithm" confusion?' [1995] 2 *EIPR* 91.
Willchon D, 'Broad Trade Mark Specifications' [2002] 24 *EIPR* 228.

Index

a priori determination of property rights 10
abuse of property rights 12
academe, *see* universities
accountability, trade secrets cases 42
ACIP 93, 106, 194
actual damage, trade secrets cases 48
Advisory Council on Intellectual Property (ACIP) 93, 106, 194
aesthetic issues in design 130, 202
agricultural processes 73, 192
algorithms, not patentable 79, 186
ALRC Report 138
  on spare parts 142, 159
  on Statements of Newness and Distinctiveness 157
amendments to patents 90
amnesty, *see* grace period for disclosures
antecedents 145
anti-piracy regimes 140
anticipation 43
appearance
  attractiveness no bar to registration 202
  in design registration 136
  innovation and 111
  intangible value of 21
  monopolies over 130
  ornamentation 164
  property rights in 14
  reproduction need not duplicate 123
  vs function and reputation 114
Apple case 176
architectural copyright 124, 167
articles, design registration for 139
artistic works
  copyright in 117
  craftsmanship in 168
  defining 170
  excluded from overlap provisions 167
  in manufacturing 120
  products incorporating 163
  vs design works 131
Atkinson, Lord 58
Australia
  compliance with international standards 87
  copyright in moulds 120

designs and patents in 114
designs law 135–150
  law of ownership of inventions 96–99
  new appearance can be registered design 112
  plant breeding in 193
  scope of patent rights in 105
Australian Law Reform Commission, *see* ALRC Report
Australian Patent Office 62
Autodesk case 180

barriers to competition 3, 19
Bastarache J 199
Baygol case 103
benign monopolies 65
Bennett J 56
Berne Convention 149
biotechnology industry 20, 65
bona fide acquisition for value 51
branding assets 141
breach of confidence actions 31–53
  against ex-employees 54–57
  aims of 30
  coverage of 25
breeder's exemption 197
Brinsden J 126
British Leyland case 161
brown-bagging 197
Buckley LJ 122, 123
buildings 167
  copyright in 117
  registered designs 164
Burchett J 185
business methods, patentability of 22, 66, 74, 187, *see also* processes
'but for' test of computer programs

Callinan J 59
casts and moulds 119
Catnic case 101, 102
certification of designs and patents 90, 135, 149
chilling effects of software patents 177
chimeric embryos 76
CIPEC case 128
circuit layouts 140, 175, 188–192

INDEX 215

can't be registered as design 136
  patentability of 23, 177
classification of designs 148
client data
  as trade secret 30
  cases involving 36
  use by ex-employees 53
co-inventors 93
Coco case 32
collaborative relationships 31
colourable imitations 124
combination patents 83
commercial value 38
common general knowledge test 84, 195
communications, in trade secrets cases 42
communications theory 2
competitive behaviour
  by ex-employees 57
  innovation and imitation as 1
  limits to 5
  regulating 10, 12
  trade secrets and 30, 52
compilations of data 26, 39, *see also* databases
complexity, patentability and 69
components, design registration 142, *see also* spare parts
compulsory licences 106
computer chips, *see* circuit layouts
computer games 184
computer-implemented processes 74
computer programs, *see also* circuit layouts; screen displays
  copyright in 116, 174, 176, 179–186
  form vs function in 110
  patentability of 186–188
  use of as infringement 185
confidence
  building 31, 32
  law of 60
  vs fidelity 56
confidentiality, *see* secrecy
configuration, *see* appearance; shapes
conservative reflex 68
constructive knowledge 51
constructive trusts 96
consumers
  attracted by innovative design 112
  distinctiveness requirement and 146
  market choices 3
  of computer equipment 191
  perception of trade marks 201
  rights under patent law 106
contextual issues 101
contract law
  confidentiality obligations in 44, 57–59
  employee's obligations under 99
  employer–employee relations 54–57
  trade secrets and 26, 52

contributory infringement 150
Coogi case 169–171
copying, *see also* imitations
  definition of 112
  deliberate vs inadvertent 127
  fraudulent imitation and 151
  need not produce resemblance 123
  of circuit layouts 190
  of engravings 119
  via manufacture 172
copyright law 116–129
  overlaps design registration 162–173
  trade secrets and 26, 39
  voluntary registration not permitted 162
corkscrew design 171
corporations
  copyright vested in 115
  secrecy within 40
  structure of viii, 12
costs of patents 67
counterclaims to patent infringement 108
'crafted' articles 170
craftsmanship 117, 167, 168, *see also* artistic works
criminal acts
  industrial espionage 34, 35
  not patentable 76
cross-licensing 64
Crown user rights 107
curiosity 2
currency representations 166
customer information
  as trade secret 30
  cases involving 36
  use by ex-employees 53

Data Access case 180
databases 26, 39
  legal protection for 18
Dawson J 181
Dean J 33, 36
decompiling code 177, 183
delay in registration 133
demarcation issues 40–42
  patents 64
  trade secrets and 29
demountable buildings 168
Denning, Lord 46
design registration 129–162
  artistic works and 164
  in Australia 23
  overlaps copyright 162–173
  published Register for 117, 158
  reforms in 13
  vs trade mark registration 201
detriment, in trade secrets cases 48–51
developing countries, impact of IPRs on 20
development 4, 18

216 INDEX

digitalisation 179
  patentability of 22, 74, 187
disclosure
  dilemma of 7
  effect on novelty 81
  grace period for 43
  information revealed by 27
  judging resemblance between 82
  of confidential information 45
  of inventions 63
discoveries, patents for 13, 79
dishonest concealment 152
distinctiveness requirement 143, 144
  in plant species 192
  inherent distinctiveness 201
  reputation and 200
Dixon J 153
doctrine of equivalents 100
documentation, importance of 42
drawings, *see also* two-dimensional works
  copyright in 118
  preliminary 172
dressmaking patterns 140
Drummond J 127, 168
duplication of effort, *see* wastage of resources
DUS requirement 192, 195
dynamic efficiency, increased by IPRs 5

economic issues, patentability and 75
EDVs 196
efficiency gains from innovation 5
eligible layout rights 189
embarrassment 49
embodiment
  meaning of 163
  of trade secrets 41
Emmett J 150, 155
employees, *see also* ex-employees
  confidentiality of 57–59
  inventions by 94–96
  knowledge held by 25, 30
  nature of duties 98
  trade secrets and 53–59
employers, entitlement to inventions 94–96
enabling disclosures 6, 63
end-point royalty systems 197
enforceable covenants 59
engravings 115, 119, *see also* three-dimensional objects
enhancements 160
equitable jurisdiction, breach of confidence actions 31
ER rights 189
essential or material features 125
Essentially Derived Varieties 196
ethical issues, *see* morality
Europe

'branding assets' 141
circuit layout designs in 140
computer programs 186
design registration in 129
grace period for disclosures 147
individual character test 144
industrial application test 71
no doctrine of equivalents 100
novelty requirement 147
patent system 69
protection of unregistered designs 133
royalty payments on saved seeds 197
utility patent model 90
evaluation and analysis exemptions 191
evergreening 86, 105
evolutionary design innovation 131
ex-employees, breach of confidence actions 54–57
ex post vs *ex ante* rights 13
examination of designs and patents 67, 90, 135
exclusive rights 16, 22, 112
existing knowledge 22
expenditure 67
experimental use exemptions 63, 106
  circuit layouts 191
  computer programs 184
expert opinions
  distinctiveness requirement and 144, 146
  in patent claim interpretation 100
  on inventiveness 84–87
exploitation
  defined 195
  rights to 104–109

fabric, *see* textiles and garments
Faccenda Chicken case 56
facsimile copying 124
failure rates of patent suits 70
fair basing requirements 70, 87
farmers
  agricultural processes 73, 192
  rights of 199
  seed saving by 192, 197
fibreglass swimming pools 167
fidelity in relationships 31
  employee's duty 54
  vs duty of confidence 56
Finkelstein J 75, 102
firms, *see* corporations
'first to file' systems 80, 134
Foggin case 150
food material, plant rights and 197
foreign publications in prior art 146
form, vs function 110
formulas not patentable 79, 186
fragmentation of knowledge 4

Franki Committee 152
fraudulent imitation 128, 152
free-riders
   in pharmaceutical industry 48
   on design innovation 111, 132
Free Trade Agreement 185
   IPRs in 19
   on confidential information 48
French J 203
function
   copyright and 122, 127
   design registration and 137
   improvements in, patenting 113
   product shape and 203
   property rights in 14
   vs appearance and reputation 114
   vs form 110
funding
   for research and development 18
   models for 9

gale of creative destruction 5
garments, *see* textiles and garments
Gaudron J 179
genetic engineering
   international obligations 194
   of plants 198
   patentability of 77, 78
Gibbs CJ 126
Gleeson CJ 55, 58
goodwill, *see* reputation
grace period for disclosures 43
   in design registration 147
   in patent law 83
Griffin case 91
Grove Hill case 88
Gummow J 151, 161, 163, 166

Hailsham, Lord 123
harmonisation of legal regimes 19
higher and lower life forms 77
history of IPRs 16
HIV/AIDS drugs 75
Hoffman, Lord 100, 101, 103, 161
horticulture 73, *see also* plants
Huffman compression tables 183
human beings, patents relating to 76–80

ideas, copyright and 127
identification
   in patent system 64
   of trade secrets 41
illegal acts 34
   industrial espionage 34, 35
   not patentable 76
imitations 1, *see also* copying; fraudulent imitation

Improver case 102
incentives to patent 63, 95
inchoate knowledge 39
incremental breeding 197
independent invention
   copyright and 122
   of trade secrets 27, 28
   possibility of 36
   vs misuse of confidential information 46
individual character test 144
individual features 157
industrial application test 71
industrial-era patents 66
industrial espionage 32, 34
   criminalisation of 35
   trade secrets acquired by 45
Industrial Property Advisory Committee (IPAC) 74, 95
industry
   artistic works in 120
   design registration in 164
   invention in 94
   mass copying in 165, 172
   products of 23
inexhaustible public good, knowledge as viii, 11
informed users 146, 158
   in design registration 156
   on replacement parts 160
infringement of copyright
   by reproduction of works 121–129
   by using a computer program 185
   of computer programs 180–181
   vs infringement of design 128
infringement of design rights 150–162
infringement of patent rights 99–104
infringement of trade marks 203
injunctions, in trade secrets cases 49
innocent commercial exploitation 191
innocent patent infringement 108
innovation patents 90–93
   design registration and 134
   for circuit layouts 188
   vs design registration 114
innovations 23
   accelerating rate of 61
   and intellectual property law 2–17
   appearance and 111
   as competitive behaviour 1
   contractual restraint on 59
   design registration for 139
   innovation matrix 9
   innovation threshold 6
   legal trends relating to 17–22, 23
   patents for 72
   property rights and 13
   reputation and 200
   the innovation dynamic 3

innovativeness test 91
integrated model of innovation 9
Intellectual Property and Competition Review Committee (IPCRC) 22
intellectual property law
 and innovation 2–17
 approaches to 2
 rights defined in 10
 trends in 17–22
 vs monopolies 15
interaction, standards of 31
interdependence, and R&D 4
International Convention for the Protection of New Varieties of Plants 176
international obligations 194, *see also* UPOV convention; Washington Treaty on Intellectual Property in Respect of Integrated Circuits; WTO/TRIPS
interoperable parts
 computer programs 183
 design registration 142
invasion of privacy 34
inventions
 disclosure of 63
 entitlement to patents of 93–96
 ownership of 54
 vs discoveries 13–14
inventiveness requirement 72, 84–87
IPCRC 22
isolation theory 78
itemisation 40–42

Jacob J 141, 144, 181
jealously guarded secrets 40

Kenman Kandy case 202
King J 153, 154
kiwifruit packs 122
know-how of ex-employees 55
know-who 30, 36, 53
knowledge, *see also* transactions issues
 contained in a patent 108
 costs of patents and 67
 demarcation of 40
 diffusion of 6–10
 ex post vs *ex ante* rights in 13
 held by employees 25, 30
 in the public domain 22
 inchoate 39
 knowledge goods 21
 of ex-employees 55
 search for 2
 tacit 7
 theoretical 14
 transactions in 64
 valuing units of 28
 with patents 64

Kruhse Enterprises case 168
Kwan case 97

language
 of patent applications 79, 99
 used in property claims 15
Law Council of Australia 156
legal regimes
 affect innovation matrix 9
 copyright 113, 115
 designs 115, 135–150
 overlapping 20, 116, 139, 162–173
 patents vs trade secrets 28
 relationships between 24
 set parameters for competition 1
 sui generis 174–204
licensing
 cross-licensing 65
 for employers by employees 99
 for non-use 63, 106
limited purpose test of confidentiality 43, 47
Lindgren J 124, 125, 128
literary works 166
 computer programs as 176, 179
living organisms 77, *see also* plants
Lockhart J 131, 156
locking system 137
Lockwood case 88, 137
look and feel issues 178, 181
lower life forms 77

'make, exercise and vend' rights 104
Malleys case 154
manipulating theory 17
manner of manufacture requirement 89
manufacturing, *see* industry
market system 3
 incentives to patent in 61
 manipulability of 68
Mason CJ 125
mass production 164
material form test 185
medals, excluded from design registration 139, 166
medical treatments, patentability of 75
Megarry J 31, 36, 46
mental processes, rights relating to 16
Merkel J 103, 156
methods or principles of construction 154, 155
Metrokane case 171
microprocessors 188
mixed secrets 50
mobility of employees 53
models
 copyright in 119
 of buildings 117, 167

monopolies
  benign 65
  'generally inconvenient' 75
  over appearance, not function 130
  pricing factors 21
  publicity obligations 60
  spare parts and 161
  Statements of Monopoly 156
  Statute of Monopolies 72
  vs IPRs 15
morality
  biomedical patents and 78
  industrial espionage and 34
  patents contravening 69, 76
Morris, William 171
Morton J 167
mosaicing 85, 108
moulds and casts 119, 172
multiple protection regimes 20
must-match components 159

National Research and Development Corporation 71
naturally occurring substances 83
New Zealand, springboarding cases 106
no monopoly without publicity 60
non-competition clauses 57
Non-Disclosure Agreements 44
non-identical designs 151
non-obviousness 28, 35
non-use, licensing for 63, 106
norm structures and principles 16, 17–22
Northrop J 189
notional public availability 36
novelty requirement 64
  for design registration 143–147
  for patents 80
  for plant breeding 195
  in *Griffin* case 91–92

object of rights 14
objective similarity test 126, 127
obligations of confidence 42–45
O'Brien case 41
obviousness 28
onus of proof, *see* proof, onus of
open markets, innovation in 3
open-source movements 20
ordinary recall 56
organisational structure viii, 12
'Orgasmatron' case 150
originality threshold 38, 125
  circuit layouts 190
  for computer programs 182
  for copyright 115
ornamentation, *see* appearance
orthodox account of patents 61

overall impression test 128, 155, 157
  for designs 129
  in design innovation 143
  statutory test of 150
overlapping legal regimes 20
  copyright and designs 116, 162–173
  textiles and garments 139
ownership
  of inventions 54
  of patents 93–99
  physical viii, 11

parallel importation restrictions 190
Paris Convention 149
particularisation
  in trade secrets cases 44
  reasons for 41
passing off, proof of 200
patent attorneys
  drafting skills 69, 87
  preliminary searches by 81
  role of 62
patent law 70–109
  computer programs and 185
  interpretation of claims 99
  knowledge transactions and 29
  limitations of 66, 68
  Plant Breeder's Rights and 198
  reforms in 13
  requirements for patentability 71–90
  trade secrets and 48
  two-level approach 90–93
  vs breach of confidence actions 25
patents 60
  for plants 193
  misuse of 65
  portfolios of 12, 27, 65
  scope of 13
  vs trade secrets 26, 27
Patent Cooperation Treaty application 81
patterns
  design registration for 136, 140
  in industry 164
peer-recognition 96
personal property, in patent system 64
personality-based IPRs 16
persons aggrieved 149
perverse side-effects 17
petty patents 90
pharmaceuticals
  evergreening attempts 86, 105
  in patent law 48, 75, 105
  trade marked names for 204
Philips case 86
philosophical theories of property 2
PhotoCure case 103

physical ownership viii, 11
Pincus J 120
pith and marrow approach 100
planning innovation 3
Plant Breeder's Rights 77, 175, 193, 195–200
plants 77, 192–200
  new varieties 175
  patentability of 23
Plix case 122
plugs, casts and moulds 119
policy context
  copyright and designs 110–115
  patents 63–70
  registered designs 129–135
  theory and 15
  trade secrets 26–31
political influences 15, 76–80
portability of employee knowledge 25
portable buildings 168
post-term competition 54–57
premiums paid to employees for inventions 95
principles of construction 154
prior art
  in design innovation 131, 143
  in design registration 145, 146
  in innovation patents 91
  inventiveness and 84
  novelty and 80–84
prior use rights 107
priority dates, significance of 80
privacy, breach of 34
private bargains 58
private sector funding 8
prize-system for patents 63
processes, *see also* business methods
  design registration and 138
  patentability of 72, 104
product innovations, *see* innovations
productivity gains 5
programming, *see* computer programs
programming style 181
progress, belief in 2
proof, onus of
  aids to 108
  in compulsory licensing 106
  in trade secrets cases 41, 45
property theory 2, 10–13, 33
proprietary rights 54
prospect theory 28
protected plant varieties 198
Protocol Questions 102
prototypes 171
provisional patent applications 81
pseudocode analysis 181
public domain, relative shrinkage of 19
public humiliation 49

public, relevant, defining 36
public sector
  funding from 8, 18, 68
  role of patents in 61
public welfare
  breach of confidence may promote 47
  designs registration better than copyright for 162
  drawbacks of secrecy 60
  patent law and 66
publication of a design, vs registration 135, 148
publicity, benefits of 28
publishing, *see also* disclosure
  incentives for 8
  overseas, in prior art 146
Pumfrey J 180
purchasers of products
  computer equipment 191
  rights under patent law 106
pure science 18
purposive approach to claim interpretation 100

quia timet, trade secrets cases 48

RAM copies 185
Rath J 167
reasonable person test
  of confidentiality 43
  of restraint on post-term competition 58
referability to obligation of confidence 44
register of designs 117, 158, *see also* design registration
register of plant varieties 195
regulation
  torts as tool for 10
  Trade Practices Act 1974 (Cth) 21
relative secrecy 36, 38
relative standard of non-obviousness 35
relevant public 36
remedies
  against patent infringement 108
  against third parties 51–52
  in trade secrets cases 48–51
  restitution for wrongs 33
  secrecy and 37
repair defence 159
replacement parts 129, 142, 159
representations, property rights in 14
reproduction, *see* copying
reputation
  design and 132
  in *sui generis* regimes 178
  innovations and 200
  intangible value of 21
  risk reduction through 4
  vs appearance and function 114

research and development
  and interdependence 4
  exemptions for 191, 197
  funding for 18
resemblance, *see also* appearance
  reproduction need not duplicate 123
  visual evaluation of 151
resource scarcity 5, *see also* wastage of resources
restitution for wrongs 33, *see also* remedies
restrictive covenants 58
retro-fitting 160
reverse auctions 74
reverse engineering
  morality of 34
  of circuit layouts 177
  of computer programs 183
  risky nature of 26
  trade secrets and 37
reverse infringement test 82
reverse mortgage case 73
Review of Plant Breeder's Rights 194
revoking a design registration 135, 149
rights, structure of ix, 13–15, *see also* exclusive rights; scope of rights
risk management
  confidential information 47
  innovation risk 3
  risk reduction 4
Root Quality case 102
royal prerogative to refuse patents 76
royalty payments 107

salary as an incentive to invent 95
Salmon, Lord 123
science
  application of 73
  innovation and 18
scope of rights 5
  designs 115
  patent system 64, 79
  plant breeding 196
screen displays 141
sculptures 115, 119, *see also* three-dimensional objects
sealing without examination 90
secondary indicators of inventiveness 85
secondary meaning, *see* reputation
secrecy 42–45, *see also* trade secrets
  confidentiality clauses 44
  drawbacks of 60
  identifying confidential information 45
  limitations of 26
  reasons for choosing 27
  relative 36, 38
  remedy and 37
  secret use of invention 89–90
  secrets improved upon 50

stifles competition 6–10
  vs patenting 89
section 40 requirements 87–89
seed saving, *see* farmers; plants
selective propagation 195
semiconductor chips, *see* circuit layouts
sets of statements, programs as 179
shapes
  design registration of 129
  monopolisation of 178
  trade mark registration of 21, 200–204
signs capable of distinguishing goods 201
simplicity, patentability and 69
social contract theory 61
social usefulness, *see* public welfare
software patents, *see* computer programs
spare parts, design registration 129, 142, 159
specialised R&D firms 18
specifications in patent claims 104
springboarding cases 49
  drug import for approval 106
  prohibition of springboarding 48
  Terrapin 37
stability requirement 192
Statements of Monopoly 156
Statements of Newness and Distinctiveness 128, 148–150, 156
  in design registration 136, 150
Statements of Novelty 156
static efficiency, reduced by IPRs 5
Statute of Monopolies 72
Stone J 201, 203
structures, *see* buildings
subconscious use of a trade secret 47
subject matter of legal regimes 11
subject matter suitable for patent 71–80
  innovation patents 93
  plant patents 199
subsistence of copyright 117–121
substantial part test 185
substantial similarity test 124, 126, 155
  in design registration 143, 162
Substantive Patent Law Theory 20
sufficiency requirement 87
sui generis regimes 174–204
supply rights 104, 107
Swish case 122
Switzerland, patent abolition in 20

tacit knowledge 7
  of ex-employees 55
  trade secrets and 30
Tamawood case
Tamberlin J 103
teaching exemptions 191
technical trade secrets 39, 43

technological innovations 23, 73
technology-neutral regimes 175, 199
technology transfer 20
Templeman, Lord 204
temporary restraining orders 37
terminology, *see* language
terms of protection for designs 115, 149
Terrapin case 50
test of anticipation 80–84, *see also* novelty requirement
testing against standards 11
tests of confidentiality 43
textiles and garments 139, 169
theoretical knowledge 14
theory of rights ix, 13–15
third parties
 remedies against 51–52
 trade secrets acquired by 32, 45
three-dimensional objects
 as reproductions 121
 infringement defence 163
 innovative appearance in 112
threshold tests for patents 69, 86
tools of trade, of ex-employees 55
torts, as regulatory tool 10
trade, customs of 36
trade mark registration
 for pharmaceuticals 105
 of shapes 21, 200–204
 vs design registration 133
trade negotiations 19
Trade Practices Act 1974 (Cth) 21
Trade Related Intellectual Property, impact of 17–22, 61
trade secrets 25–59, *see also* secrecy
transactions issues
 costs of patents 67
 firms and viii, 12
 with patents 64
 with trade secrets 29
true and first inventors 93
trust arrangements for financial returns on invention 96
trust, building 31
Turbo Tek case 154
'twists' 38
two-dimensional works
 copyright in 118
 infringement defence 163

uncertainty in innovation decisions viii, 10
unconscionability, restitution and 33
underlying concepts 153
uniformity requirement 192

unintended side-effects 17
unique disability of confidees 46
uniqueness 38
United Kingdom
 ownership of industrial patents 94–96, 97
 screen displays registrable 141
 terms of protection 149
United States
 circuit layout legislation 189
 computer program patents 176
 doctrine of equivalents 100
 Free Trade Agreement 19
 grace period for disclosures 147
universities, *see also* public sector
 cost recovery by 18
 focus on patents in 96
unknowability problem 31, 47, 52
unregistrable designs 165
UPOV convention 176, 194
usefulness, *see* utility requirement
utility requirement
 difficulties with 66
 doesn't imply social benefits 69
 implicit in manner of manufacture requirement 89
 innovation patents 92
 not limited to patents 21

valid covenants 58
valid designs 136–143
value-free patent system 69
vendible products 73
very senior employees 98
video games 184
visual expression and features, *see* appearance

Washington Treaty on Intellectual Property in Respect of Integrated Circuits 140, 176, 189
wastage of resources
 due to competition 3
 from patents 60
 in monopolies 15
 resource scarcity 5
 trade secrets and 28
Wham-O case 119, 120
Whitford J 123
Wilcox J 125
World Intellectual Property Organization (WIPO) 17–22
World Trade Organization (WTO), *see* WTO/TRIPS
wrongful conduct, restitution for 33
WTO/TRIPS, impact of 17–22, 62

For EU product safety concerns, contact us at Calle de José Abascal, 56–1°,
28003 Madrid, Spain or eugpsr@cambridge.org.

www.ingramcontent.com/pod-product-compliance
Ingram Content Group UK Ltd.
Pitfield, Milton Keynes, MK11 3LW, UK
UKHW021813080825
461487UK00038B/1308